Columbia Essays in International Affairs

VOLUME VI

The Dean's Papers, 1970

Columbia Essays
in International Affairs

VOLUME VI

The Dean's Papers, 1970

BY STUDENTS OF THE

FACULTY OF INTERNATIONAL AFFAIRS

COLUMBIA UNIVERSITY

EDITED BY ANDREW W. CORDIER

DEAN OF THE FACULTY

NEW YORK AND LONDON

Columbia University Press

1971

Copyright © 1971 Columbia University Press
Library of Congress Catalog Card Number: 66-14078
International Standard Book Number: 0-231-03550-0
Printed in the United States of America

Foreword

Each year, members of the Faculty of International Affairs, who provide instruction for the School of International Affairs and its Regional Institutes, select a number of student essays representing a large degree of originality and high quality of scholarship for possible inclusion in the annual volume of *Essays on International Affairs: The Dean's Papers*. The papers are presented to a review committee, appointed by the Dean, by the faculty member who originally encouraged the paper. The review committee selects the best papers for publication. It is a source of great satisfaction to the students whose papers are selected, to their instructors, and, indeed, to the entire Faculty to see these research efforts brought to fruition in published form. Readers of these volumes have often expressed great surprise at the quality of research and individual comprehension which these essays frequently demonstrate.

The range of topics represented by these papers attests to the scope of concerns of students in the School of International Affairs and its regional institutes. They reflect an interest in the problems of establishing new governments, of social change in the third world, of international economic relations, of strategic and technological aspects of the international world with particular reference to the Non-Proliferation Treaty and problems of historical research concerning peasant revolts.

Miss Bette Knapp's discussion of "The Establishers—A Comparative Analysis of Adenauer and Nehru" examines the critical role these two leaders played in establishing regimes in Germany after the debacle of World War II and in India before and after the stormy and disruptive achievement of independence. Miss Knapp argues the importance of the political style and personal characteristics of these leaders in setting the tone and institutional practices now characterizing the politics and governance of both countries. Personal and political biography and institutional analysis are here combined as she compares the lives, circumstances, and creative accomplishments of these two leaders.

Patricia Reynolds' discussion of "Developmental Change in San Blas, Panama: A Comparative Community Study" looks at social, institutional, and political change from a different angle. Her method is mainly anthropological as she examines the approach to social and political change of two Cuna Indian villages on islands off the coast of Panama. One village has shown notable readiness to accept and adapt to innovation, the other more successfully resisting change. She identifies a number of significant variables, including the unique factor of personal leadership, contrasting historical experiences as well as a number of institutional differences in seeking to explain these contrasts.

In the field of international economics, Glenda Rosenthal has analyzed the complex relationships between "The EEC and the Maghreb." She examines economic advantages to Maghrebian countries of entering the Common Market, the difficulties of the negotiations, and the significance of relationships between Tunisia, Morocco, and Algeria in participating within this system of preferences. She raises a warning about growing United States opposition to the proliferation of discriminatory trade arrangements which are increasingly working against the interests of those outside the Common Market.

Strategic problems are considered by two authors who use quite different methods. Janusz Wisniowski applies a rigorous systems analysis approach to "Problems of Political Equilibrium in the Soviet Proposals for a European Security Conference." Taking the Soviet proposals for such a conference as his main focus, he illustrates a systems approach to analyzing their probable intentions and general strategy. He argues that Soviet moves designed to hasten U.S. disengagement from Western Europe while keeping Western European states divided represents a thought-out, dynamic systems model, while American and Western European policies tend to be simply defensive, usually static, stop-gap, and episodic. He warns that unless Western policy makers use more systems-oriented analysis and planning, Soviet policy-makers will succeed in their design.

Keith Sours' "Italy and NATO: The Policy of the Italian Communist Party" is a more conventional discussion of the interaction between foreign policy and domestic politics as it affects the fortunes of Italy's Communist Party. The Party has to advocate policies which will win it support at home within Italy. At the same time, as part of the international Communist movement, it should also support policies designed to weaken the Common Market and NATO and strengthen ties with the Eastern European Communist states. He finds that the events in Czechoslovakia in 1968 posed this familiar dilemma particularly sharply to the Italian Party. He points out that there are numerous domestic grievances within Italy which can be used to strengthen the voting support for the Party but that the Brezhnev doctrine poses grave difficulties to the Party when foreign policy issues become salient.

Growing concern over the unrestrained development and proliferation of nuclear weapons is represented by three papers. In an effort to understand one set of arguments leading states to choose the nuclear option, Charles Bethill examines the "Nonmilitary Incentives for the Acquisition of Nuclear Weapons." Nonmilitary arguments, though admittedly less weighty than "security" and "prestige" reasons, may provide that extra margin of argument should strategic considerations be indeterminate. His examination of the nature of the state system leads him to conclude that even if direct use of nuclear weapons is not envisaged there are a number of diplomatic justifications often marshaled to accelerate the acquisition of nuclear weapons. Whether one is attempting to go it alone or seeks to work within an alliance system, nuclear weapons are thought to improve one's bargaining position. Advancing nuclear technology by using the security argument may have certain domestic political advantages for its proponents, as well as the more obvious technological and "spill-over" effects and economic advantages, particularly in the field of power generation, where other sources of energy are lacking. By indirection—and by intent—the paper demonstrates the very broad range of interests to be answered and disincentives to be mounted if proliferation is to be successfully discouraged.

Gertrud Svala presents to American readers a perspective we do not often see, namely "Sweden's View of the Non-Proliferation Treaty." Sweden had been an advocate of a peaceful world. Yet Sweden had been a strong critic of the NPT. In brief, the Swedes believe that the NPT as presently drafted and agreed to will have substantial commercial and economic disadvantages for those countries not already possessing nuclear capabilities. Sweden also doubts the effectiveness of the treaty to stop proliferation and holds that security for those not so equipped will be threatened by the exclusive possession of nuclear weapons on the part of the Superpowers the NPT seeks to perpetuate. Sweden has proposed an alternative package which lays greater stress on parallel nuclear disarmament by those already possessing nuclear weapons.

Accepting the NPT as playing a constructive role in contributing toward establishing the nuclear arms situation, Darioush Bayandor discusses "Maintenance of the NPT in the 1970s: The Asian Dimension." He first analyzes the ambiguities in the NPT itself, stressing the obligations the nuclear powers have undertaken in efforts to encourage others to sign, and assesses the unlikelihood that the Superpowers will be able to fulfill the obligations they have undertaken. He then examines the policy approaches and nuclear programs of Israel, India, and Japan. Comparing and contrasting the programs themselves, he also assesses the likelihood of each going ahead to the point of actually developing and testing nuclear weapons. His conclusion is not reassuring to the proponents of non-proliferation.

Traditional historical analysis is exemplified by Paul Shapiro's study of "The Horia Rebellion in Transylvania, 1784–1785," as he examines a phenomenom of growing contemporary interest in parts of the developing world, i.e. peasant rebellions. The revolt led by Horia was not a nationalist uprising of Romanians against Magyar landowners; rather, it represented an effort to ease the exactions and uncustomary oppression imposed on the peasantry by state agents of the Crown on Crown estates. As the protest gained momentum, open conflict forced state functionaries on Crown lands to reduce their exactions, with the apparent support of the Emperor. But as the rebellion expanded, conventional military action repressed the uprising. It represents an early effort to demand land reform and improve cultivation and tenancy conditions. In this "social rebellion," as Shapiro terms it, deteriorating economic conditions were the main precipitants; religious and nationalist issues were only marginal.

The selection of these nine essays for publication in *The Dean's Papers, 1970,* was based upon careful review in three stages. After being recommended by their sponsoring professors, the studies submitted were examined by committees appointed by the regional institutes or, in the case of subjects of a functional or nonregional type, by a committee designated by the Committee on Instruction of the Faculty. The final selection was made by a committee of the Faculty of International Affairs, consisting of Howard Wriggins, Chairman, Professor of Government, and Director of the Southern Asian Institute, J. C. Hurewitz, Professor of Government, and Bruce L. Smith, Associate Professor of Government. It is a pleasure to express my appreciation to this committee for the care they took in fulfilling this responsibility. I am happy, also, to express my thanks to Marguerite V. Freund,

Administrative Assistant of the European Institute, who again provided very efficient liaison between student contributors, faculty, the
selection committee, and the Press. I wish likewise to thank Phyllis
Holbrook of the Columbia University Press, who edited and super-
vised proofreading of *The Dean's Papers, 1970.*

Andrew W. Cordier
Dean

June 1971

Contents

Columbia Essays in International Affairs

VOLUME VI

The Dean's Papers, 1970

The Establishers: A Comparative Analysis of Adenauer and Nehru

BETTE KNAPP

Future histories may well list among the chief political characteristics of the last quarter century not only the nation-state explosion but the high mortality rate of infant democracies. The fact that most democratic governments, christened with the glowing hopes of new independence, have failed to endure much beyond their founding, suggests that the period of establishment following the inauguration of a democratic system is crucial to its survival. Political scientists have made little attempt, however, to analyze on a comparative basis the functioning of the political process during this limited time span, which may coincide with the period in office of the first head of government. Moreover, though the importance of the national leader in the period of transition to a new political structure has been generally recognized, there appears to have been no study specifically focusing on the role of the leader in infusing the democratic process into constitutionally provided institutions. Here is a preliminary attempt to investigate this gap in knowledge of the establishers, as contrasted with the founders and maintainers, of political democracy.

Two establishers who successfully navigated new democracies through the trials of transition have left their images indelibly imprinted on the history of the period: Konrad Adenauer, first Chancellor of the Federal Republic of Germany; and Jawaharlal Nehru, first Prime Minister of India. During the period 1947–64 the names Adenauer and Nehru became almost world-wide synonyms for Germany and India. The remarkable impact which the two countries had on international affairs so soon after acquiring independence from foreign occupation and colonial rule (in 1949 and 1947 respectively) was due as much to the towering personalities of the two men, their ability to win the confidence of other nations, and their proved politi-

cal acumen in national development as it was to the strategically piv-
otal positions of the countries themselves in an era of mounting
East-West tension. Despite predictions that societies with strong authoritarian traditions, and little or unsuccessful previous experience
in democratic practice, would reject democratic implants and despite
the pressures of East-West conflict, for which each has been an important target, the Federal Republic and India today stand as perhaps the principal examples of stable, modern democratic political
systems to have emerged since 1945.

Can the survival of democracy in both countries attributed to the
sustained leadership of Adenauer and Nehru be corroborated by empirical evidence? Did each as head of government and leader of his
political party, play a decisive role at critical junctures which determined the substance and direction of the development of the political
system? If they did not perform as "democrats" in the classical sense,
did they employ the political skills and provide the infrastructure
necessary for the infusion of the democratic process and its continued evolution?

Studies in comparative politics have thus far tended to concentrate
on either technologically advanced nations or emerging states of Asia
and Africa, but the twain seem rarely to meet. Further, they tend to
attribute the failure of "instant democracy" to an inadequate gesta-
tion period, low literacy rate, cultural incompatability, and underdeveloped economies, instead of considering that democratic institutions originated in the West through an evolutionary process which
only today has culminated in highly educated, urbanized industrial
societies. Comparison confined to Asian and African states, however, does not avoid cultural contradictions, contrasting experience
under colonial rule and various levels of political organization prior
to colonial domination. The failure of Weimar and other post-World
War I European experiments with democracy indicates that emana-
tion from European civilization is not a sure formula for democratic
durability. Conversely, India's success (as well as that of Japan and
the Philippines) suggests that Asian culture may be sufficiently fertile to nurture democratic growth. The question arises whether democracy is, indeed, a uniquely Western system of government or
whether, though originating in the West, it is a culturally and economically neutral process for arriving at agreement, the success of
which may, however, be dependent upon the existence of certain

political conditions which are equally unrelated to a specific culture or level of technological development. Though it is often stated that democracy depends on a high level of political sophistication among the electorate, it may be more appropriate to say that the national leader's practice of leadership must be congruent with various levels of political sophistication within the society at its successive stages of evolution.

An analysis of the methods employed by Adenauer and Nehru might reveal common characteristics which could suggest requisites for leadership in the period of democratic establishment, as well as indicating whether cultural and technological differences did, in fact, have any direct bearing on the way in which they functioned as national leaders. As both the Indian and German democratic systems are of recent origin and were established following the similarly "traumatic" and humiliating experience of colonial rule or total national defeat and military occupation, the results of such a comparison might be relevant for other new states.

In comparing the performance of Adenauer and Nehru during the establishment of the German and Indian democracies, the writer is operating on the basic assumption that the establishment of a democratic political system depends primarily on the prior existence and interaction of organized political institutions (including a nationwide representative political party) and a dominant political leader whose personal ambition is directed toward the establishment of such a system. Though at a later stage institutions may assume the burden of maintaining a democratic system, in the initial period it is the national political leader who is crucial in determining its success or failure. We shall consider: 1) each leader's family background and personality as they relate to his functioning as a politician, 2) his previous political experience, 3) his style of leadership and political philosophy, and 4) the ways in which he influenced the development of the democratic political process in creating a new national image, mobilizing political strength, expanding participation, providing national equilibrium, stimulating an opportunity for choice. In all of these areas, except the first, the growth of dissent, criticism and opposition is implicit.

The Setting

SOME COMMON CHARACTERISTICS OF GERMANY AND INDIA
IN THE ADENAUER-NEHRU ERA, 1947–1964

The striking contrast of India and the Federal Republic is of such magnitude that one is tempted all too easily to dismiss the possible usefulness of a comparative study of the national leaders of two states which appear to have so little in common. Closer inspection, however, reveals a number of similar features which form substantial background for a study of national leadership focused on the particular time when both were attempting to assimilate a democratic political system.

India and the Federal Republic both stepped into independence as portions of divided countries. The influx of refugees prompted by division placed heavy burdens on already staggering economies, as well as creating additional problems for social and political integration and a readily ignitable fuse to forces of irredentism. Fortunate that the major industrial areas remained within their national boundaries, they were, on the other hand, separated from major sources of food located in the predominantly agricultural severed part: while the raw jute for India's important jute industry was now in East Pakistan, West Germany's reviving industry was deprived of natural markets in the East. Pressures of the intensifying East-West split, of which its division was a consequence, created a high incidence of interaction between international politics and the internal politics of the Bonn Republic. India for its part was subjected to the fluctuating pressures of Soviet-U.S. competition in the emerging world at a time when foreign economic aid was essential to launch widespread socioeconomic modernization. Thus Nehru and Adenauer not only were confronted with the rigors of transition in government under difficult socioeconomic conditions but were buffeted by the forces of growing East-West conflict.

The problems which confronted the Chancellor and the Prime Minister as they assumed authority were compounded by similar divisive factors which stemmed from their respective histories and the fact that both countries are amalgamations of previously distinct political units: regionalism, minorities, religious division, linguistic differences.

But if there were strong centrifugal forces, India and Germany also possessed several attributes considered principal requisites for national unity and the evolution of stable democracy. Both had well-defined national borders; although India had first to integrate the Princely States within the new state, and the Federal Republic, regarding its current borders as temporary, looked to the 1938 frontiers of a united Germany. They both had long histories including peaks of glory, a cultural heritage shared by a majority of the people, achievement in the arts in which citizens could take pride, and long religious traditions which bound (as well as divided) the majority of their populations.

The constitutions of both countries, on the drafting of which Adenauer and Nehru exerted considerable influence, set up governmental systems which permitted a high concentration of power in the offices of Prime Minister and Chancellor. Both adopted federal, parliamentary systems of government. But though India's federalism gives vent to regional expression, it is unitary in fact,[1] with fiscal and revenue powers, plus those for national planning, vested in the Centre and thus strengthening the position of the Prime Minister. At the same time, with provisions for implementation of national plans constitutionally seated in the States, the system is conducive to Centre-State bargaining. In the Bonn Republic, on the other hand, the Basic Law (adopted in 1949) attempted to balance the federal relationship. The office of Chancellor, however, was greatly strengthened in comparison to that of Prime Minister in the British Cabinet system (on which India's is based) or Weimar: It is impossible for a Chancellor to be removed through a vote of confidence unless the majority vote "no" and a successor is immediately nominated.[2] Moreover, his position is further strengthened by the fact that the Chancellor is responsible for foreign policy decisions and the general formulation of policy.[3] Thus both Nehru and Adenauer occupied po-

---

[1] For studies of centralizing effect of fiscal provisions and planning, see Chanda Asok, *Federation in India: A Study of Union-State Relations* (London, 1965); K. Santhanan, *Union-State Relations in India,* The Indian Institute of Public Administration, (London, 1960); Richard L. Park, *India's Political System* (Englewood Cliffs, N.J., 1967); and "The Centre and the States: A Symposium on the Balance of Power in Our Federal System," *Seminar,* No. 111 (November, 1968). The best study of State-Centre bargaining is Marcus Franda, *West Bengal and Federalizing Process in India* (Princeton, N.J., 1968).

[2] Federal Republic of Germany, *Basic Law,* Article 65.

[3] *Ibid.,* Articles 67 and 68.

sitions with potentially great concentration of power; but whereas in Germany this power potential was inherent in the office itself, in India it could be largely derived from manipulation of the division of economic power in the federal system.

Both countries have multiparty systems. In Germany, this has tended increasingly toward a two-party system (with the CDU and the SPD the major parties) and coalition governments. India, on the other hand, has a dominant party (the Congress Party) system at the national level, but growing party competition at the state and local levels.[4] Although participation in elections has been high, the people of both countries have also shown general apathy toward politics. If India's largely illiterate, agrarian-based population with little experience in political democracy were politically naïve and apathetic during most of the Nehru era, Germany's urban-centered, industrially advanced citizens, reacting to the failure of Weimar and twelve years of regimentation under Nazi totalitarianism, assumed a skeptical "count me out" attitude toward political participation while they concentrated on more immediate personal needs of economic recovery.

India and Germany also have certain traditions in organization and attitudes toward authority which are similar. Both have strong bureaucratic traditions which have produced a tendency to look to the bureaucracy for expected services from government rather than to organize political strength and work through political institutions. Hero worship and the tendency to look to a strong leader has been an important force in each country, though in Germany this may be expressed in a father image or knight-soldier; whereas in India [5] it is the prince or king whose combined power and wisdom will assure the citizen's well-being and security.

Perhaps the most significant common feature of India and the Federal Republic is that both in 1947/49 had in their heritages elements of democratic thought or practice interwoven with predominantly authoritarian traditions; that they had had limited experience with practical democracy prior to 1947/49; and that democracy came as a result of organized internal demand over a period of at least two gen-

[4] Studies of the growth of political parties may be found in Myron Weiner, *Party Politics in India: The Development of a Multi-Party System* (Princeton, N.J., 1957) and Philip Mason, ed., *India and Ceylon: Unity and Diversity*, Institute of Race Relations, London (New York, 1967).

[5] W. H. Morris-Jones, *The Government and Politics of India* (2d ed.; London, 1967), p. 15.

erations, though outside forces (the Western Allies in Germany; the British in India) also exerted an influence. In India the traditional *panchayat raj,* the customary Indian practice of arriving at decisions through consensus after long discussion, the evolution and struggle of the Indian National Congress from its inception in 1885 as an elite group seeking home rule to a mass democratic party dedicated to independence and socioeconomic development, the Congress' internalized democratic conflict-resolution technique, and the gradual devolution of government to Indian control with nationwide elections and state autonomy provided more than a minimal speaking acquaintance with democratic practice. Germany's century-long liberal tradition and struggle for parliamentary government, the object lesson in the pitfalls of democracy under the Weimar Republic, political parties with roots in the previous century, and the outcropping at the close of World War II of Christian political groups, determined to see a workable democratic system adopted similarly provided a background of some depth on which to found a new democratic government. Thus both India and Germany had gone through what Rustow, in his dynamic model for transitions to democracy, has called the *Preparatory Phase,* during which

the dynamic process of democratization itself is set off by a prolonged and inconclusive political struggle . . . [in which] the protagonists must represent well-entrenched forces . . . and the issues must have profound meaning to them.[6]

While external forces did contribute to the establishment of both systems, it must also be remembered that it was the Indians and Germans who made the decisions and worked out the compromises which produced their constitutions. The British made a rapid departure from India with the transfer of authority; and although the Allies carefully reconstructed local and *Land* governments on democratic lines during 1945–49, had final approval of the German Basic Law, and maintained a veto over certain aspects of German affairs until sovereignty was granted in 1955, the Allied occupation lasted only ten years. In both cases the democratic process could have eroded once they were gone.

Perhaps the most striking contrast politically in 1947/49, which might be interpreted to have somewhat righted the disequilibrium between the two countries, should be cited: India made the transfer to

[6] Dankwart A. Rustow, "Transitions to Democracy: Toward a Dynamic Model," *Comparative Politics,* II, No. 3 (April 1970), p. 352.

independence with functioning democratic political institutions at both the Centre and in the States, based on the 1935 Government of India Act; West Germany's independence followed close on the heels of the Basic Law's ratification, almost concurrent with the setting up of the central government, and thus may more closely represent a case of "instant democracy."

Political Prelude

The performance of the national leader in the primarily political function of heading a democratic government is conditioned not only by contemporary circumstances and institutional framework but by his personality and previous experience as well. For this, childhood and early public life may well constitute the prelude to the main political performance.

CHILDHOOD AND FAMILY

Although armchair excursions into psychoanalysis may be risky, for the political scientist to ignore the man and concentrate exclusively on leadership in relation to its political context comes dangerously close to eviscerating the politician and might be equally prone to distortion of ultimate conclusions. Without succumbing to tendencies toward "oddity makes the leader" theories, one might simply observe the obvious: the interaction of personality with reality largely determines the individual's expectations and hence influences his performance in any specific situation. For the individual the route from cradle to grave may be viewed as a continuing political process of multiple interaction on various levels. The process may thus start in the childhood home, not merely with transmission of attitudes and values, but more importantly, through daily interaction with family members in the informal, rudimentary acquisition of expectations, approaches and techniques for dealing with authority, assembling power, confronting those who differ and circumventing obstacles. The thesis put forth by Storr [7] holds that for the child's innate aggressive drive to develop creatively rather than pathologically the relationship with the parents must allow disciplined assertion of independence and expression of difference without threat of personal rejection or loss of his security in the family, also contains significant

[7] Anthony Storr, *Human Aggression* (New York, 1968).

implications for democratic politics. Similarly, Almond and Verba [8] illustrate the significance of the family in political socialization, with adult attitudes such as trust or apprehensiveness of strangers, willingness to express one's views in political discussions, and response to opposition (essential ingredients for democracy) closely related to home experience.

Comparison of the family environment and early public life of Adenauer and Nehru with their conduct as Chancellor and Prime Minister reveals that methods and approaches in dealing with political situations, as well as social attitudes and political philosophy, can be traced to influences in this period. Although distinctly different in personality, with sharply contrasting family backgrounds, there are certain similarities in both which had a perhaps more significant bearing on the way in which the two men functioned as political leaders.

The Adenauer-Nehru family environments contrasted not so much in the element of East and West as in their social, economic, and cultural content. Yet in many respects this difference peculiarly suited each man for his role as head of government in the socioeconomic circumstances of his country at independence. Born in Cologne in 1876, Konrad Adenauer was the third son (and one of four children) of a solid, middle-class Rhineland family. His father, a secretary at the district court in Cologne, had received only primary education and worked as a farm hand and in a brickyard before enlisting in the Prussian Army in order to qualify for the Civil Service. Distinguishing himself in the Battle of Königgrätz, he was one of two privates honored by promotion to lieutenant, but later had to leave the service to marry because his future bride's father, a bank clerk in Cologne, could not afford the bond required of an officer's bride.[9] By sharp contrast, Jawaharel Nehru, twelve years younger than Adenauer, was born into the Indian aristocracy, the only son (and oldest of three children) of an affluent, influential, and politically prominent Kashmiri Brahmin family. His father, Motilal, a prominent barrister, "dean" of the Allahabad High Court legal profession, a leader of the Congress Party, and one of its important financial contributors was

[8] Gabriel A. Almond and Sidney Verba, *The Civic Culture—Political Attitudes and Democracy in Five Nations,* The Little, Brown Series in Comparative Politics (Boston, 1965), pp. 284–87.

[9] Paul Weymar, *Adenauer—His Authorized Biography,* tr. Peter DeMendelssohn (New York, 1957), p. 17.

an urbane, cultured man who had amassed a fortune and made his home a center of social and political activity.[10]

Whereas the Adenauers lived modestly in Cologne in a small house three windows wide and supplemented the family income by renting half of the first floor and all of the second to various tenants,[11] the Nehrus lived lavishly (until joining Gandhi in the 1920s) in a palatial home (with indoor swimming pool and electric lights—"an innovation for Allahabad in those days" [12]) located in a predominantly British section on the outskirts of Allahabad. An admirer of the British,[13] Motilal adopted a life style more British than Indian, and Jawaharlal, who did not wear Indian dress until he joined Gandhi at thirty, was educated at home by English governesses and tutors until, at fifteen, he went to England to attend Harrow, graduate in natural science from Trinity College, Cambridge, and read law at the Inner Temple, London. Though the Adenauers' three sons received university educations, this was achieved through personal sacrifice by the parents, frugal planning, careful management, and the cooperation of the sons, who were expected to place in their mother's housekeeping fund money earned at coaching and tutoring while attending the Gymnasium.[14] Even so, shortage of funds by the time Konrad was ready to go the university and his father's belief that he was better qualified for business, almost dashed his hopes of becoming a lawyer. His obedient but painful attempt at apprenticing in a banking firm convinced his father of his error,[15] and the family managed a meager allowance to support his study for three years at the universities of Freiburg, Munich, and Bonn.

Aside from material aspects, Nehru's environment was a cosmopolitan blend of East and West, with a strong secular orientation, while Adenauer's was parochial, Rhineland-centered, and devoutly Catholic. Though the chief intellectual influence of the Nehru home politically was British liberalism, the chief cultural influence was Moghul. Motilal knew Persian and Arabic better than Sanskrit and Hindi (which he disdained), and Jawaharlal grew up more proficient in Urdu than Hindi,[16] though English was in fact his "mother tongue."

[10] For a fuller account of Nehru's family see Michael Brecher, *Nehru: A Political Biography* (London, 1959) and Jawaharlal Nehru, *An Autobiography* (orig. ed. 1936; Bombay, 1962).

[11] Weymar, p. 15.   [12] Nehru, *An Autobiography*, p. 12.

[13] Brecher, *Nehru*, p. 37.   [14] Weymar, p. 16.   [15] *Ibid.*, pp. 20–21.

[16] Brecher, *Nehru*, p. 42.

He was liberally educated in Indian history and classics, both Sanskrit and Moghul, as well as the philosophy, history, and science of the West. Before becoming Prime Minister in 1947 Nehru had not only visited historical centers in India and spent seven years as a student in England, but had also lived almost two years in Switzerland during the 1930s, traveled extensively in Europe several times, and visited the USSR. Adenauer, on the other hand, traveled little in Germany, except for studying at Freiberg and Munich plus a year working in Berlin, while his only reported travel beyond Germany before becoming Chancellor at seventy-two was for vacations in Switzerland and to Northern Italy and Austria when he was a student in Munich.

The broadly secular atmosphere of Nehru's childhood, encouraged by the mix of Hindu and Muslim culture, was reinforced by the combined effects of his father's relaxed attitude toward religion and his mother's Hindu orthodoxy. Though religious rites and festivals were observed, and his father followed Hindu family and social customs in respect for his wife, the lack of formal religious orientation left Nehru free to explore religion for himself. His observations produced a distaste for the "superstitious practices and dogmatic belief" of organized religion and an " [incapability] of thinking of a deity or of any unknown supreme power in anthropomorphic terms," [17] which led in adult life to a profoundly spiritual agnosticism. Adenauer by contrast came from a devoutly religious family which joined in morning and evening prayers daily (as well as in family tragedy),[18] and attended church twice on Sundays. Moreover, those closest to him seem also to have been religiously oriented: his only close friend in school became Abbot of the Monastery of Maria Laach (where Adenauer spent some time in hiding during the Nazi regime); his brother, Hans, became influential in the Rhineland Catholic Church as Dean of the Cologne Cathedral; and a neighbor with whom he engaged in political discussions during the "Rhöndorf interlude" of isolation under the Nazis, held firm convictions that politics must be related to Christian principles.

The free-ranging nature of Nehru's early education, plus the fact

[17] *Ibid.*, p. 600.

[18] See Adenauer's account of the death of his youngest sister: His father's conduct seems to have made a deep impression on the six-year-old boy and is reflected in his own behavior during the death of an infant son in 1920. Weymar, pp. 18 and 60.

that the aesthetically inclined boy was exposed to both Indian and Western history, literature, religion, as well as science and socioeconomic thought, not only through the educational process but in his home environment, had three major consequences for the future politician. It encouraged, first, an eclectic tendency to combine not only elements of East and West but those of different doctrines and beliefs as well, which was subsequently reflected in his approach to religion, economics, and political philosophy. Second, his outlook combined a synthesis of East and West, tradition and modernity, which made him part of two worlds but never quite at one with either and placed him at the leading edge of the new India from the late 1920s until shortly before his death in 1964, after seventeen years as Prime Minister. And, third, raised in an atmosphere of British–Moghul-Hindu culture with a minimal emphasis on religion, he developed a strongly secular outlook which enabled him to stand above the communal conflict which accompanied partition to become the major champion of India's Muslims and symbol of India as a secular state.

The impact of home environment is equally evident in Adenauer's behavior as politician and Chancellor. Just as family life was planned and ordered so that seemingly impossible goals might be attained, Adenauer as Chief Mayor of Cologne established the famous "green belt" and revitalized the city's cultural and economic life to make it a German showplace. Patience, one of the first lessons learned from his father and early experimentation with horticulture,[19] determination to succeed in any task undertaken, and careful budgeting of time and energy were all traits learned in youth which became characteristic of his later conduct, whether in office or during the twelve years (in retirement at Rhöndorf, in hiding or prison) under the Nazi regime. Finally, for Adenauer religion not only became an inner resource in personal and public life but also provided the basis for his political philosophy.

Despite the more obvious dissimilarities, Adenauer's childhood family experience was surprisingly similar to Nehru's in certain respects which could have been the genesis of their attitudes and modes of operation as democratic political leaders. A lively concern for the child's best interests was a distinctive characteristic of both families. The atmosphere of security, acceptance as an individual, love, pride in family and its members' accomplishments, and responsibility to others (approximating conditions suggested by Storr and Almond/

[19] *Ibid.,* pp. 15–16.

Verba) was conducive to creating self-assurance, respect for authority, and tolerance of opposition in political life.

The father was dominant in both households, but the mother exercised considerable influence, exhibited strong character and played a
significant supportive role for husband and children. Though Adenauer and Nehru looked to their fathers as models, they viewed them
as examples, not "idols." The relationship between father and son
was constructive in both cases; there is no evidence of suppression or
abnormal tension, fear, antagonism, jealousy. The quiet, matter-of-
fact courage in personal tragedy, the self-control and resilience, the
devotion to family, and the sense of responsibility of the elder Adenauer made a deep impression on the son. When, as Chief Mayor of
Cologne (with the city in chaos after the 1918 rebellion and Germany's World War I defeat), Adenauer made the statement that
"Times of political catastrophe are especially suitable for new creative ventures," [20] he not only reflected the object lessons learned from
his father but prophesied the posture of the future Chancellor in establishing the Bonn Republic.

In his autobiography, Nehru relates having "admired [his] father
tremendously" and yet being "afraid" of his fierce temper: to the
small boy

He seemed . . . the embodiment of strength and courage and cleverness,
far above all other men I saw; and I treasured the hope that when I grew
up I would be rather like him. But much as I admired and loved him I
feared him also. I had seen him losing his temper at servants and others
and he seemed to me terrible then and I shivered with fright, sometimes
mixed with *resentment*, at the *treatment* of a servant.[21]

But "fear" did not alienate him; Motilal (and later Gandhi) became
his closest confidant in adult life. Perhaps the key is in the words *resentment* and *treatment;* the boy's resentment shows refusal to be
cowed, and its direction against the *treatment,* rather than the *father,*
is characteristic of the future national leader's ability to distinguish
adversary from act in any dispute. Of a more sensitive nature than
his father, Jawaharlal was also heir to his volatile temper, a fact which
might have constituted a bond of understanding. Moreover, Motilal's
"amazing love for his children," [22] "his exquisite and delightful
deference to youth," and his "tolerance toward his political

[20] *Ibid.*, p. 63.   [21] Nehru, *An Autobiography*, p. 7. Italics added.
[22] Krishna Nehru Hutheesingh, *With No Regrets*, pp. 95–97, cited in
Brecher, *Nehru*, p. 40.

enemies," [23] (words which could later have described India's first Prime Minister) encouraged a close, but politically at times combative, comradeship between father and son.

Though the fathers were dominant, they were not tyrants; though the sons were obedient and respectful, they did not lack spirit and minds of their own. Available evidence indicates an atmosphere conducive to the development of independent thought and expression. The example of the Adenauer family council to decide whether or not to forgo meat on several Sundays in order to afford a Christmas tree and candles; the fact that Nehru was able to differ with his father on political issues without jeopardizing their personal relationship; the strong supportive roles of the mothers (Adenauer's mother earned extra money sewing; Nehru's—petite, beautiful, and fragile —participated in nonviolent demonstrations), and the fact that the family members were expected to work together; all suggest a disciplined freedom of expression and participation which might have predisposed both men to a type of leadership which encouraged open dissent, bargaining, conciliation, and cooperation under strong leadership.

EARLY PUBLIC LIFE

Both Adenauer and Nehru practiced law after completing their university studies. While this period proved a further training ground and steppingstone for the future Chancellor, Nehru's experience had no significant impact on his subsequent career. Although entering practice in 1912 under the aegis of his father (who was "acknowledged leader" of the Allahabad High Court and envisioned his son's succeeding him), Nehru did not distinguish himself during seven years of practice and rarely pleaded a case before the court.[24] After London he found the law and lawyers in Allahabad stultifying, while his natural reticence to speak in public made the arguing of cases which did not capture his imagination uninviting. Adenauer, on the other hand, "loved his work" and won an impressive reputation for his success in pleading cases within a few years after being offered a position in the offices of *Justizrat* Kausen, one of Cologne's most distinguished civil lawyers and leader of the *Zentrum* (Catholic Center Party) in the Cologne City Council. It was during this period that

[23] Extracts from an unpublished memoir of Sir Frederick James (Finance Member, Viceroy's Executive Council), cited in Brecher, *Nehru,* p. 39.

[24] Brecher, *Nehru,* p. 53, and Nehru, *An Autobiography,* pp. 28–29.

Adenauer learned—primarily from Kausen—to present a complicated issue in simple terms with an argument based on a massive
compilation of facts. According to an observer at the time:

He had no brilliant oratory but . . . an enormously effective way of convincing people with the sheer weight of his sober and factual arguments
. . . this peculiar eloquence . . . worked like quiet and persistent rain
which gently and stubbornly soaked every objection and counterargument
until they simply disintegrated.[25]

Perfected during his years as Chief Mayor of Cologne, this technique
became his stock-in-trade after 1945 both in domestic politics and in
negotiating with the Allies.

Adenauer and Nehru entered politics with influential backing. But
whereas Adenauer's political career was launched as a result of his
own bold initiative, Nehru moved gradually into the politics of the
Indian National Congress as the result of the politicized home atmosphere and the increasing personal appeal of the Nationalist movement. As an assistant judge in the Cologne district court, Adenauer
learned, in 1906, that the office of adjunct in the Cologne city government was open and that a young judge from Saarbrücken was
being considered. With the self-assurance bordering on audacity
which became characteristic, Adenauer walked into the office of his
former employer, Kausen, (who "practically dominated the city parliament" as leader of the *Zentrum*) and asked: "Why not take me,
Herr Justizrat? I'm sure I'm as good as the other fellow." With powerful *Zentrum* backing through Kausen's sponsorship and good
connections with the Liberal Party through the influential Wallraf
family to whom his wife of four years was related, Adenauer was
elected Junior Adjunct by the Municipal Council with a vote of 35
out of a possible 37.[26]

But while Adenauer's move into Cologne politics had an aura of
rational calculation and decisiveness which were to become trade-
marks, Nehru's plunge into active participation in the Indian Nationalist movement contained an emotional component which was also
evidenced in his conduct as Prime Minister. The congruence of two
events (plus his boredom with law practice) provided the impetus
which prompted Nehru at thirty to give up law and take an increasingly active and vital part in the Congress Party. The Amritzar Mas-
sacre following promulgation of the repressive Rowlatt Act of

[25] Weymar, p. 25.   [26] *Ibid.,* p. 28.

1919, which assaulted much of the liberal philosophy he had learned from the British, and the emergence of Gandhi on the Indian political scene with his concept of *Satyagraha,* combined to crystallize Nehru's more revolutionary inclinations and provide an acceptable means of expression which was feasible in the Indian context.[27] But when he took the plunge, he began "at a fairly high level," [28] with the support of Motilal and Gandhi.

Comparison of Adenauer's experience as Chief Mayor of Cologne (1916–33) [29] and Nehru's as an architect of the Indian struggle for independence (1919–47) shows patterns for meeting political situations and managing people which were later applied when they became heads of government. Though their experience differed in scope, specifics of circumstance and tactics, their techniques of political contention within the constitutional or institutional framework were basically the same.

Called by his critics "Utopian" and a "reckless and wild speculator," Adenauer's greatest achievement as mayor—the conversion of Cologne into a modern cultural, educational, and commercial center —was accomplished by sheer political craftmanship through persistent engagement with a cost-conscious, reluctant city parliament. Success in winning parliamentary support for his programs rested on his resourceful blending of personality attributes with his most outstanding skill to accomplish political ends. First: "his real strength," according to a life-long critic, "lay in his ability to influence individuals . . . generally considered cold, reserved and unfeeling . . . Rather, he possesses the remarkable gift of generating warmth and friendliness in precisely the direction where he senses his own advantage." [30]

[27] Brecher, *Nehru,* pp. 62–67; and Nehru, *An Autobiography,* pp. 40–41.

[28] Nehru to M. Brecher in New Delhi on January 30, 1958; Brecher, *Nehru,* p. 1.

[29] Summary of Adenauer's political activity: 1913/16, Bürgermeister, Cologne; 1915/33, Oberbürgermeister, Cologne until dismissed by Nazis; 1926/33, President, Prussian States Ministry; 1926, twice considered for Chancellor but he rejected bids on grounds not politically feasible to function under conditions proposed. Post-World War II: 1945, Oberbürgermeister, Cologne, for brief period (appointed by Americans as they took Rhine area but dismissed by British); 1945–49, devoted time to organization of CDU and reestablishment of German Government, chairman Rhineland CDU and British Zone CDU, representative on British Zone Advisory Council; 1948–49, President, Parliamentary Council (which drafted Basic Law), negotiator with the Allies.

[30] Robert Görlinger, Socialist opponent of Adenauer, later Mayor of Cologne, cited in Weymar, p. 72.

Second: employing the style of advocacy which had brought success at court, he "contrived to get his views accepted, using perfectly constitutional means in gradually reducing a reluctant or hostile majority and winning it over to his side." [31] But he did not stop there; Adenauer, the master of "parliamentary artistry," [32] was also the master politician: Municipal councilors were invited individually for a glass of wine, accompanied by his persuasive arguments; "a special point" [33] was made to invite opposition members to his house, where they were exposed to his "hard to resist" personal charm; debate on legislation was skillfully stage-managed; and favors were accorded the faithful. The action was kept within constitutional confines, but the limits were subject to perhaps more than a two-way stretch; the contest was goal-oriented (Adenauer managed the goals) and persistently pursued, but utilized accepted democratic political procedures. "Occasionally his patience snapped" [34] and Adenauer presented parliament with a *fait accompli* (e.g., the "green belt"); but one's impression is that Adenauer the politician so enjoyed the sportsmanship of the political game that "Adenauer the autocrat" did not assume the upper hand.

By the time he received the reins of government from the British in 1947, as Vice President of the Interim Government's Executive Council, Nehru had held every major office in the Congress Party (more than once),[35] served similarly on the Provincial level, had been a member of the Congress Working Committee (High Command) for almost twenty years, taken part in election campaigns and acquired some practical experience in local government as chairman of the Allahabad Municipality. He had formed the Congress Center Party and, with Jayaprakash Narayan, led the formation of a socialist group within Congress. A skillful reconciler of divergent views, he effected the compromise between the No-and-Pro-Changers in 1923 and was mediator between the Left and Right from the mid-1930s on. If Gandhi established the methods and built the bond between urban workers and peasants, it was Nehru who set the large goals, brought the middle class, intellectuals, and youth to the Congress, and

[31] Dr. Willi Suth, Adenauer's brother-in-law (City Treasurer of Cologne), cited in Weymar, p. 63.
[32] Görlinger, *ibid.,* p. 70.   [33] *Ibid.,* p. 72.   [34] Suth, *ibid.,* p. 64.
[35] General Secretary, 1924, 1928; President, 1929, 1930, 1936, 1946; member, Working Committee, 1923-on, except for a brief period when he resigned; also held presidency of All-India Board Volunteer Organization and All-India Trades Union Congress.

organized the peasants. Favored of Gandhi, yet critical of him at times,[36] Nehru opposed him on Dominion Status in 1929–30 and led the forces which brought about adoption of full independence as the Congress goal, as well as on defense measures in World War II. He had the vision to place India's independence struggle in a global context and became Congress foreign policy spokesman. Owing to Nehru's foresight in the 1930s India (unique among developing countries) entered independence with a commitment to and an embryonic plan for social and economic modernization. He represented Congress in negotiations with the British between 1942 and 1947 and it was largely due to him (with the support of Sardar Patel) that the Attlee Plan and Lord Mountbatten's suggestion for Partition were finally accepted in 1947.

Revolutionary in objective, Congress was democratic and evolutionary in methods. Its organization was highly centralized and disciplined (although discipline periodically broke down—to Nehru's lament—under pressure of dissident groups, leading to a cyclical pattern of fission and fusion); but the process was democratic, characterized by reciprocal action of pressure and resistance between dissidents and High Command which ultimately gave way to bargaining, negotiation, concession, compromise, conciliation, and consensus. The struggle with the British, moreover, was one of political confrontation and endless negotiation, compatible with the democratic process. Not only was Nehru exposed to the Congress system, he in large measure contributed to its development. And though his rise to the pinnacle of Congress leadership was eased by being the favored of Gandhi, he ran the tortuous course through contending forces of conservatives, liberals, and Gandhi to secure adoption of his views and ultimate leadership after independence.

Thus both men had accumulated thirty years of practical political experience before assuming office as chief executive in new democratic states. Nehru, leader of the underdeveloped Asian nation, had had more extensive experience at the national level, in political mobilization, party organization, and extension of political participation, than had the Western Adenauer, the major portion of whose experience had been provincial and who engaged in party organization only in establishing the CDU between 1945 and 1949. Adenauer, on the other hand, had had more intensive experience with executive-

[36] Jawaharlal Nehru, *A Bunch of Old Letters* (Bombay, 1958), pp. 56–58, 74–75, 254–56, and *An Autobiography*, pp. 504–28.

legislative interaction. In both cases, personality traits combined with approaches and skills learned through past experience were converted during this period into effective instruments for persuasive political combat.

The National Leader

"A true Renaissance Man": with Nehru the description referred to the aesthetic, many-faceted political intellectual; with Adenauer it was used by critics in a Machiavellian sense. Though such caricatures do not represent the whole man, they do spotlight the points at which the Chancellor and Prime Minister differed most. More important, however, were politically significant, convergent personal characteristics.

PERSONAL CHARACTERISTICS, POLITICAL THOUGHT, AND STYLE

Contrasts in personality tended to affect the tone, emphasis, and effectiveness of action rather than mode of operations. An austere, taciturn, and sturdy Chancellor starkly contrasted with a suave, spontaneous, almost-charismatic Prime Minister. Adenauer was self-assured, emotionally controlled, disciplined in personal and public life, decisive in thought and action. Rare to exhibit emotion, he became "icy when furious." Instances of "tantrums" are said to have been acts for effect.[37] A more complex personality, Nehru was a collection of contradictions. He was self-assured, but reticent; disciplined in ordering work and private life, but unable to bridle a mercurial temper; an admirer of rationality, yet apt to respond emotionally; tolerant of political opponents, but impatient with lack of order in coworkers; lucid in thought, decisive on major policy directions, he was also indecisive and vacillating (as procrastination over linguistic States reorganization illustrated). Whereas Adenauer could separate personal relationships from evaluation of a man's usefulness under changing political imperatives (e.g., his dismissal of Gustave Heinemann, Minister of the Interior), Nehru's heart was apt to rule his head (only great public pressure forced him to reassign Defense Minister Krishna Menon after the Chinese invasion of India).

Both Adenauer and Nehru shared characteristics which might have

[37] A Federal Republic official who wishes to remain anonymous; in interview, January 17, 1970, New York City.

significantly influenced their orientation as establishers of new democratic systems of government. Both men blended a high degree of optimism with a basically realistic, pragmatic approach to life and politics. Strong characters, individualistic, with dominant personalities,
they displayed courage, stamina, adaptability, and resilience in political situations. Initiators, synthesizers, and experimenters, they held
strong views, but were flexible, if forceful, actors. Aloof and de-
tached, they were intensely involved. Capable of affability, warmth,
and disarming charm, they could withdraw to a cool armor of re-
serve, had few friends, and found sanctuary and emotional satisfaction in close family relationships. Devoted to wives and children,
strict allotment of time for family was balanced with an acute sense
of public responsibility. Though economical in emotional expenditure outside the family, they were keenly attuned to human need and
spent emotional energy on larger groups or issues rather than individuals. They enjoyed verbal sparring and respected strong men with
realistic, firmly held ideas. Ambitious in the sense of seeking satisfaction in successful accomplishment of tasks undertaken, they
seemed to find personal extension and expansion in politics; neither
appeared in quest of power for itself or for self-aggrandizement.
Imaginative and practical, their vision transcended immediate problems and they were adept at meshing future vision with present political reality.

Political philosophy may provide the basis for a national leader's
political action, may be the pattern for the design he wants to work
out through politics, or may constitute the window dressing to project
an image which will magnetize popular support. Or it may be an as-
semblage of values, standards, and convictions—derived from observation and experience, molded by inclinations of personality—which
form touchstones for flexibly developed policy and a framework for
action beyond the margins of which authority must not encroach.
Adenauer and Nehru fall within the last category. Both had firmly
held but generally defined political values, but they were not doctri-
naire in their beliefs. They held firm, broadly sketched, long-range
goals and intermediate objectives about which they could be more
flexible. More concerned with action in terms of urgent, concrete
realities than with the profundities of ideology, neither had a systematic *Weltanschauung.* It has been said of Nehru: "Pragmatism looms
very large in his thought, as it does in his approach to his decisions,
[he] does not cling to ideas *per se* but views them in a social setting

. . . [and] is brilliant in adjusting them to different circumstances." [38] The same could have been said of the German Chancellor.

Konrad Adenauer was a political realist guided by broadly defined Christian and humanitarian principles. Two main influences seem to have molded his political thought: 1) his devout religious background and 2) his optimistic, pragmatic realism. The religion rooted in childhood blended with the experience of the practical politician dealing with the realities of city government were molded during the Nazi period (at Rhöndorf and Maria Laach) by reflection on religion and politics. He believed that the highest value must be placed on the individual; that Christian ethics, to which the individual is central, must form the basis of political democracy; that "democracy was the only political system allowing the individual a maximum of freedom and initiative." [39] But if religion formed a broad frame of reference, he was not dogmatic: Guided by Terence's "I am a man; I count nothing human indifferent to me," [40] he also believed that God gave man a mind to think with and hands and arms to use; that

If one does not want to go from failure to failure in politics, one must keep to what is possible. It would be absurd to neglect the possible because it did not correspond to high-pitched ideal demands.[41]

As an optimist, he believed life could gradually be improved, obstacles circumvented, goals approximated; as a realist, he accepted existing conditions and institutional limitations as the framework for action; and as a pragmatist, he manipulated conditions, maneuvered limitations, accepted half-loaves which would approximate major objectives. Fiercely anti-Communist, he was widely flexible in combining elements of socialism with free enterprise, though rigid in his conviction that power should not be amassed in any one center.

Freedom of the individual was similarly central to Nehru's thought, though he arrived by a different route. The socialist, agnostic symbol of a modern, secular India, came remarkably close to the German Christian Democrat when he said:

ultimately it is the individual that counts . . . the idea that appeals to me without belief, the old *Hindu idea* that *if there is any divine*

[38] Brecher, *Nehru,* p. 601.   [39] Suth, quoted in Weymar, p. 64.
[40] Adenauer, quoted, *ibid.,* p. 11.
[41] Adenauer, quoted in "Deutsche Korespondenz," December 22, 1964, Archives, German Information Center, New York City.

essence in the world every individual posesses a bit of it . . . and
*he can develop it. Therefore, no individual is trivial. Every in-
dividual has importance and he should be given full opportunities to
develop.*[42]

His political thought [43] was a Smorgasbord of ideas drawn from
classical liberalism, humanism, Fabian Socialism, Gandhism, Marxism, the Hindu *Vedanta,* and Buddhism, as well as study and observation of Indian and European historical and contemporary realities.[44] Strongly attracted to Marxism, an admirer of Soviet rapid
development, he summarily rejected Communism for its totalitarianism and use of violence.[45] Social and economic improvement could
and must be reached through democratic means to preserve individual freedom of initiative and choice. "Temperamentally and by training . . . an individualist and intellectually a Socialist," [46] he believed
planning and state-ownership should be used to advance socioeconomic development, but socialism *per se* was not the goal. He saw,
with Adenauer, danger in overconcentration of power: he "[did] not
want State Socialism of the extreme kind in which the State [47] is all
powerful. . . . The State is very powerful politically. If you . . .
make it very powerful economically also it would become a mere
conglomeration of authority." He found doctrine intellectually con-
fining and unrealistic; above all, he was skeptical, experimental: "We
have to learn from practical experience and proved in our own
way." [48] Like Adenauer, he was committed to representative democracy,[49] not through sentimental or Utopian idealism but for the practical reason that no other system had proved capable of both maxi-

[42] Nehru, quoted in Brecher, *Nehru,* p. 607. Italics added.

[43] See M. N. Das, *The Political Philosophy of Jawaharlal Nehru* (London,
1961); and Brecher, *Nehru,* pp. 125–26 and 598–608.

[44] See, for example, Jawaharlal Nehru, *The Discovery of India* (New York,
1948); *Glimpses of World History* (New York, 1948); and *An Autobiography.*

[45] Das, pp. 105–6; Nehru, *Glimpses of World History,* pp. 820–27; 843–50;
851–65; and Brecher, *Nehru,* p. 126.

[46] Brecher, *Nehru,* p. 606.

[47] For discussion of Nehru's views on "The State, Government, and the Individual," see Das, pp. 168–88.

[48] Nehru, quoted in Brecher, *Nehru,* p. 532.

[49] For discussion of Nehru's views on democracy, see Das, pp. 94–124;
Brecher, *Nehru,* p. 602; and *Jawaharlal Nehru's Speeches,* March 1953–
August 1957 (The Publication Division, Ministry of Information and Broad-
casting, Government of India, 1958), III, 154–58.

mizing individual freedom and achieving social and economic modernization.

When they assumed the helm of government and responsibility for navigating new democratic systems through the formative years, Nehru and Adenauer were equipped with a full complement of political techniques, attitudes, and approaches which could be adjusted to evolving circumstances. Moreover, neither was burdened with an excessive amount of ideological baggage. Their styles of leadership, remarkably similar in major respects, reflected their personalities, previous experience, and political thought in the way they interpreted their roles as chief executive and related to the individuals, institutions, and circumstances forming the framework within which they functioned. Combining strong, authoritative leadership with bargaining politics, they had fixed objectives, maintained tactical flexibility, and saw themselves in contention with other forces for adoption of policies. Emphasis was on persuasion through accepted political processes; both scrupulously acted within constitutional limits to reach consensus, though they interpreted their powers broadly. Criticized for by-passing Party, Cabinet, and Parliament as policy-forming organs, it is more significant for democratic development that they regularly used Cabinets as consultative councils and sounding-boards for hammering out policy directions (though they reserved the right to make final decisions); and that both regularly engaged in parliamentary debate and exposed themselves to often scathing criticism. Though they relied on outside advisers, rather than solely on their ministers, Adenauer respected ministers who were hard fighters with cogent arguments,[50] while Nehru was influenced by intellectual prowess of men such as Krishna Menon. Politicians and manipulators rather than charismatic leaders, they derived major support from their parties; but whereas Adenauer held firm (if not absolute) control over the CDU as chairman, Nehru used his indispensability as a Congress vote-getter to bend the conservative-controlled party machine. Consequently, Adenauer stressed behind-the-scenes negotiation with elites [51] (in the CDU, government coalition and nongovern-

[50] A Federal Republic official who wishes to remain anonymous; in interview, January 17, 1970, New York City.

[51] Lewis J. Edinger, *Kurt Schumacher: A Study in Personality and Political Behavior* (Stanford, Calif., 1965), p. 217; Edinger, *Politics in GERMANY— Attitudes and Processes.* The Little, Brown Series in Comparative Politics (Boston, 1968), p. 212.

mental groups) and limited public appeals in press interviews in instances when such pressure seemed necessary to move elites; whereas Nehru reaffirmed his mass popularity in frequent talks with peasant and other groups to reinforce his position. Both aggregated power by acting as reconcilers and mediators among divergent groups.

The blending of authoritative leadership with marketplace politics conducted within the established institutional framework, constituted a synthesis of traditional attitudes toward authority with new democratic institutions. It infused the new system with basic democratic processes, but also provided a bridge between past habits and future attitudes for acceptance of the political system. Thus it satisfied both the need for authority and the need to perform in a manner which would habituate political actors and citizens to the ways of democracy.

The Action: Stability and Dissent

As chief executives of new democracies Adenauer and Nehru faced the paradox of reconciling two immediate needs: to establish national political stability and to guarantee free expression of dissent. A sustained period of dynamic stability is required if democracy is to survive; for only through proved performance in satisfying pressing economic and social needs can public expectations be met and citizens become accustomed to the democratic process as an acceptable means of improving their lives. Yet, as Rustow points out,

Only by means of dissension can democracy become a learning and a problem-solving process, a way of finding proximate solutions to insoluble questions. Only through continual expression of disagreement by sharply rivaling groups can political participation be maximized and political equality thus approximated.[52]

As a safety valve for potential political frustration, expression of dissent may, in fact, contribute to stability [53] in the period of establishment; but habits learned in opposing the old regime, combined with

[52] Dankwart A. Rustow, *A World of Nations—Problems of Political Modernization* (Washington, D.C., 1967), p. 234.

[53] For discussion of democracy and political development, see Lucian W. Pye, *Aspects of Political Development,* The Little, Brown Series in Comparative Politics (Boston, 1966), pp. 71–88.

fragmentation of political opposition, may inhibit growth of a responsible dissent-compromise-consensus pattern, obstruct enactment of urgent socioeconomic measures and lead to political instability and discredit of the system. The democratic establisher thus faces a third "imperative" [54] equally fertile with seeds of democracy's destruction: the consolidation of sufficient power to manage the forces of stability and dissent and remain in power long enough both to effect his primary objectives and establish identity with the democratic system, not merely state or nation. In order to attempt to determine how they may have contributed to the establishment of democratic systems in Germany and India let us focus on Adenauer's and Nehru's performance in six areas, all democratic requisites, the management of which could have substantially influenced growth of stability and dissent.

NEW NATIONAL IMAGE

How its citizens perceive the political system of a new state depends largely on the imprint made by the "establisher." In this respect Nehru and Adenauer performed dual functions: the embodiment of national tradition, they linked past to future hope; formulators and principal conveyors of a new national image, they set the direction the political system would take.

A solid, middle-class product of the Empire, successful Weimar politician, untainted by Naziism, Adenauer represented to the bulk of older Germans the best of a shaken tradition. In "Der Alte" the majority could see the father image compatible with German patterns of authority confidently embarked on a second German democratic experiment; his fortitude and belief in the future provided a steadying influence at a time of social, economic, and political uncertainty. With Empire roots, Adenauer was also a twentieth-century politician. His engagement in the political marketplace of democracy, advocacy of the Common Market, and sights set on a new Germany as an integral force in a United Europe gave youth twin goals of dynamic economic progress and a significant stake in the future. His emphasis on pride in the German people (rather than state or nation), their courage, industriousness, and capacity for economic ac-

---

[54] For discussion of the need of leaders of new states to stay in power with enough authority to carry out their programs, see W. Howard Wriggins, *The Ruler's Imperative—Strategies for Political Survival in Asia and Africa* (New York, 1969).

complishment, as well as on Germany as an outpost of Western democracy, deflected the old urge toward nationalism to a new pride in economic achievement and identity with the democratic West European community.

Nehru's syncretic personality, aristocratic bearing, and role in leading India to independence similarly provided the formula necessary to link the past to the future in order to stabilize the changing present. He was the modern "prince" of Indian tradition, the symbol of Western science, humanism and secularism, the architect of Indian modernization. His complex personality was a magnetic binding force for diverse strands of Indian political life. Older politicians of the independence movement, youth, businessmen, peasants, intellectuals, conservatives and liberals, traditionalists and modernizers, Hindus and Muslims, all found something with which to identify. The "single personal focus of loyalty, symbolic of national unity," [55] he used this power to project the new image of India. His "conversations" with the masses (or political actors) [56] urged them to draw strength from Indian tradition, including democratic elements, in order to build together a modern, secular democratic India as part of a new world order.

A NATIONAL HETEROGENEOUS POLITICAL PARTY

If the "essence of democracy is the reconciliation of dissension" [57] and the democratic process is to work, the field of conflict must be channeled so that bargaining which will lead to agreement can effectively take place. To avoid the debilitating donnybrook of multiparty systems seen in Weimar and the French Fourth Republic, the existence of at least one political party which encompasses politically significant heterogeneous segments of society could satisfy the dual needs for dissent and stability by narrowing the range of political choice while providing a vehicle for participation.

The Congress Party in India and the Christian Democratic Union (CDU) in Germany are such amalgams of disparate political and social interests. National parties organized to the local level, they are

[55] Rupert Emerson, citing the apparent need "of newly rising people" for personal leadership, in *From Empire to Nation—The Rise to Self-Assertion of Asian and African Peoples* (Boston, 1967), p. 281.

[56] See, for example, speech to Lok Sabha, March 28, 1957, in *Jawaharlal Nehru's Speeches*, III, 156.

[57] Rustow, *A World of Nations*, p. 234.

essentially conservative-moderate, but have significant liberal-left and less influential right wing components. They constitute umbrellas for state organizations with different socioeconomic and regional interests.

Nehru and Adenauer contributed to the nature of the parties in the formative years and, by acting as mediators and aggregators of diverse groups after becoming chief executive, helped to offset the fissiparous tendencies characteristic of both countries. Both sought to maintain broadbased, nonideological parties attractive to forces which might otherwise lead to an atomized, ineffectual multiparty system. Nehru's tolerance of intraparty opposition, emphasis on cooperation, and ability to find common ground for action reconciled factions which might have added to India's party proliferation.[58] Moreover, the fact that Nehruvian socialism (pragmatic rather than ideological) was pressed to a lesser or greater extent as circumstances allowed and gradually grafted to a conservative Congress machine [59] (never pushed as the sole goal to the point of rupturing the Party), reflects the Prime Minister's determination to use socialist methods where appropriate to achieve socioeconomic development, but at the same time to avert India's potentially destabilizing factionalism by maintaining a comprehensive Congress base.

Similarly in binding together autonomous CDU *Land* parties as he rose to national leadership [60] during the organizational years 1945–50, Adenauer not only outmaneuvered and isolated his chief

[58] Most of the political parties had existed before independence as part of the Congress. Fourteen ran against Congress at the national level in the first general election and an additional 51 ran in the States. Weiner, *Party Politics in India,* pp. 17 and 19.

[59] Prior to the death of Sandar Patel (Congress "strong man," an extreme conservative, and Nehru's only rival for power after 1948) in 1950, a compromise program was worked out between the Nehru-Socialist group and the industrialist-conservative wing headed by Patel. "A socialist pattern of society" was not adopted as a Congress goal until the Avadi Resolution of 1955, although socialist principles date back to the Karachi Resolution of 1931, which laid down Fundamental Rights for the constitution of an independent India and was inspired by Nehru. The first Five-year Plan made clear concessions to the private sector and during most of the Nehru era the goal was a mixed-economy and social welfare.

[60] For detailed study of Adenauer's rise to CDU leadership, consolidation of the Party, and his influence on party objectives, see Arnold J. Heidenheimer, *Adenauer and the CDU—The Rise of the Leader and the Integration of the Party* (The Hague, 1960).

rivals, but effected party cohesion by building alliances with politically significant former rivals [61] and regional CDU groups. Exacting
in efforts to build a broadbased party, he united Catholics and Protestants, trade unionists and industrialists, businessmen, farmers, ex-
pellees, and former petty Nazis. He contained *Land* parties which
would have led the CDU toward Christian Socialism, nationalism,
and an Eastern orientation (Berlin, Frankfurt, Hesse) and aligned
with those which strengthened his stand favoring a social market
economy/united Western Europe/cooperation with the Allies (Bavarian CSU, North German CDU groups). Striking a middle course
through major ideological differences he was instrumental in the
adoption of a program which avoided the extremes of socialism or
conservatism but could accommodate both. As Chancellor he acted
as arbitrator of party differences, curbed the influence of the Catholic
clergy, and in public speeches mimimized [62] the "Christian" Democratic basis of the CDU to broaden its appeal.

OPPOSITION, CRITICISM, AND DISSENT

Perhaps the most distinctive characteristic of democracy,[63] the existence of opposition and dissent can be easily determined: less
obvious is the role of the establisher of a new democracy in its development. Adenauer influenced the emergence of a competitive party
system by molding a clearly distinguishable new major political party
and by taking action, as opportunity arose, which sharpened CDU-
SPD competition and ultimately cast the SPD in the role of opposition party. Nehru's influence was primarily that of fostering an atmosphere in which dissent and opposition could freely develop and be
channeled into the political system.

The Federal Republic, unlike India, came into being with two
major political parties: the CDU (which, with its Bavarian counterpart, the CSU, the Free Democrats, and the German Party, formed
the government coalition) and the Social Democratic Party, which
formed the major opposition party. Although the intransigence of
SPD leader Kurt Schumacher [64] and the existing federal electoral

[61] *Ibid.,* pp. 61–107.

[62] Catholic-clerical association was minimized to attract non-Catholics.

[63] Robert A. Dahl, ed., *Political Oppositions in Western Democracies* (New Haven, 1966), p. xviii.

[64] For the role played by Schumacher and the SPD in postwar German political development, see Edinger, *Kurt Schumacher.*

laws [65] were also contributing factors, the fact that Bonn was able to skirt the pitfalls of ideological and class cleavages characteristic of past German politics and develop a dominant two-party system with a stable government and responsible opposition can be attributed largely to steps taken by Adenauer prior to and after becoming Chancellor.

First: By welding a cohesive national party and blocking CDU dominance by the Christian-Socialist/trade unionist/Eastern-oriented wing favoring coalition with the SPD, Adenauer shaped the second distinctly different major party needed for the development of a competitive party system. Second: In deliberate steps taken between 1946 and 1948 regarding CDU-SPD coalition, he not only sharpened the identity of the CDU but forced the SPD into the opposition. His refusal (in 1946) to place the fledgling British Zone CDU in a role secondary to the stronger SPD, when Schumacher offered cooperation "on the condition . . . that [the CDU] recognize the SPD's claim to leadership," [66] cast the die for a highly competitive relationship between the two leaders and their parties. His formation of a coalition "administration" in the Frankfurt Economic Council (1947) left the SPD in "opposition" and set the pattern for the Bonn Republic. His adroitness in maintaining CDU cohesion in the Parliamentary Council [67] (September 1948/May 1949) strengthened the image of CDU-SPD competition. Finally, at the meeting which he called at Rhöndorf [68] after the 1949 election, to consider formation of the new government, he managed through skillful politicking and stage-management to override pressure within the CDU for a "grand coalition" and won support for a CDU/CSU-Free Democrat-German Party coalition, which left the SPD as the principal opposition.

That a CDU-SPD coalition was ever a realistic hope might be questioned in view of Schumacher's self-image as rightful leader of the new Germany and his contempt for Adenauer.[69] More important,

[65] The federal electoral laws provide that a party cannot seat a deputy in the Bundestag unless it has received 5 percent of the vote. The Communist Party, which contested the first election, was eliminated because it did not win the required 5 percent.

[66] For report of incident by Dr. Paul Otto (who was present), see Weymar, p. 190; also mentioned in Heidenheimer, *Adenauer and the CDU*, p. 149, and Edinger, *Kurt Schumacher*, p. 221.

[67] Heidenheimer, *Adenauer and the CDU*, pp. 134–36, 155, 162.

[68] For account of meeting, see Weymar, pp. 264–69; also mentioned in Heidenheimer, *Adenauer and the CDU*, pp. 179–83.

[69] See Edinger, *Kurt Schumacher*, p. 221.

however, is the fact that Adenauer, more than most, realized that such a coalition would produce a weak government with no party capable of forming an effective opposition. Influenced by the example of Weimar and the French Fourth Republic, he "did not believe in democracy of constantly shifting majorities, but one within a set framework." [70] By consolidating CDU strength as Chancellor and continuing to avoid a fragmented opposition, he not only created the political stability necessary for the system to be effective in carrying out social and economic reconstruction, but laid the groundwork for a democratic two-party system.

Although India's party system has yet to spawn a second party large enough to challenge Congress dominance and make the system competitive on the national level, minor party representation in the *Lok Sabha* [71] during the Nehru era and dissident groups within Congress provided an embryonic official and an informal opposition. Effective opposition, however, developed, first, on the state [72] and local levels and, second, between state governments and the Centre. Although Congress controlled most state governments, when it lost an election the response was not to suppress opposition but to retrench and strengthen the party machinery for the next general election. Congress loss of Andhra [73] to the Communists in 1955, followed by its victory in 1959 elections, is an early example of effective competitive politics in India. The most dramatic example of State-Centre bargaining is that of the Congress-controlled West Bengal government, which on three occasions obstructed, reversed, or modified New Delhi's original policies due to its strong bargaining position gained through use of the State Party organization, deals with "key men" and mobilization of a highly politicized electorate.[74]

The fact that the Centre's emergency power to take over state gov-

[70] A Federal Republic official, who wishes to remain anonymous, in an interview on January 17, 1970, New York City.

[71] In 1956 there were 33 parties represented in the Lok Sabha, Weiner, *Party Politics in India*, p. 224.

[72] For development of state party politics, see Myron Weiner, ed., *State Politics in India* (Princeton, N.J., 1968); Weiner, *Party Politics in India*; Selig Harrison, *India: The Most Dangerous Decades,* (Princeton, N.J., 1960); and Mason, ed.

[73] For full account of Andhra elections, see Harrison, *India*.

[74] For case studies of State Reorganization in 1956, establishment of the Damodar Valley Authority, and Land Reform, see Franda, pp. 8–179.

ernments was sparingly used,[75] that obstreperous Congress opposition was dealt with by accepted disciplinary procedures, that increased competition and criticism with the growth of new parties (and organized interest groups) on the state and local levels was contested by Congress through the electoral process, can be largely credited to the tone set by Nehru's leadership. "I believe completely in any government . . . having stout critics, having an opposition to face," he said in 1957, "Without criticism people and government become complacent. The whole parliamentary system . . . is based on such criticism. It would be a bad thing . . . if people were not allowed to speak and criticize government fully and in the open. . . . It would not be proper democracy." [76]

A look at both men in relation to their Cabinets indicates that they welcomed free discussion, although their dominant personalities tended to discourage dissent. Adenauer discounted Cabinet members he considered weak, of questionable judgment, or "do-gooders"; [77] Nehru "respected critics if they had the courage of their convictions and did not seek favors." [78] Adenauer once asserted: "The most successful man in politics is he who can outsit the rest." [79] Both used long meetings to wear down opposition or divergent views and were adept at producing common formulas for agreement. The outcome when there was disagreement depended on how strongly they felt on

[75] President's rule has been exercised in Andhra, Kerala, Punab, and Rajasthan. See Weiner, *State Politics in India.*

[76] *Jawaharlal Nehru's Speeches,* III, 152.

[77] A Federal Republic official, who wishes to remain anonymous, in an interview on January 17, 1970, New York City.

Franz Joseph Strauss (former Defense Minister) has stated that he and Adenauer had had sharp differences and long discussions, but that it was within a framework of Adenauer's "respect" for him and his "admiration" of the Chancellor: In an interview with Ed Newmann, *Speaking Freely,* on WNBC-TV, Sunday, January 18, 1970.

Edinger notes that "Most major policy decisions were made by Adenauer alone or in consultation with a small 'kitchen cabinet' of his most trusted ministers, key civil servants, and parliamentary deputies; the regular cabinet, the Bundestag, national CDU organs, and the electorate ratified rather than determined government policy." *Politics in GERMANY,* p. 274.

Brecher says that two or three Cabinet members played decisive roles, *Nehru,* p. 463.

[78] A. B. Shah, ed., *Jawaharlal Nehru, A Critical Tribute,* Indian Committee for Cultural Freedom (Bombay, 1965), p. 21.

[79] Suth quoting Adenauer in Weymar, p. 64.

the issue; each had an order of priorities ranging from foreign affairs (over which they kept almost exclusive jurisdiction) down to subjects others could decide completely. Nehru might make an impassioned plea for a position on which he felt strongly; Adenauer, who remained dispassionate even at the height of controversy,[80] waited until all arguments had been expended, then devastated his opponents with his courtroom technique. Though they have been criticized for discouraging democratic growth by their dominance,[81] it must also be recognized that a leader with a keen sense of political advocacy and will to win the game, will "dominate" if others do not engage in the game. Conversely only by action which will evoke strong response can a leader spark democratic growth.

How the leader of a new democracy responds to public disclosure of political scandal could be another indication of his contribution to the development of opposition and the establishment of the democratic process. Although it must be said that Adenauer did not acquit himself as well in *"Der Spiegel* Affair" (1962) as Nehru in the "Mundhra Affair" [82] (1957), the full exposure of both cases through the press and nationwide discussion, which incurred severe criticism of the government, pointed up parliamentary responsibility and accountability to the public. Implicit in the intensity, breadth, and duration of the public debates, moreover, is the fact that neither leader made a serious attempt to suppress discussion of an issue which was both damaging to the image of his regime and placed public limits on government.

ELECTIONS

Regular elections, honestly conducted, based on universal suffrage with secret ballot and contested by more than one party are a prime requisite of democracy to enable citizens to identify with and participate in government, choose among differing policies and candidates,

[80] Edinger, *Kurt Schumacher,* p. 221.

[81] "Under the weight of his personality, the Chancellor extensively stifled the free play of democracy, the establishing and strengthening of which was so largely his own achievement," Alfred Grosser, *Die Bonner Demokratie* (Düsseldorf, 1960), pp. 419 ff., quoted in Gordon A. Craig, *From Bismarck to Adenauer, Aspects of German Statecraft* (rev. ed.; New York, 1958, 1963), p. 103.

[82] For an account of *Der Spiegel* Affair, see Richard Hiscocks, *The Adenauer Era* (Philadelphia/New York, 1966), pp. 241–51; and for the Mundhra Affair see Brecher, *Nehru,* p. 460.

and express acceptance of the political system. In insisting on intensive, countrywide campaigning during the first four general elections [83] to bring issues and candidates to the largest number of the electorate, Adenauer and Nehru (both indefatigable campaigners) not only utilized elections for political education, but set the pattern and character of future elections. Adenauer's vigorous campaigning despite his age, and Nehru's refusal to postpone India's first general elections [84] in 1951, which (because of communal strife, social and economic dislocation) came at a bad time for Congress and the new government, demonstrated the importance they placed on regular elections. The high percentage of the electorate which voted and the nature of subsequent elections indicates that the national leader may influence popular participation and choice in the way he relates to the electoral process. In a functioning democracy one takes for granted that politicians are eager electoral contestants, but in the beginning, before the democratic system is established, someone must start the contest. If the national leader risks his prestige in verbal combat, other candidates—particularly the opposition—are prodded to active engagement.

THE MARRIAGE OF POLITICAL POWER AND PUBLIC NEEDS

Both leaders were keenly perceptive in identifying politically significant social and economic issues. They were equally adroit in working out formulas which satisfied their minimum standards while incorporating concessions adequate to win support from differing but politically important groups. Thus support was gained through alliance to enact legislation which answered pressing needs and, in so doing, strengthened public support not only of the party but of the political system itself.[85] In view of the tendency in India and Ger-

[83] General elections (state and national) were held in India in 1951/52, 1957, 1962, and by-elections in some states between 1952 and 1955. With 199,519,188 eligible voters and 120,822,487 votes cast in 1957, India had the world's largest democratic elections. See Norman D. Palmer, *The Indian Political System* (Boston, 1961), pp. 215–34. German elections were held in 1949, 1953, 1957 and 1961, with 78.5 percent of the electorate voting in 1949 and 86.0 percent in 1953. For analysis of the 1953 elections, see James K. Pollock, ed., *German Democracy at Work—Selective Study* (Ann Arbor, Mich., 1965).

[84] Brecher, *Nehru*, pp. 438–39.

[85] Although as the dominant party in the Lok Sabha Congress could be assured of votes necessary for enactment of legislation, divergent interests within Congress and those represented by them had to be reconciled.

many for people to expect services from government, had Nehru and
Adenauer not acted promptly to answer social and economic needs
the credibility of the democratic system would have been placed seriously in doubt.

Although Ludwig Erhard was the "architect" of the German "economic miracle," Adenauer picked Erhard as Minister of Economic
Affairs (though he had little respect for him as a politician) and mas-
terminded politically sensitive economic and social legislation which
helped to legitimate the regime. He confined his interest in economics to questions which were politically important.[86] Recognizing
that "the broad masses of people would have to be economically and
socially content" [87] he concentrated on wages, prices, or other matters which affected living standards and hence might influence the
government's popularity and prospects at the polls. His programs
tended to be a mixture of human and political considerations which
would improve the individual's lot while producing the social har-
mony needed for political stability. Thus comanagement in the coal
and steel industry avoided nationalization, but satisfied the unions'
demand for a voice in management; the restoration of pensions to
former civil servants who were lesser Nazis and those who had been
disqualified by the Nazis won support of groups which might have
been disruptive forces; tax concessions were made to private home
owners; and "one of the most important pieces of social legislation"
sponsored by his government (in 1957) ensured workers and employ-
ees that their pensions would retain their value in purchasing power.[88]

Nehru similarly emphasized social reform and economic development, in a democratic context, in areas which were politically sensitive, and could have led to instability. Thus he emphasized secularization and abolition of barriers against untouchables (Harijans), for without full integration and equality for India's Muslims
and Harijans there could be no democracy. He encouraged adoption
of the *Panchayati Raj,*[89] with control over community development
programs, to give the villager a sense of participation in and control
over government. Moreover, he was responsible for India's "democratic planning," the fact that the Planning Commission (of which he
was chairman) was set up early in 1950, shortly after the Indian

[86] Hiscocks, pp. 49–50.

[87] A Federal Republic official, who wishes to remain anonymous, in an interview on January 17, 1970, New York City.

[88] Hiscocks, pp. 43–50.   [89] Palmer, pp. 173–77.

Constitution became effective; and that the first Five-year Plan was launched in 1951.

"AFTER . . . WHO?"

The ability of the system to provide a successor to the first chief executive may be a significant indicator of the degree to which he was able to establish the democratic process. Nehru and Adenauer made no preparations for successors; yet succession was handled in an orderly manner, by democratic procedures through established political institutions.[90] The popularity of both men began to wane after reaching peaks in 1957 (though both won electoral victories after that) and restlessness (particularly in the CDU) began to mount. Nehru suggested resignation twice, but remained at the Congress High Command's insistence. Despite widespread "after-Nehru-who?" talk, he left the decision to chance and the Party in the belief that the people, if accustomed to expect certain things of government, would demand appropriate leadership. Adenauer's postponement of retirement only strengthened CDU pressures for his departure. His behavior in considering the presidency then remaining Chancellor, as well as his attacks on Erhard (favored to succeed him), not only dramatically spotlighted a potential abuse of office but crystallized the demand that he step down.[91] It may not be totally far-fetched to speculate whether the conduct of both men was not in part calculated to stimulate the forces necessary for democratic selection to operate. Although each might have groomed a leadership group from which a successor could be selected, the designation of an heir-apparent would not have been in keeping with democratic establishment.

That Adenauer and Nehru managed stability and dissent sufficiently to permit infusion of the system with an infrastructure of democratic attitudes, practices, expectations, and responses, may be inferred from subsequent elections and changes in government. India's second succession crisis (1966), 1967 elections with Congress' state losses, and Syndicate-Indira Gandhi power struggle, all adhered

[90] For analysis of the Congress process in selecting Lal Bahadur Shastri to succeed Nehru, and Indira Gandhi (Nehru's daughter) to succeed Shastri, who died January 11, 1966, see Michael Brecher, *Succession in India: A Study in Decision-Making* (London, 1966).

[91] For discussion of succession struggle in the CDU, see Heidenheimer, *Adenauer and the CDU*, pp. 221–29.

to democratic means. The Federal Republic's two national elections, change of Chancellors, experiment with a "grand coalition," and first change of government parties in 1969, showed competitive democracy at work. Indian and German democracies thus survived their establishers; whether they had actually become "habits" with their citizens is still too early to assess.

Conclusion

If one assumes that politics is a dynamic process of multiple relationships, then democracy might be viewed as a political system in which dynamism is accelerated; one which incorporates both stability and change as products of conflict resolution. During the period of establishment, however, the management of stability must be stressed so that change and *habituation* [92] to the new system may take place and the system's self-equilibrating mechanisms take effect. Viewed in this context, the study of Adenauer and Nehru indicates that their authoritative-manipulatory-negotiating style of leadership operating within the institutional framework was congruent with the demands of the system, the socioeconomic conditions, and the varying levels of political sophistication and competence in both public and political elites. It linked past to present while projecting to the future by merging traditional attitudes and practices with those required for the evolution of new democratic institutions. Adenauer and Nehru thus managed to balance the reality of populations largely inexperienced in political democracy and societies containing significant nondemocratic elements with the ideal of popular participation which contributes to the system as well as seeks something from it.

The Adenauer-Nehru experience further demonstrates that in pluralistic, polarized societies the establisher's primary task may be that of *multiple reconciliation;* [93] of competing interests, political power, and responsiveness to public demands, old habits and new forms, expectations and realities. His role as arbitrator places high priority on aloofness from close identity with specific groups (particularly within the party) while being intensely involved (at times highly partisan) in the political process. It places higher priority on his political acu-

[92] Term used by Rustow for the fourth phase of his "dynamic model" in "Transitions to Democracy," p. 358.
[93] Borrowed from Rustow, *A World of Nations*, p. 153.

men, adroitness, and flexibility as strategist and tactician, as well as his perceptiveness and vision in relating future goals to present realities, if time is to be gained to allow democratic institutions to take root.

As the ultimate authority in the decision-making process, as well as the link between the government, legislature, party, and other agencies, the chief executive in a new democracy has the capacity at critical junctures to deflect the course of political forces toward strengthened democratic development or its erosion. Instrumental in lessening the dangers of the multiparty systems by stressing CDU and Congress heterogeneity, while fostering conditions conducive to opposition, Adenauer and Nehru also adeptly balanced power aggregation with social responsibility. Perhaps the most hazardous factor for infant democracy is that the seeds of its destruction are inherent in requirements for its growth to maturity. In the period before institutions are entrenched, stability, dissent, and the power necessary to manage them can as easily lead to authoritarian rule as democratic growth. If democracy is successfully to take root, study of Adenauer and Nehru suggests that the conditions require a strong leader with a firm commitment to the democratic process and a highly developed sense of self-restraint, who can utilize power or restraint to manipulate situations as they evolve. Although it is true that beliefs can be adjusted to actions, it seems equally apparent that the leader buffeted by the need for rapid development, obstructed by dissent and the aggravating slowness of the democratic system, with ready access to power, could turn to authoritarian, coercive measures unless he has a firm grip on democratic guidelines. Pragmatism, individualism, and flexibility alone can easily lead to expediency unless moderated by respect for the individual, commitment to the democratic process, and awareness of the costs risked in resort to nondemocratic methods.

Comparison of Adenauer and Nehru, moreover, confirms the importance of previous political experience to successful implantation of democratic institutions. If the democracies were new, the establishers were not "instant." Though their genesis might have been childhood family experience, the techniques, attitudes, and approaches which made it possible for Adenauer and Nehru to cope with the exigencies of democratic establishment were developed (as personality traits and political philosophy were molded) during the thirty years of political experience which preceded their becoming

heads of government. The striking similarity of their modes of operation indicates, however, that the impact of cultural / economic differences on leadership is more one of nuance in image projected than in
substance of method. Adenauer and Nehru were primarily political
men, advocates by training; neither had had bureaucratic or military
experience (in fact, both were antimilitarist); both were what Deutsch
might call *outside-insiders:* [94] They had vision beyond that of their
political contemporaries, were not from the heartland of their countries' traditions, yet far from being alienated were steeped in tradition; they were synthesizers and adapters of ideas and methods; and
they sought power to effect radical, democratic change which would
include continuity with the past but in the context of new international relationships. [95]

[94] An adaptation of the term used by Karl Deutsch in *Political Community
and the North Atlantic Area* (Princeton, N.J., 1957), p. 88.

[95] Readers interested in a further investigation of the subject of this article
may wish to consult:

Adenauer, Konrad, *Memoirs 1945–53,* tr. Beate Ruhm von Oppen (Chicago, 1966).

Alexander, Edgar, *Adenauer and the New Germany—The Chancellor of the Vanquished* (New York, 1957).

Barber, James D., "Adult Identity and Presidential Style: The Rhetorical Emphasis," *Daedalus,* American Academy of Arts and Sciences (Summer, 1968), pp. 938–68.

Bölling, Klaus, *Republic in Suspense—Politics, Parties and Personalities in Postwar Germany,* tr. Jean Sternberg (New York, 1964).

Clay, Lucius D., *Decision in Germany* (Garden City, N.Y., 1950).

Dahl, Robert A., *A Preface to Democratic Theory* (Chicago, 1963).

Erler, Fritz, *Democracy in Germany* (Cambridge, Mass., 1965).

Heidenheimer, Arnold J., *The Governments of Germany* (New York, 1966).

Hoffman, Stanley, and Inge Hoffman, "The Will to Grandeur: de Gaulle as Political Artist," *Daedalus,* American Academy of Arts and Sciences (Summer, 1968), pp. 829–87.

Kapur, Narinder, "On Selection of Congress Candidates," Fourth General Elections in India, *Political Science Review,* VI, Nos. 3 & 4 and VII, Nos. 1 & 2 (July–Sept / Oct–Dec 1967; Jan–Mr / Ap–Jn 1968), pp. 75–84.

Kissinger, Henry, "The White Revolutionary: Reflections on Bismarck," *Daedalus,* American Academy of Arts and Sciences (Summer, 1968), pp. 888–924.

Lasswell, Harold D., *Power and Personality* (New York, 1962).

Moraes, Frank, *Jawaharlal Nehru* (New York, 1956).

Nehru, Jawaharlal, *Independence and After* (New York, 1950).

Park, Richard L., *India's Political System* (Englewood Cliffs, N.J., 1967).

Park Richard L., and Irene Tinker, eds., *Leadership and Political Institutions in India* (Princeton, N.J., 1950).

Rustow, Dankwart A., "Atatürk as Founder of a State," *Daedalus,* American Academy of Arts and Sciences (Summer, 1968), pp. 793–828.

Schuster, Sir George, and Guy Wint, *India & Democracy* (London, 1941).

Smith, M. Brewster, "Opinions, Personality and Political Behavior," *The American Political Science Review,* LII (March, 1958), 1–17.

Spitz, David, "Power and Personality," *The American Political Science Review,* LII (March, 1958), 84–97.

Wilcox, Wayne, "Politicians, Bureaucrats, and Development in India," New Nations: The Problem of Political Development, *The Annals,* The American Academy of Political and Social Science, Vol. 358 (March, 1965).

Nonmilitary Incentives for the Acquisition of Nuclear Weapons

CHARLES D. BETHILL

To formulate effective and acceptable international arms control arrangements, it is necessary to identify and analyze all factors that might account for an affirmative decision on the acquisition of nuclear weapons. My purpose here is to explore some of the neglected issues in the various national debates about the possession (development or receipt) of modern systems of mass devastation.[1] Political leaders and defense intellectuals [2] have devoted most of their attention to the overtly military and quantifiable problems of deterrence and possible use. The peripheral functions [3] of the maintenance of nuclear weapons have received insufficient study by those seeking to

[1] Attention is directed toward the debates in those countries which have exercised the nuclear option (United States, Soviet Union, Britain, France, China) and those which might be expected to do so in the near future (Japan, India, Israel, Canada, Germany, Sweden, Switzerland, Italy). Certainly, there are other states which will probably be capable of producing nuclear weapons in the next decade or two but the level of the debate in these countries is as undeveloped as are the programs. See Leonard Beaton, *Must the Bomb Spread?* (Middlesex, England, 1966), ch. 4, "The Probable Rate of Proliferation."

[2] Primarily the academic strategists (Brodie, Huntington, Kahn, Schelling, Wohlstetter, *et al.*) who have usually preceded their military counterparts in recognizing the radical implications—dangers and opportunities—of new weapons systems.

[3] The term *peripheral functions* is used to designate all those uses of a nuclear weapons program that are not directly associated with the *ostensible functions* of such arms: deterrence and defense. Peripheral functions should not be equated with *peripheral reasons* for undertaking such a project. Often, the central consideration in an affirmative decision to exercise the nuclear option is a desire to realize a peripheral function, e.g., great power status or prestige and influence. In the course of this essay, many such affirmative deci-

comprehend why a state decides to exercise its option. An appreciation of the full range of incentives for nuclear armament, however, is a prerequisite for any progress in the revision of policies and attitudes so as to achieve a reduction in global tension. The destructiveness and management uncertainties of nuclear weapons make such understanding and action imperative.

In the contemporary nation state, there is hardly a major public or private activity which does not bear upon the security of the polity in some respect. A country's ability to preserve its sovereignty and freedom of maneuver in the international arena derives from a complex compound of strength in its military, diplomatic, political, and economic affairs. Nuclear weapons may be acquired by one state for strictly military reasons while another undertakes the effort to gain advantages not immediately associated with defense or deterrence. Nevertheless, security considerations are involved in either case as long as the decision was motivated by a desire to advance the international stature or general well-being of the country. It must be clearly stated that no nation has yet determined to equip itself with nuclear weapons for what can be labeled irrational, that is, totally unrelated to security, reasons, and it is doubtful whether this will ever occur. There are many dimensions—not all of them are necessarily obvious or complementary—along which the decision to exercise the nuclear option may be analyzed.[4] The distinction that has to be made is that between the military and nonmilitary aspects of secu-

sions based upon peripheral functions are discussed in an effort to indicate the broad range of nonmilitary reasons that states have elected or might elect to exercise their nuclear option.

[4] For example, were India to develop a strategic nuclear-weapons system, it might improve its military position vis-à-vis China, but there would be severe costs in other areas. Pakistan would feel threatened and would probably attempt to increase its military strength. The great powers would be unhappy with this act of nuclear proliferation and with the effect it would have on other states contemplating such action. The nonaligned bloc might construe such an undertaking as an abdication of leadership of their group. There might well be a fierce reaction from a population that is exceedingly anti-atomic and pacifistic and which would prefer that priority be given to dire domestic problems. Economically, such a program would impose a severe financial strain on a country as poor as India. It appears evident, therefore, that while the acquisition of nuclear weapons would seem sensible if analyzed along a single dimension, i.e., military relations with China, there are an overwhelming number of counterarguments if several other dimensions are investigated.

rity. Nuclear weapons, though usually associated with the former, very often can be justified in terms of the latter.

Although the military arguments for acquiring nuclear weapons are well publicized and understood, it is also necessary to uncover and explain what other reasons might be advanced for joining the atomic "club." However, debates about the relative importance of the military and of the nonmilitary components of the decision are not particularly useful, and no effort is made in this essay to establish a mechanistic order of precedence.[5] Briefly, the range of opinion on this matter includes the following possibilities: 1) defense and deterrence requirements govern nuclear weapons policy;[6] 2) prestige and influence is the "decisive issue";[7] 3) nonmilitary considerations operate as marginal values which direct the choice when the strategic argument is indeterminant.[8]

In any event, the observation of Robert Rothstein seems appropriate, "The impact of nuclear weapons on international politics has been so extensive that the decision to become a nuclear power can be justified in a variety of ways. Ultimately, however, that decision must at least appear rational on military grounds."[9] All the nonmilitary issues examined here can, in an extended manner, be related to military security and it is up to the individual analyst to make a subjective judgment as to what is the prime rationale behind a specific nuclear arms policy.

The nonmilitary arguments for nuclear weapons acquisition can be divided, for the sake of convenience, into the following categories: international politics, alliance politics, domestic politics, and the politics of illusory security. The meaning of these terms for my specific purposes are provided during the substantive discussions, but

[5] For an interesting general survey of the military and nonmilitary arguments which are critical or supportive of American arms policy, see Robert A. Levine, *The Arms Debate* (Cambridge, Mass., 1963).

[6] As in Bernard Brodie, *Escalation and the Nuclear Option* (Princeton, N.J., 1966), or J. K. Ray, *Security in the Missile Age* (Bombay, 1967).

[7] Beaton, ch. 3, "What Countries Want."

[8] "Examined solely in terms of military security, analysis suggests that on margin, the utility of nuclear weapons for the remaining non-nuclear powers is not likely to be high. But when we add political and psychological factors to the analysis, the calculus of utility has to be adjusted." Robert L. Rothstein, *On Nuclear Proliferation,* School of International Affairs, Columbia University, occasional papers (New York, 1966), pp. 47–48.

[9] *Ibid.,* p. 16.

basically the terms describe the various levels of relations that a national political elite maintains: 1) with its adversaries, 2) with its friends, 3) within itself, and, 4) with its general population. It must, of course, be emphasized that such compartmentalization has no place in the complex and integrative real world, but is only intellectually useful as a way to organize analytical material.

International Politics

International politics may be said to refer to the competitive relations among nations which view each other as adversaries or potential rivals. Whereas friendly states can communicate frankly and cooperatively among themselves, countries which feel mutually threatened deal with each other through symbols, signals, and exemplary actions.[10] The possession of nuclear weapons functions as just such a useful diplomatic tool which can be manipulated to encourage caution and respect. In international politics, resort to nuclear weapons is the ultimate implied sanction; however, countries having the capability capitalize on this asset through skillful, complementary foreign policy rather than through warnings and threats of holocaust. In spite, and paradoxically because, of the immense destructiveness of atomic weapons, the advantages (if any) that are to be exacted from enemies result from their possession rather than from their use.

GREAT POWER STATUS

The most obvious motivation for acquiring nuclear weapons is to assert a position of primacy in the community of nations.

Great Power status has become so synonymous with nuclear capability that no nation can aspire to international leadership without strategic nuclear armament. . . . A nation seeking to lead in international politics must therefore eventually face the choice of either developing nuclear weapons or renouncing its aspirations.[11]

[10] Adversaries, of course, often do engage in what are described as frank and cordial discussions. These consist largely of exchanged messages, warnings and probes rather than conversations in the commonly understood sense of the term. In any event, they are subsidiary to the actions taken by the participants as indicators of essential attitude. However, it must also be noted that relations between nominal allies often degenerate into cryptic and abrasive interchange.

[11] Ciro Zoppo, "France as a Nuclear Power," in R. N. Rosecrance, ed., *The Dispersion of Nuclear Weapons* (New York, 1964), p. 113.

It is quite revealing that just those countries proclaimed great powers at the close of World War II and rewarded with seats on the Security Council of the UN are the ones currently in possession of atomic arsenals.[12] There assuredly is an element of self-fulfilling prophecy in this coincidence of image and weapons procurement. It is an historically valid observation that no state desiring a major role in world affairs has permitted itself to be militarily outstripped through a voluntary decision not to pursue the latest innovations in arms technology.

An analysis of the configuration of force in the contemporary world suggests that there are really only two world powers in the international arena. Relative to the military strength of the United States and the Soviet Union, the aggregate capacity of all the other states that aspire to this status is insignificant. For them—Britain, France, China—the development of nuclear weapons is an easy way to reassume the trappings of the preeminence they once enjoyed. Richard Rosecrance perceptively notes,

Great Power status is assumed to be confirmed or conferred by autonomous nuclear capability, and states desirous of such recognition may want the nuclear bomb as a talisman of greatness. The need may be more insistent when events have called a state's primacy into question.[13]

World power aspirations are formed by national pride, history, resources, and organization, and so it is not unreasonable to expect the nascent powers Germany and Japan to be carefully examining these incentives for entrance into the nuclear club.

PRESTIGE AND INFLUENCE

In addition to those nations that seek positions of international leadership, there are a host of middle-level states which believe that the acquisition of nuclear weapons will confer upon them some degree of prestige and respect. These technologically advanced countries [14] would exercise their option in order to gain some influ-

[12] Technically, of course, China is supposed to be represented at the UN by the Nationalist government although it is the mainland regime, the People's Republic, that developed and controls nuclear weapons. This diplomatic quirk does not alter the point that the nations adjudged to be great powers twenty-five years ago now all lay claim to a nuclear capability of some degree.

[13] R. N. Rosecrance, "Introduction," in Rosecrance, p. 4.

[14] Those which come immediately to mind include Canada, Germany, India, Israel, Italy, Japan, Sweden, Switzerland.

ence and stature without attempting to go so far as to challenge the recognized and de facto great powers. Leonard Beaton suggests that an analytical distinction be made between the motivations of the great powers (world leadership and defense) and other states that possess nuclear potential (prestige and influence.)

On the whole, most countries are interested in prestige and influence but have no real tradition of orthodox military strength. Nuclear weapons for defence rather than prestige are mainly the concern of European countries with a strong military tradition plus Israel (which might in a sense be said to fall into this category.) Prestige has been and is likely to remain the decisive issue.[15]

To the political elites of many countries, nuclear weapons have come to be considered "virile symbols" [16] of modernity and strength.

The temptation to pursue this mark of status is compelling even when such activity may seem to be financially counterproductive. Ciro Zoppo aptly comments that "Prestige considerations may, in fact, be deemed important enough by some national leaders to induce them to set about acquiring nuclear weapons even when economic considerations are inhibiting and their strategic usefulness is open to question." [17] It must, however, be remembered that reputation and image are extremely important components of the diplomatic arsenal of a nation and can often be used to greater effect than violent techniques of obtaining compliance.

In general, nuclear capability is widely assumed to enhance international stature which in turn results in a more successful foreign policy. Whether the individual country is striving for great power status or just for increased prestige and influence, atomic arms are commonly thought to be the most convenient method by which to improve its position relative to other states, that is, those which do not or cannot undertake to negate this advantage through similar programs. Of course, nuclear weapons acquisition for the purpose of gaining prestige will very likely be a strategy of very transient benefit because other countries will naturally be inclined to take appropriate action to rectify the imbalance. The dynamic which works to equalize any prestige differentials is very much the same as that described by

[15] Beaton, p. 66.

[16] William Bader, *The United States and the Spread of Nuclear Weapons* (New York, 1968), p. 71.

[17] Zoppo, "France as a Nuclear Power," in Rosecrance, p. 113.

analysts evaluating the ultimate strategic (military) consequences of
nuclear proliferation.

EXCLUSIVE INTERNATIONAL COUNCILS

Integral to the fabric of international diplomacy are a variety of
select, multinational organizations established to deal with the basic
political, military, and economic problems which concern both the
participants and all other countries. Two crucial characteristics of
such bodies are: 1) they choose their own members and 2) their importance often extends far beyond their originally prescribed limits
of interest. To be included in these select councils, therefore, is indispensable to a country's self-esteem and its efficacy in the world
arena. Some states (most notably China) have been rather ostenta-
tiously barred from assuming a place at these tables of discussion
and negotiation. Where logic and equity fail, however, the acquisition of nuclear weapons may very well serve to secure entrance for
such countries into those organizations from which they have been
summarily excluded.

The case of China is exemplary and most instructive. Since the accession of the Communists to power, the People's Republic has been
relegated to a condition of extreme isolation and diplomatic ostra-
cism. Partly because of its own unorthodox rhetoric, xenophobia, and
preference for self-reliance but mostly due to the excesses of the
Cold War, China has been denied a seat at the UN [18] and refused a
voice in the various disarmament conferences.[19] Though there continues to be some doubt that the ruling elite would accept offers of participation if now tendered, the evidence suggests that the compulsion
to be recognized as a great power with all of its perquisites would result in a positive response.

One goal of the Chinese nuclear program seems to have been to
rectify this lack of appreciation for the sensibilities and importance
of the Middle Kingdom. It has been persuasively reasoned that the
supposed danger of an atomically armed China will compel other
states to invite it to talks at the major established forums to avoid a

[18] See A. M. Halpern, ed., *Policies Toward China: Views from Six Conti-
nents* (New York, 1965), Appendix B, pp. 503–7, for a summary of votes on
the China question in the UN.
[19] Most notably the Eighteen Nation Disarmament Conference which has
been meeting in Geneva.

catastrophe due to a lack of understanding and communication. Morton Halperin states the argument this way:

The political use to which China will put her developing nuclear capability is likely to be general, within the context of her claim to being a great power whose views cannot be ignored in the settlement of Asian or disarmament and arms control problems. She can base her right to participate in international conferences or to be recognized as having an important part in the settlement of disputes on the fact that she is now one of the world's five nuclear powers; she can then attribute whatever success she does attain in political conferences at least partly to the fact that she has a nuclear capability.[20]

It is sad and vaguely macabre to contemplate the inescapable irony that it requires a force of nuclear weapons to explode open doors previously closed to normal relations with a pariah state like China. Yet, it is undeniably true, as Michael Yahuda observes, that "deterrence involves interaction," [21] and that cooperation may very well be the ultimate result of bellicosity.

It must be pointed out that China is not unique in its acquisition of nuclear weapons partly in order to exact from the ranking great powers offers for participation in select international bodies. Both Britain and France, for example, have explicitly stated that at least one purpose of their respective nuclear programs was to gain "influence in the arms control negotiations that determine so many other aspects of international affairs." [22] No independent nation can suffer decisions involving its status and safety to be made by other states when it can possibly avoid this encroachment on its sovereignty by undertaking the development of modern instruments of destruction. An atomic detonation becomes the guarantor of inclusion—an international rite de passage—in the important multinational conferences and agreements of the times. Other parties may perhaps be invited to participate if they have the potential to develop a meaningful nuclear capability or if their presence will lend an aura of international de-

[20] Morton H. Halperin, *China and the Bomb* (New York, 1965), pp. 131–32.

[21] Michael B. Yahuda, "China's Nuclear Option," in *China After the Cultural Revolution: A Selection from The Bulletin of the Atomic Scientists* (New York, 1969), p. 198.

[22] Michael E. Sherman, *Nuclear Proliferation: The Treaty and After* (Ontario, Canada, 1968), p. 36.

mocracy to what must essentially be a process of negotiation among the global elite. Still, it is only the actual possession of atomic arms that establishes standing in diplomatic conclaves and assures consideration in the calculations of other states.

IDEOLOGICAL COMPETITION

Any discussion of the utility of nuclear weapons as a policy instrument in foreign affairs must be guided by the realization that international politics at the present time is very much a product of the broad competition between the predominant ideological blocs. Geographical, historical, cultural, and opportunistic considerations are powerful—perhaps determinant—factors shaping the configuration of forces in the world arena but it is the conflict of alternative models of development and government that provides an element of fluidity. The formally nonaligned states which were brought into existence by World War II, nationalism, and the disintegration of coionialism are the primary objects of ideological proselytizing (though some effort is made to direct propaganda at the populations of the great-power adversaries.) The educated elites of these emergent countries have a unique opportunity (within certain limits of realpolitik) to choose which model to emulate in whole or part. The phenomenon of consciously adopting a given system of production and authority is unparalleled in the history of incrementally evolving nation states.

The two criteria by which a political philosophy can be judged involve assessments of values and performance. Values refer to the quality of life, the degree of freedom in the system and the amount of popular approval of the prevailing arrangements. Performance concerns the condition and size of the economy, the level of employment and the capacity for continuous technological innovation. Without question, performance, which can be quantified, is a more convenient basis of judgment than values, which can only be subjectively interpreted. The competition between ideological blocs, therefore, is largely reduced to a contest of material output with only perfunctory attention paid to the rationality and justice of the underlying political theories. One aspect of performance—a barometer which has achieved excessive emotional and symbolic importance—is the existence of a complete nuclear program which includes the fabrication of advanced weapons. Though it would be simplistic to equate nuclear weapons with the success of an ideological system, the possession of these devices is a necessary though not a sufficient condition for respect. Capitalist and Socialist powers feel bound to match each other's arsenals at least in part to demonstrate to the yet uncommitted states that their respective economies and technologies have the capacity and vigor not to be outclassed. An innovation which really does represent a triumph of superior ability on the part of one ideological bloc will place the other at a considerable disadvantage in the struggle for allegiances (to say nothing of the struggle to maintain military security.)

As the science and engineering of nuclear weapons becomes more public and less expensive, however, the development of these armaments will naturally cease to be considered a major accomplishment and indicator of the vitality of a given ideology in operation. At some time in the future, it might very well be possible for underdeveloped countries of unarticulated political philosophies to construct several devices if they can assemble some physicists, technicians, critical materials, and capital. But for now, the creation and refinement of a nuclear capability continues to be a crucial psychological pawn in the nonmilitary global competition between ideological blocs for the respect and cooperation of the presently uncommitted states.[23]

Alliance Politics

Alliance politics involves relations among states which are formally committed to agreements of friendship, mutual assistance, and collective defense. They maintain institutionalized processes for resolving internal disputes and for formulating a shared policy toward nonmembers. This formalization of status distinguishes an alliance from a situation of simple nonantagonism. Although allies are supposed to be governed in their common affairs by principles of cooperation, respect, and equality, they are, in fact, prone to engage in independent undertakings and self-serving maneuvers aimed at advancing their relative position within the nominally united group.

[23] The use of the possession of nuclear weapons by a state to exact regional concessions has been omitted from this catalogue of possible nonmilitary reasons of international politics for acquiring atomic arms. Even when there is almost no chance that these weapons will be employed—because of tactical inapplicability, e.g., U.S.–Vietnam or because of great power strategic coverage, e.g., India-China—the threat of their use is an aspect of psychological warfare which can better be considered a military function of nuclear weapons and thus beyond the scope of this essay.

Entrance into an alliance hardly alters the dynamic of a country's external policy—the protection and advancement of state interests—but merely adds a new sub-arena within which it can pursue its goals.

Just as the acquisition of nuclear weapons serves certain functions in international politics, that is, in relations with adversaries, so too can it be used to great effect in alliance politics, that is, in relations with colleagues. Essentially, there are three ways to use the possession of nuclear weapons in respect to alliance politics: 1) to secure entrance into such an organization, 2) to gain a greater voice in the consultative councils of the alliance, and, 3) to sever membership in the group. These functions can be illustrated by examining representative case studies.

ADMISSION

Israeli leaders and defense specialists, aware of the precarious nature of the Middle East security situation, would like nothing better than to enter into a Western-oriented bilateral or multilateral military alliance.[24] While Moshe Dayan and others have repeatedly asserted that their country would never request the assistance of foreign troops,[25] they would like to conclude an agreement whereby they would obtain allies committed to supply their hardware needs while extending strategic protection against overt Russian intervention. Although the United States and Britain have indicated their determination not to countenance the destruction of Israel and have sold arms to the Jewish state, Jerusalem, guided by the memory of France's reversal, is wary of such voluntarism. A signed accord with the United States or inclusion in the NATO alliance would constitute the guaranteed support that the Israelis feel would deter the Arabs (and the Russians) or defeat them if a test of arms developed.

Neither of these desired arrangements seems likely to be approved —given present circumstances—by any of the proposed partners.

---

[24] "Privately and publicly applying for a mutual defense arrangement with the United States only to be rejected time and again, Israel made few political efforts to become a member of the Third World in formation, but it made many and determined efforts to keep, deepen and even put on an exclusive basis her friendship with the United States." M. S. Arnoni, *Rights and Wrongs in the Arab-Israeli Conflict* (Passaic, N.J., 1968), p. 24. The author presents the Arab viewpoint, but the foregoing assertion would be accepted by most observers.

[25] See Ruth Gruber, *Israel: On the Seventh Day* (New York, 1968), p. 49.

The United States is wary of concluding a formal commitment to the military defense of Israel for a number of obvious reasons: 1) fear of becoming implicated in an embroilment similar to that in Vietnam (especially if the war in Southeast Asia continues), 2) fear of being maneuvered into a confrontation with Russia as a result of the uncontrolled actions of their respective client states, 3) desire not to further alienate the Arabs who are not yet regarded as irreconcilable enemies and with whom substantial commerce (investment and trade) is still conducted, and 4) desire not to give the Soviet Union the impression that an attempt is being made to threaten its southern flank through the interjection of American troops in the Middle East.[26] Similarly, the member states of NATO are unwilling to extend membership in the organization to Israel for a variety of pragmatic reasons: 1) fear of purposefully seeking to become involved in a volatile situation which could very easily spread to Europe, 2) fear of angering the Arab countries from which the nations of Western Europe purchase their oil, 3) desire not to enlarge the area of territorial responsibility of NATO (some original members are still upset about the accession of Greece and Turkey to the Treaty), and, 4) desire not to erode further the cohesion of the alliance through internecine quarrels about the wisdom of associating with Israel.[27] Thus, there is seemingly little reason to believe that Israel can gain entrance into either a bilateral or a multilateral alliance.

However, there is one development that could alter present circumstances sufficiently to make irrelevant those arguments against concluding a pact with the troubled Jewish state: the creation of an autonomous Israeli nuclear force. A good deal of evidence suggests that the super powers regard proliferation—particularly in so explosive a region as the Middle East—as the single most destabilizing threat to peace and Soviet-American detente. Both sides are anxious to avoid the introduction of atomic arms into this battle zone because of the very real danger that this would make it impossible to con-

[26] The existence of such formations as NATO, CENTO, and SEATO (pacts of differing characters) in addition to bilateral agreements is disturbing to the Russians who feel that the United States and its allies are attempting to construct a series of hostile defense groups along the periphery of the Soviet Union in fulfillment of a policy of containment. A pact with Israel would inescapably give added credence to this notion.

[27] For an interesting discussion of Israeli policy in regard to the United States, the NATO countries and the Middle East in addition to other matters, see Theodore Draper, *Israel and World Politics* (New York, 1968).

tinue to limit hostilities to this area. The super powers may very well be willing to make certain concessions and commitments to their respective friends in the Middle East in return for a prohibition on independent nuclear forces. Since Israel is the region's most technologically advanced country, the United States would be first to face this choice.

In brief, a hypothetical situation could develop as follows. Israel acquires, or announces that it will soon do so, nuclear weapons. This disturbs the United States and the Soviet Union; both believe that a dangerous element has been added to the Middle East conflict that threatens the stability of the region and increases the likelihood of an unwanted Soviet-American confrontation. At this point, Israel—whose real goal is to secure an alliance rather than to deploy more destructive arms systems—offers an exchange. In return for a mutual defense treaty with the United States, Jerusalem will surrender its atomic arsenal or accede to a dual control arrangement with the Americans. This trade-off might very well be found acceptable to both the United States and the Soviet Union (which would probably reciprocate by negotiating parallel agreements with the Arab states it supports) because the supposedly more responsible super powers would thereby avoid the diffusion of control over nuclear weapons and preserve their own preeminence. (France and China continue to be problems in any event.)

In effect, as this projection upon the Israeli case suggests, a very plausible reason for acquiring nuclear weapons is to give them up in return for a formal alliance which would provide greater security for the "extortionist" state. The super powers involved may not be enamoured of this pressured liaison but find it preferable to the powerlessness of possibly becoming implicated in a nuclear war against their inclination. This use of nuclear weapons can justly be termed *a nonmilitary function* because there is no intention of coordinating nuclear arms into a defense or deterrence strategy. It is simply their existence—or the belief in their existence—that is sufficient to gain the desired diplomatic objective which, in turn, is directly related to the country's security position.

RESPECTED VOICE

While it was possible in the preceding paragraphs only to speculate about how the acquisition of nuclear weapons might be motivated by a desire to gain entrance into a formal alliance, there is a good deal of empirical evidence that another reason a country might develop these devices is to assure itself a respected voice in the councils of an alliance of which it is already a recognized member.

The British experience, in this regard, is very instructive.[28] Despite her major contribution to the wartime atom-bomb project (particularly in the early theoretical stages), Britain discovered itself in 1945 to be without the bomb and prevented by American administrative and legislative restrictions from obtaining complete knowledge of the requisite processes. Because the British continued to consider themselves a great power, the decision was soon taken to construct atomic weapons.[29] As its independent nuclear program progressed, Britain was coming to realize just how costly the war had been. The disintegration of the Empire and the stagnation of the metropolitan economy indicated that Britain had lost its position of strength and was unlikely to regain its former elevated standing.

On April 4, 1949, the North Atlantic Treaty—with its crucial clause stating that an attack upon one would be considered an attack against all—was signed thereby guaranteeing Britain and the other European signatories American participation in the event of an armed conflict. This major security development, however, had little visible effect on the British decision to acquire an independent nuclear force. Work continued apace and a successful atomic device was tested on October 3, 1952. (A thermonuclear bomb was exploded five years later.)

The question naturally arises as to why Britain, assured of U.S. military intervention and cognizant that it did not have the resources to develop a deterrent credible to either of the super powers, chose

[28] There are very informative and helpful essays on Britain and nuclear weapons in the collection edited by R. N. Rosecrance previously cited. See chs. II and V by H. A. DeWeerd and chs. III and IV by Rosecrance. Much of the following material can be found there and in Leonard Beaton and John Maddox, *The Spread of Nuclear Weapons* (New York, 1962).

[29] Aside from considerations of status and prestige, there does seem to have been some concern at this time (the late Forties) about the country's military security. Relations with Russia had deteriorated with the onset of the Cold War and the intentions of the United States did not become clear until the establishment of NATO in 1949. As Attlee reflected years later, "It (the development of nuclear arms) had become essential. We had to hold up our position vis-à-vis the Americans. We couldn't allow ourselves to be wholly in their hands and their position wasn't awfully clear always. . . . We had to look to our defense—and to our industrial future." Quoted by R. N. Rosecrance, "British Incentives to Become a Nuclear Power," in Rosecrance, p. 56.

to pursue an atomic ambition. One explanation, discussed previously and particularly valid in the immediate aftermath of World War II, involves lingering self-conceptions of great-power status and prestige. Another, more enduring, reason is that the British felt that the possession of nuclear weapons was necessary to assure themselves a respected voice in an alliance which might otherwise be quite thoroughly dominated by the powerful United States.

When there is more than one political unit controlling strategic armaments within an alliance, all the states which are so equipped, regardless of the relative disparity of their forces, must consult and cooperate together in determining a common policy. Discussion and coordination are of the utmost importance among those pact members which have the separate capacity to instantaneously implicate the entire group in a thermonuclear exchange with an adversary. For example, it is revealing to compare the difference between U.S.–British and U.S.–Danish relations within the context of NATO. Britain has the explosives and delivery systems necessary for a serious attack on the Soviet Union whereas Denmark has no such offensive capability and is even dependent upon her stronger friends for territorial defense. Obviously, the United States must treat Britain with greater deference that it does Denmark because the former has both the status symbol of a great power as well as the very real ability to cause catastrophic harm to the United States as a result of an ignorant or petulant provocation or attack on the Soviet Union.[30]

Thus, the British nuclear program since the conclusion of the North Atlantic Treaty may reasonably be thought to have been aimed at gaining influence on the United States within the alliance rather than to have been meant to intimidate the Russians.[31] In this case, the acquisition of nuclear weapons serves the nonmilitary func-

[30] There is no suggestion here that Britain would directly and calculatedly try to influence American policy and action in this manner.

[31] The original (pre-DeGaulle) French decision to construct nuclear weapons may very well have been motivated by the same factors that guided British policy-makers, i.e., a desire for great-power status and a respected voice in NATO. Witness this observation by Lawrence Scheinman, "Diplomatically, France had discovered during the preceeding several years (before 1957) that her nuclear inferiority had markedly affected her capacity to play a major role in the strategy-direction and decision-making councils of NATO." Lawrence Scheinman, *Atomic Energy Policy in France Under the Fourth Republic* (Princeton, N.J., 1965), pp. 189–90.

tion of an instrument of alliance politics whereby a weaker partner is able to secure the attention, respect, and consultation of the leader.[32]

SEVERANCE

Finally, the possession of nuclear weapons can enable a country to reduce its commitments to an alliance or withdraw entirely. The example of France and NATO is instructive on this point. President DeGaulle maintained very different attitudes toward each of the two aspects of the alliance: 1) the collective defense treaty and 2) the organization established to integrate military planning. The Treaty was an agreement between sovereign, independent, and nominally equal states which were reciprocally pledged to join with an attacked member against an external adversary. The Organization, with its civilian and military councils to coordinate policy and preparation, was inherently hierarchical and discriminatory. To the French leaders of the Fifth Republic, adherence to a mutual defense pact was prudent and honorable while participation in its operational apparatus was undemocratic and demeaning. France had joined NATO when it was particularly weak and in need of the protection and assistance of the United States. Subsequent developments—postwar reconstruction, extrication from Indo-China and Algeria, formation of the Common Market—completely altered this condition and laid the groundwork for the reassertion of French pride and autonomy.

To obtain the approval of officials and citizens for his plan to withdraw France from the organizational dimension of NATO, DeGaulle had to convince them that such a course was not only gratifying but also feasible in regard to security. Atomic weapons were the ideal symbol of technological sophistication and military strength; the substantial fact that a French nuclear force was practically useless in deterring or defending against the Soviet Union was psychologically irrelevant.[33] The development of a supposedly viable nuclear-weap-

[32] It might also be mentioned in this regard that West Germany has raised the specter of its acquiring nuclear weapons in order to bring indirect pressure on its allies not to evade the reunification issue in their dealings with the Soviet Union.

[33] The military rationale for a French *"force de frappe"*—as developed in the writings of General Gallois and others—is basically unconvincing because of its overestimation of the capability of a medium power to affect a super power. Certainly, it was not Gallois's theories that dictated French nuclear decisions. As Rothstein observes, both France and Britain "developed nuclear

ons system gave the French the confidence to lessen their dependence on NATO and its Anglo-Saxon leadership. The very existence of the *force de frappe* was seen formally to elevate France once again to great-power status and to provide it with at least the illusion of meaningful strength in the international arena. Of course, real security continues to rest in the American guarantee expressed through commitment to the North Atlantic Treaty pledge that an attack upon one would be considered an attack upon all to be dealt with appropriately. For France, the possession of nuclear weapons has, in reality, played a significant psychological rather than military role. Acquisition of these arms made possible the renewed self-esteem and international respect that enabled France to reduce its involvement in that part of an alliance which was subjectively regarded as superfluous and oppressive.

Domestic Politics

The decision to acquire nuclear weapons often depends on a compound of domestic political factors in addition to an objective evaluation of the security position of the state. Interest group conflicts and economic projections must be recognized and appreciated to understand fully the whole range of influences which bear upon the calculations of policy-makers. While strategists may theoretically isolate and examine the military problems and opportunities confronting their nation, political leaders are unable to concentrate solely on this component, but find it necessary to consider a variety of nonmilitary, internal matters. This is true regardless of the basic ideological principles by which the particular government is structured. The leadership of both the United States and the Soviet Union (as well as that of any country which must face the nuclear choice) is compelled to take a multiplicity of (often conflicting) pressures into account in determining a course of national policy and action.[34] (In the five coun-

---

weapons and then sought a strategy which would justify their acquisition." Rothstein, p. 41.

[34] After judging how the acquisition of nuclear weapons will bear upon their areas, spokesmen for major interest groups can be expected to lobby for their special positions and benefactors, competing for the attention and trust of the decision-makers. The implications for a society considering a nuclear weapons project are so extensive and yet so inadequately understood that there is bound to be intense argument about its probable effects. The feedback

tries which have exercised the nuclear option, the decision to do so was basically made by the top political elite with a minimum of public discussion.[35] There is every reason to believe that this will continue to be the pattern should other countries choose to join the nuclear club.)

INTRA-ELITE CONFLICT

As members of the political elite consider the question of nuclear weapons, one of their primary concerns is how the decision taken will affect their own individual positions and careers. Though the circumstance is scarcely appreciated, the acquisition of nuclear weapons is largely a resultant of intra-elite conflict. Factions within the leadership circle argue and maneuver to see the adoption of their recommendations as well as the strengthening of their own sector of responsibility. These elite factions, of course, have experts and allies distributed throughout the society on whom they can call for needed advice and support in the high-level struggle. Not enough cross-national empirical research has been done to determine whether there is consistency in which groups urge nuclear weapons development and which groups oppose it. Three factions within the elite are generally assumed to favor atomic arms programs for self-serving (as well as patriotic) reasons. These supposed proponents are: 1) the military, 2) the political hardliners (civilian and military), and 3) the heavy industrialists.

It is to be expected that the military, understanding its mandate to be that of maintaining maximum preparedness with the best possible arms, will agitate for increased [36] expenditures in the field of nuclear

---

of information and opinion from those studying the likely consequences of a proposed program of atomic development is inevitably incorporated into the decision-equation fashioned by those with the ultimate responsibility for evaluating and comparing the available options. This is not to imply a pluralistic model of atomic policy decision-making. As will shortly be discussed, only the most powerful political, military, and industrial groups—representing a small fraction of the people—are involved to the extent of forming opinions and giving advice.

[35] Describing the French case, Scheinman defines this elite as "a relatively small group of people well situated in authoritative positions and operating through informal channels of communication outside the mainstream of political activity." Scheinman, p. xvi.

[36] The word *increased* is very significant in this context. Experience shows that the armed services in the countries that have exercised the nuclear option

weapons acquisition. Aside from concern for defense, the attention, money, and technical innovation inherent in the manufacture of new weapons redounds to the power and prestige of those people who lead the military establishment. Contrariwise, the argument is also made that nuclear weapons improve the relative position of the civilian leadership over the military. The nature of atomic warfare puts a premium on the ability to manage political crises without resort to the strongest instruments in the country's arsenal, but if they are to be used, the decision is that of the civilian head of state assisted by his closest counselors. Nonmilitary leaders can control a nuclear-war situation as their counterparts have never been able to do in respect to conventional war. (All of this, of course, is mercifully only in the realm of speculation and hypothesis.) It is unclear, therefore, whether one can generalize as to whether it is the military or civilian factions within the political elite which profits by a decision to acquire atomic arms. What is important is that these factions will operate in accordance with their perception of how such a program will affect their position. Without discounting the ostensible primacy of security considerations, when the utility of a nation's possession of nuclear weapons is not either overwhelmingly clear or patently absurd, it can be expected that the various factions within the elite will advance proposals which are seen to benefit their particular interests.

A second elite faction which generally does urge the acquisition of nuclear weapons is that of the political hardliners consisting of similarly inclined civilians and military men. This group strengthens its relative position within the leadership through the process of the self-fulfilling prophecy. First, dire warnings are made regarding the threat posed by hostile states to the security of the country. This danger can be relieved, it is claimed, through increased military preparedness, that is, nuclear weapons or whatever else is new and destructive. Such an undertaking inevitably induces a reaction from that state against which the armament program was directed. The politi-

---

were often very hesitant to enter the era of nuclear-equipped armed forces. In many cases they opposed or passively accepted the recommendations made by civilian defense specialists. Cautious and conservative military leaders were not always willing to invest in new weapons systems and modes of control at the expense of familiar and well understood methods of organized warfare. Therefore, while the military has usually been a proponent of increased expenditures, it was often opposed to *initial* appropriations in the years when nuclear weapons were a novelty.

cal hardliners, however, point to this reaction as proof that other states are seeking to undermine the military safety of their own country. It is in this way that they guarantee the correctness of their own predictions and thereby improve their standing with the elite. At the cost of an ever expanding arms race, the political hardliners seek continually to extend their influence. Even without questioning the personal sincerity of the members of this group, it is clear that the dynamic which has been described does benefit their relative power position and in a close case can not fail but to influence their recommendations.

Another group within the elite which is credited with being advocates of nuclear-weapons acquisition is that of the managers of industry (particularly heavy industry), in both capitalist [37] and socialist economies. These men prosper politically as the investment and expansion in their sector is increased. The creation of a viable weapons system (as opposed to a few ceremonial detonations) involves tremendous outlays of money and manpower for research, scientific facilities, production factories. Great benefit, of course, is also reaped from the effects of technological spin-off. Little wonder that the elite members of this background would prefer resource allocation to this area—through an affirmative decision on nuclear weapons—than to other parts of the economy with which they are less directly associated. As already noted in regard to other groups within the leadership, it is not that industrial managers selfishly put their own welfare above the best interests of the state—that would ultimately be self-defeating—but that when the objective arguments for and against are closely balanced, elite faction self-interest becomes determinant.

NATIONAL ECONOMY

The intent of the preceding paragraphs was not to suggest that the sole basis of elite decision-making is the conflict of factional ambitions. Self-interest is decisive when national interest is obscure. In appraising basic national interest regarding the acquisition of nuclear weapons, one of the domestic nonmilitary factors which must be considered is the effect that such a program will have on the economy.

---

[37] In capitalist countries, finance capitalists in addition to industrial capitalists favor the commencement of nuclear weapons programs and their related enterprises because maximum investment and stock profits are to be made in a (government-fueled) expanding economy in which dynamic, innovative growth industries are flourishing.

In this respect, we are not considering the sectarian interests of the industrial managers as expressed in intra-elite argument and manipulation; rather, we are concerned with the attitude of the policy-makers toward the relationship between the acquisition of nuclear weapons and the status of the national economy.

An analysis of the affirmative decisions taken by the 5 great powers and of the content of the debates raging in a host of other countries today indicates that many politicians and experts consider an atomic-arms program which is rationally planned and patiently implemented to be economically beneficial to their respective countries. The common assertion that nuclear weapons are wasteful while commercial nuclear plants are useful appears, in practice, not really to be valid (at least so far as policy-makers are concerned). An atomic-arms program contributes to the economy in three ways: 1) provides a general stimulus, 2) results in increased electric power generation, and 3) leads to a variety of theoretical and practical advances through technological spin-off.

The development of a credible nuclear-weapons system involves the expenditure of substantial amounts of money as well as the mobilization of scientific talent and industrial resources. Never has a civilian program been able to command the investment and commitment that can be gotten by programs justified by national defense needs. Despite strain on governmental budgets, there is no evidence that the acquisition of nuclear weapons has adversely affected the financial condition of the people in the United States, the Soviet Union, Britain, France, and China. While it may be logically argued that any large-scale innovative task will result in increased jobs and incomes from constantly expanding related industries, the historical point is that this has most often occurred in the case of making instruments of warfare. The likelihood of this situation changing, that is, conversion, is improbable even if it is desirable. Many countries now contemplating the exercise of their option are inspired by expectations of economic benefits rather than financial sacrifice for the sake of national security. Even Japan, whose postwar economic miracle is commonly credited to the relative absence of defense spending and the concentration of resources on the peaceful applications of technology, is examining the incentives for constructing nuclear weapons including that of "the stimulus it would give to the economy." [38] If it is

---

[38] Bader, p. 80. It must be pointed out that the author goes on to say that it is still extremely doubtful that the Japanese actually would develop nuclear

true (or thought to be true by the country's decision-makers) that the construction of these weapons is financially useful, then the acquisition of atomic arms may increasingly come to serve the nonmilitary function of bolstering the domestic economy.

Even if one does not accept the proposition that the manufacture of atomic-arms and modern-delivery systems is beneficial to the entire economy, it is clear that a military nuclear program inevitably assists some sectors, most notably the country's gross electric-power generating capacity. Every state contemplating the nuclear decision is aware of the complementary relationship between atomic explosives and power reactors. In order to construct a fission bomb, it is necessary to accumulate and process substantial (as measured by time and equipment) amounts of plutonium. The most abundant source of this critical material is as a by-product of uranium-fueled electric-power generators.[39] Although they are more promising than conventional plants, atomic-power reactors are still very expensive and not really accepted by cost-conscious budget officials and ordinary citizens. Political leaders who are convinced of the necessity of increasing the amount of electric power generated and of using nuclear reactors to do the job can overcome such hesitancy through a policy of benign deceit. By asserting that the national defense requires atomic arms or the capability to make them on short notice, support can be obtained for these power reactors that would not have been forthcoming if only their commercial utility had been emphasized. In short, a program can almost always be assured of official and popular approval if it can be related (truthfully or speciously) to security. In the period 1952–60, for example, the French civilian program had to be justified in terms of military potential. Scheinman observes:

Within this industrial framework, military applications of atomic energy received an increasingly greater emphasis, partly as a result of the assessment of French security requirements, partly because peaceful applications were not economically feasible enough to warrant a large-scale industrial effort.[40]

Thus, another domestic nonmilitary reason for acquiring nuclear weapons is that it provides the rationale and unassailable cover for

---

weapons since any advantages would be "outweighed by the restraints imposed by the country's physical circumstances, its relationship to the United States, and to its national psychology." *Ibid.*

[39] See Beaton, ch. 5, "Plutonium."   [40] Scheinman, p. 202.

developing the peaceful (though perhaps not immediately profitable) uses of atomic energy.

A final economic reason that a country might undertake to construct a nuclear-weapons system is that such programs are closely associated with modernization and material well-being. A great deal of attention is paid to the possibilities of technological spin-off and the unforeseen benefits which the 5 nuclear powers have received as a result of their military programs. Even before the first atomic test, it was known that nuclear energy could be harnessed as a source of electric power, but few predicted the wide range of scientific, medical, and commercial discoveries that would follow.[41] Ideally, a country would directly pursue those nonmilitary advantages of nuclear energy. However, the pattern has been (and there is little expectation that it will soon be changed) that such benefits were subsidiary effects of a weapons program upon which most effort had been expended. The assumption of benefits from technological spin-off, therefore, is a minor economic reason for proceeding with a nuclear-weapons program but some cognizance should be taken of its influence on decision-making.

The Politics of Illusory Security

Before concluding this essay on the nonmilitary reasons that nations acquire atomic weapons, some mention must be made of the ill-considered, reflex causes of nuclearization. There is a dangerous tendency to proceed to stockpiling weapons of mass destruction due to strategic misconceptions and an absence of thought about possible consequences. Arguments are often advanced in favor of atomic-weapons development which purport to be derived from military considerations, but are actually rooted in instinct and supposition.

As discussed earlier, security is an incredibly complex condition which can be upset by actions simplistically intended to provide greater safety for the individual country. When a decision which is ostensibly based on a military analysis is really based on misinformation and ignorance, it seems appropriate that it be discussed separately from valid military arguments. Those nations which have already joined the nuclear club did so for logical, if sometimes subtle,

[41] See Arnold Kramish, *The Peaceful Atom in Foreign Policy* (New York, 1963), ch. 9, "The Quiet Revolution."

reasons of military security, international politics, alliance politics, and domestic politics (the last three have been discussed above). The possibility exists—happily diminishing as nuclear-weapons strategy becomes as widely disseminated as nuclear-weapons technology— that a state may in the future acquire these bombs for outmoded or irrelevant reasons.

STRATEGIC NAÏVETE

One (non-)reason for acquiring nuclear weapons is the belief that more and better arms naturally improve security. The example of the Soviet-American arms race demonstrates that this contention is not necessarily true. At best, the constant uncritical search for improved weapons leads to a costly, stalemated arms spiral; at worst, it results in a situation of disequilibrium which tempts the stronger to strike or compels the weaker to preempt. In the atomic era, the dogma that an independent state must strive to possess the most advanced arms technologically and economically available is obsolete and dangerous in its lack of appreciation for politics, strategy, and the death-potential involved.

"INEVITABLE" PROGRESSION

A second (non-)reason for acquiring nuclear weapons involves what Bader terms "this very natural drive" [42] and what Rosecrance describes as the "well-understood psychological mechanism of task completion." [43] Essentially, this pertains to the somewhat metaphysical notion that a certain dynamic exists in a nuclear program that causes an inevitable progression toward the development of the bomb. In a rationally inexplicable manner, the internal technical and political logic of atomic science supposedly must lead to its development for destructive purposes. The truth of this proposition can not be discussed intellectually, but must be tested empirically. The United States, the Soviet Union, Britain, France, and China do not disprove (or necessarily affirm) it. Japan, India, Israel, Germany, Sweden, Switzerland, and Italy are indeterminate cases. Canada alone among the countries capable of producing nuclear weapons seems to have conclusively demonstrated its intention not to do so and thereby has shown that under certain conditions the nuclear option may be discarded. In this essay, an attempt has been made to identify some nonmilitary reasons why nations acquire nuclear weap-

[42] Bader, p. 85. [43] Rosecrance, "Introduction," in Rosecrance, p. 4.

ons. It would be a disavowal of what has been said previously to accept the claim that no reason is needed at all and that nuclear weapons are a natural and inevitable consequence of atomic experimentation. Insane though the situation may sometimes appear, never has a decision to develop nuclear weapons been made that was not supported by complex and sometimes contradictory estimations of the military and nonmilitary interests that would thereby be served. There is every likelihood that this will continue to be the case.

Concluding Note

Critical to any agreement on arms control and disarmament is a thorough understanding of all possible reasons for the acquisition of nuclear weapons. If the underlying motivations are not identified and analyzed, little progress can be expected in dealing with their effects. Considerable attention has been devoted to the military considerations which necessitate (or justify) the development of atomic arms. However, in order to fashion truly effective arrangements, the nonmilitary factors involved in the decision to obtain nuclear weapons must also be closely scrutinized.

This essay represents a preliminary effort to examine some of the nonmilitary reasons that nations have constructed atomic-weapons systems or might be tempted to do so in the future. The issues which are discussed need not be iterated or belabored here; they are presented to stimulate thought rather than to support specific conclusions. Obviously, the formulation and acceptance of meaningful diplomatic accords on arms control and disarmament is possible only if the diverse incentives for nuclear-weapons acquisition are recognized and if suitable provisions are made to alternatively satisfy the military and the political functions of these arms.

The Horia Rebellion in Transylvania, 1784-1785

PAUL A. SHAPIRO

Pîn-a fostu Horia împĕratu
Domniĭ nu s-aŭ descultatŭ,
Nicĭ în patŭ nu s-aŭ culcatŭ
Prândŭ la masă n-aŭ mâncatŭ;
Craiu finu Niculescu
Pe car' Horea numescŭ . . .

[As long as Horia was emperor
The lords didn't take off their shoes,
Nor did they sleep in their beds
Nor eat their dinner at the table;
Our fine king Niculescu
Whose name they call Horia. . . .]

—1879: Cărpeniş [1]

Peasant rebellions in the Habsburg Monarchy had not been uncommon in earlier times, but they were perhaps never so numerous as in the eighteenth century. In Hungary alone there were eight major uprisings between 1735 and 1790.[2] By far the greatest and most ferocious of these was the revolt which began in Transylvania in 1784,

[1] Nicolas Densuşianu, *Revolutiunea lui Horio în Transilvania şi Ungaria, 1784-1785* [The revolution of Horia in Transylvania and Hungary, 1784-1785] (Bucharest, 1884), p. 465. This poem was recited to Densuşianu in 1879 by Gheorghe Gligoră and Ursŭ Coroiŭ of the village of Cărpeniş.

[2] Hungary here is intended to include Royal Hungary, Croatia, and Transylvania, though Transylvania was administratively separate during most of these years. For an outline of the constitutional structure of Hungary see Béla K. Király, *Hungary in the Late Eighteenth Century* (New York, 1969), p. 241.

under the leadership of Horia, Cloşca, and Crişan.[3] It is difficult to say whether the Horia Rebellion, as I call it, was "typical" of peasant rebellions in the Habsburg dominions, for many have been called *typical* while only the element of some sort of peasant discontent was common to all. The rebellion bore some resemblance to the Bohemian Nywelt-Chvojka Revolt of 1774–75 which erupted when, prior to the issuance of the Robot patent of August 13, 1775, the rebels claimed "that a patent had been issued which freed them of all robota, but that the seigneurs had suppressed it" and that "they were . . . the soldiers of the Emperor merely taking what he had demanded for them." [4] Despite his sympathy with the plight of the Bohemian peasants, Emperor Joseph II, at this time co-Regent with his mother, had the rebellion subdued by Imperial troops. The Horia Rebellion also resembled the 1735 Pero Segedinác Revolt which took place in the Békés County of Royal Hungary and which Béla Király describes in the following terms:

Its causes were many and complex, but above all was the traditional cause of unrest—the misery of the peasants . . . . Religious grievances also played a part. The rebels' main weakness was their lack of modern weapons in contrast to the fairly well equipped standing army. The rebels sought only to free the peasantry from the harsh burdens of their urbarial obligations and the *portio;* they did not aim to alter the feudal social system. It was a peasant revolt par excellence, doomed to failure, as such revolts usually were, when confronted by the superior forces of the organized state.[5]

Finally, the Horia Rebellion bore considerable resemblance to "the most notable and most typical Croatian peasant rebellion," [6] the Matija Gubec Rebellion of 1573, of which Tomasevich writes:

The slogan of the rebellion was "For Old Rights" (za stare pravice). This slogan is met very often where conflicts between the peasantry and the feudal lords appear. The content of the old rights cannot be defined. What they generally denoted was the earlier, the traditional, and for the

---

[3] For an enumeration of eighteenth-century Hungarian peasant revolts, see *ibid.,* p. 213.

[4] William E. Wright, *Serf, Seigneur, and Sovereign: Agrarian Reform in Eighteenth Century Bohemia* (Minneapolis, Minn., 1966), p. 49.

[5] Király, pp. 212–13.

[6] Jozo Tomasevich, *Peasants, Politics, and Economic Change in Yugoslavia* (Stanford, Calif., 1955), p. 67.

serfs more favorable burden of obligations toward the feudal lord, to which the peasantry tenaciously clung, especially in times when the feudatories tried to increase their obligations and reduce their rights. The leaders . . . planned to free the peasants from serfdom and to establish a peasant government in Zagreb responsible directly to the Emperor, in whom the peasants believed as a protector against the rapacious feudatories. They also advocated equality among classes and payment of taxes . . . by all classes.[7]

But while the Horia Rebellion shared some common characteristics with each of these previous rebellions, it was not the same as any single one of them.

As in so many other cases, it is worthwhile here to point out what the Horia Rebellion was not. It was not simply a feudal rebellion in the strict sense of the term. Nor was it a religious or a national rebellion, though it has often been characterized as both. The revolts in Bohemia, Royal Hungary, and Croatia mentioned above were all feudal revolts of serfs against their local feudal lords. The Horia Rebellion, on the other hand, began in 1782 [8] not as a general revolt of feudal serfs against their landlords, but as a protest by fiscal "serfs of the state" living on crown lands in the Zarand, Metalici, and the Apuseni Mountains against the general deterioration of their economic situation and more specifically against the excesses of the Imperial functionaries administering these districts from the town of Zlatna. Although the rebellion rapidly grew to encompass many of the serfs, both fiscal and feudal, of the counties of Zarand (Zaránd), Hunedoară (Hunyad), Alba (Fehér), Turda (Torda), Cluj (Kolozs), and Arad (Arad), and even of Maramureş (Mármaros)—counties of the "Land of the Hungarians" in Transylvania [9]—both Hungarian and Romanian historians agree that, at its inception at least, the rebellion was a local affair within the emperor's direct fiscal domain. Ladislas Makkai writes:

---

[7] *Ibid.*

[8] I reckon the beginning of this rebellion from the Câmpeni incident, discussed later in this essay.

[9] See Király, Appendix A. Transylvania was divided into the Land of the Hungarians, the Land of the Székelys, and the Land of the Saxons. In order to maintain uniformity of nomenclature, I use Romanian place names for all Transylvanian counties, cities, and towns referred to in this essay. Where Hungarian or German place names are well known, I include them in parentheses immediately after the first appearance of the place name.

It was in the state property of Zlatna that the movement broke out: the Treasury was for its serfs a lord perhaps even more cruel than the Hungarian or Saxon landlord.[10]

and his Romanian contemporary Nicolae Iorga concurs:

It was a matter only of a local movement, of interest to the fiscal peasants and directed against revenue farmers and not principally against the nobles . . . for there were no feudal nobles on this territory.[11]

The ranks of the fiscal state serfs of Zlatna produced the three major chieftains of the rebellion, Ursŭ Nicola, alias Horia, Ion Oargă, alias Ion Cloşca, and Gheorghe Marculu, alias Gheorghe Crişan.[12] Horia was a state serf born in 1730 in the village of Albac in the Abrud mining region of the Apuseni Mountains. Despite claims by some Romanian nationalist historians that he knew how to read and write and that he spoke "fluent German," [13] it is unlikely that Horia possessed any of these capabilities. It is uncertain whether the two letters in Romanian (in Cyrillic script) attributed to Horia and now located in the Jankowitz Archives in Cluj (Kolozsvár, Klausenburg)— letters from Horia to György Bisztrai, the subprefect of Câmpeni— were actually written by the revolutionary leader.[14] On the other hand, it is known that his letter of November, 1784, to Lieutenant Hoffmann of the First Regiment of Romanian Border Guards was written for him by a Romanian nobleman of Câmpeni, one Alexandru Chendi,[15] that the petitions which he carried to Vienna in 1779 and 1780 were written by an ennobled Romanian of Abrud, Samuel Marţi (later a revolutionary captain for this district),[16] and that the petition

[10] Ladislas Makkai, *Histoire de Transylvanie* (Paris, 1946), p. 281.

[11] Nicolae Iorga, *Histoire des Roumains de Transylvanie et de la Hongrie* (Bucharest, 1915, 1916), II, 170.

[12] The names by which these rebel leaders are remembered, Horia, Cloşca, and Crişan, were given to them by their families in the first two cases— Horia from *hora*, 'a dance,' and Cloşca from the word meaning 'sprightly'— while the origin of the name Crişan is less certain. It perhaps came from the White Criş River which flows through the Zarand Mountains of the Zlatna district.

[13] Georges Moroïanu, *Les Luttes des Roumains Transylvains pour la Liberté, et l'Opinion Européenne* (Paris, 1933), p. 54.

[14] See Densuşianu, p. 137.

[15] *Ibid.*, pp. 149, 413. Chendi served Horia as a secretary in both Latin and Hungarian during the rebellion, according to his declaration to Vice-Colonel Karp in Abrud on January 5, 1785.

[16] *Ibid.*, pp. 105 ff.

The Horia Rebellion, 1784–1785

of late 1782 was written by István Ferenc Enyédi, the Imperial agent who, perhaps as interpreter, accompanied Horia at his audience with the Aulic Chancellery during his 1782 visit to Vienna.[17] As an additional proof in this matter, Horia himself, during his interrogation by Count Jankowitz following the demise of the rebellion, denied being able to either read or write.[18]

Whatever his education or degree of literacy, however, Horia was considered a social leader by the local population of the Zlatna region as early as 1779, when they first sent him to Vienna, and, as early as October, 1782, he was considered the most dangerous agitator of the Abrud Mountains by the administrators of the Zlatna district.[19] Ordering the arrest of Horia on October 5, 1782, Administrator György Devai wrote:

in these mountainous areas people put great faith in Horia, and put all their hope in him . . . . I fear that if he arrives once more at Vienna it is likely that in the spring the mountain people will begin an uprising greater than that of Sofronie.[20]

Born in the village of Cărpeniş in the Abrud district in 1744, Ion Closca, the youngest of the three captains, was also a state serf. He accompanied Horia to Vienna in 1779, 1780, and 1782, but apparently not in 1783–84. Wealthier than either of his fellow commanders, he owned a house and both cultivated and pasture lands on the main road from Abrud to Câmpeni.

Gheorghe Crişan, also a state serf, was born in Cărpeniş in 1732. He made no voyages to Vienna, and little is known of his life prior to 1784 except that he served for several years in the Transylvanian military regiment of Count Ferenc Gyulai.[21] In 1784 he was to prove the most violent and destructive of the three revolutionary leaders,

---

[17] *Ibid.*, pp. 108 ff.   [18] *Ibid.*, p. 138.

[19] *Ibid.*, p. 106. Only Densuşianu of all the sources cited gave any indication of how the representatives financed their journeys to Vienna. Closca apparently testified to Count Jankowitz that the money was provided by the local villages of the Zlatna region. He said that in 1782 he received 20 florins each from Bucium, Abrud, and Cărpeniş. The representatives traveled on foot, he said, the journey taking four weeks each way.

[20] Al. Neamţu, "Din antecedentele răscoalei lui Horia" [Concerning the antecedents of the Horia uprising], *Anuarul Institutului de Istorie din Cluj,* IX (1966), 264. Neamţu cites this passage from the *State Archives of Cluj,* Maria Theresa doc.nr.586/1782. The Sofronie uprising is discussed later in this essay.

[21] Densuşianu, p. 141.

the only one who seriously advocated the extermination or exile of all non-Orthodox, non-Romanian elements, noble and serf alike, of the lands engulfed by the rebellion.[22]

Even when the rebellion spread beyond the state domain and into truly feudal lands, for the most part under the suzerainty of Hungarian nobles in these regions of the Transylvanian Grand Principality, it still remained more social than religious or national. In this respect, as well as in the nature of its leadership, it was very different from any of the Transylvanian movements in which the Romanians of this region had participated in earlier decades of the eighteenth century. The two most important of these earlier movements had been those led by Bishop Micu-Klein and by the Orthodox priest Sofronie.

The eighteen articles of the Leopoldian Diploma of December 4, 1691, had established the legal-constitutional structure of Transylvania upon its reincorporation into the Habsburg Empire after over one hundred fifty years of rule by native princes tributary to the Ottoman Porte. The articles enumerated 4 "recognized" religions in the principality—Catholicism, Lutheranism, Calvinism, and Unitarianism—and 3 recognized nationalities—Hungarian, Saxon, and Székely. Those individuals not members of these religions or nationalities had no constitutional rights within the principality, but were simply "tolerated" groups. The Greek Orthodox Romanians formed the largest such group and constituted over 50 percent of the total Transylvanian population.[23] Subjected to the pressures of the Counter-Reformation and basing their action on the promise of material

---

[22] There is no evidence that Horia or Cloşca ever addressed the serfs or their masters in terms similar to these. Crişan, who was commander of the troops which actually began the violent stage of the rebellion on November 2, 1784, first advocated these goals under the following circumstances. On October 31, he addressed a gathering of 500 or 600 peasants from the districts of Zarand and Hunedoară at the Church of Meştecan, telling them that the emperor had given them the choice of enlisting in the border regiments or remaining serfs, with reduced feudal obligations. The local Orthodox priest confirmed the validity of Crişan's statements, and the entire body of peasants decided to go to Alba-Iulia to enlist. En route the peasants killed 2 subprefects sent from Alba-Iulia to halt their progress toward the city. At this point, fearing for their own and their families' safety, the peasants threatened to disband and return home. It was to prevent this that Crişan told the peasants that the emperor had sanctioned the execution of all the nobles and Hungarians which the peasants could lay their hands on.

[23] Makkai, p. 275.

advantages for the church hierarchy and perhaps for all converts to the new faith, the Orthodox Bishop Theophile and the Metropolitan Athanase Anghel accepted a Union of the Orthodox and Roman Catholic Churches in 1697–99, thereby creating the Uniate Church of Transylvania.[24] Innocent Micu-Klein, during the twenty-two years (1729–51) of his tenure as the Uniate Bishop of Transylvania (between 1699 and 1783 there was no Orthodox Bishop of Transylvania), led a movement aimed at the dual establishment of the Romanians as the fourth "recognized" nationality of the principality and of the Uniate Church as the fifth "recognized" religion. He also sought the end of personal serfdom (Leibeigenschaft) and the reduction of the robot obligations (compulsory feudal labor service) of serfs to two days per week.[25] Despite the fact that the Catholic-Orthodox Union was very unpopular and had made little headway among the Romanians of the South, because of its national and social aspects the movement was popular in both northern and southern regions of the principality. The leading role of the church hierarchy and the importance of ecclesiastical issues, however, clearly differentiate the Micu-Klein movement from the Horia Rebellion.

The 1759 peasant uprising led by the Orthodox priest Sofronie, an uprising which took place in the same southern regions around Abrud and Zlatna as the Horia Rebellion, was concerned exclusively with religious matters. As a result of the uprising many Uniates were reconverted to Orthodoxy, the endemic persecution of those who refused to accept the Union, common up to this time, was forbidden by the Gubernium of the principality, and, in 1762, the Orthodox population of Transylvania was placed under the jurisdiction of the Serbian Bishop of Buda.[26] Both the Micu-Klein and the Sofronie movements were largely ecclesiastical and exclusively Romanian. These were not characteristics of the Horia Rebellion.

"The most important part in putting down the rebellion of 1784," writes Nicolas Densuşianu, "was played by the leaders of the Romanian Orthodox Church of Transylvania."[27] While several local priests

---

[24] For more on the Uniate Church see Makkai, pp. 272–75.

[25] The goals of the Micu-Klein movement are explained in some detail in Constantin Daicoviciu and Miron Constantinescu, eds., *Brève Histoire de la Transylvanie* (Bucharest, 1965), pp. 149–51.

[26] R. W. Seton-Watson, *History of the Roumanians from Roman Times to the Completion of Unity* (Hamden, Conn., 1963), pp. 181–83.

[27] Densuşianu, p. 277.

supported the rebellion, the leaders of the Church opposed it from the outset. The first Orthodox Bishop of Transylvania since the founding of the Uniate Church in 1699 was the Croatian cleric Gideon Nichitici, appointed on November 6, 1783, and was installed at Sibiu (Nagyszeben, Hermannstadt) on July 12, 1784. Owing his new position to Vienna and unwilling to jeopardize it, he was ready to use his ecclesiastical authority to help subdue the rebellion which was aimed, at its inception, primarily against the Viennese administrators of the royal domain. In August, therefore, prior to the actual outbreak of violence and only weeks after his arrival in the principality, Nichitici wrote to the priests of Zarand urging them to quiet the people and to persuade them to perform their feudal and fiscal obligations.[28] In November, he traveled with Michael Brukenthal, a nephew of the governor and special commissioner of the Transylvanian government, to the disturbed areas—specifically to Miercurea, Alba-Iulia (Gyulafehérvár), Orăscia, and Deva—for the purpose of urging the peasants to return to their homes. During this journey he issued a circular to the local clergy ordering them "to travel in their communes, to read the circular of the bishop to the people, to make propaganda against Horia, and to convince the peasants to stay home." [29] Part of the bishop's circular was the following:

Horia, the captain of the rebellion, has not ceased performing evil deeds and perpetrating lies against God and against the Emperor and against the laws of the Church and the priestly blessings . . . . Therefore we order in the name of the Emperor that not a single Romanian dare to listen to the lies of Horia nor to go with him nor with his bands, nor to aid him or his men openly or secretly.[30]

The bishop's order was sufficient to put the whole upper clergy and a substantial part of the local lower clergy into action against the rebellion. As proof of the important pacification role of the Church, we find that in January, 1785, Ion Marişu, the priest of the Țebea commune in the Zarand district, was awarded a gold medallion and a salary boost of 200 florins per year because he had kept Țebea from participating in the rebellion (this was the only commune in Zarand County not to participate); in addition, all members of the commune were exempted from state taxes for one year.[31] Nichitici, who in early December traveled with the Imperial army and convinced several

[28] *Ibid.*, pp. 252–53. Densuşianu presents the text of this message.
[29] *Ibid.*, p. 278.   [30] *Ibid.*   [31] *Ibid.*, p. 481.

groups of peasants to disband without fighting, received a 1,000-florin reward from the emperor; this was the largest single amount paid to any individual for helping to suppress the rebellion.[32]

All of this, of course, does not disprove the fact that there was considerable religious hatred aroused among the peasants. In several places the peasant soldiers forced conversions, under penalty of death, on Uniates, Catholics, and Protestants, but even Densuşianu admits that this was done almost exclusively to members of the nobility and without orders from the revolutionary commanders.[33] The motives of the revolutionary leaders were social rather than religious; religious hatred, while it accounted for some of the rebellion's brutality, was only a secondary repercussion of social outrage. Thus, while accepting Makkai's assertion that "the violation undergone by the Greek Orthodox faith, social misery, and hatred of the nobility played the preponderant roles in the awakening of the passions of the masses," [34] any valid explanation of the rebellion should emphasize the roles of the last two factors more than that of the first one. However, none of the positive demands of the rebels concerned religious questions.

If it was not a religious uprising, neither was the Horia Rebellion essentially national in character. There were no demands made in the name of "the Romanians" per se, but only in the name of the serfs of Transylvania. There was no repetition of Bishop Micu-Klein's demand that the Romanians be recognized as the fourth legitimate nationality of the principality. But more positive proof of the non-national nature of the rebellion is also available. For instance, many Magyar peasants, especially from the more heavily Magyar districts around Cluj, and many Magyar mine workers fought on the side of the predominantly Romanian rebels, while many Romanian nobles took the side of the predominantly Magyar landowners. Concerning the plundering of Abrud by the rebels, Alexandru Sterca-Suluţiu, in his mid-nineteenth century *History of Horia,* writes:

[32] Even the capturers of Horia, Cloşca, and Crişan received only 300 florins and a medallion from the emperor. On rewards see Densuşianu, p. 480, on the role of Bishop Nichitici, p. 385.

[33] In the towns of Abrud and Roşia, for instance, the conversions of 548 Unitarians, 468 Reformed Protestants, 65 Catholics, and 41 Lutherans were recorded; see Densuşianu, p. 205. In Brad, several Jews were executed by the rebels.

[34] Makkai, p. 282.

Here, miraculously and unspeakably, many Magyars of the city dressed in Romanian clothes and . . . helped destroy the archives of the city and release the prisoners held there.[35]

"In villages of mixed population, Hungarian serfs rose up under leaders like Mihály Rátz, János Járai, and János Csonka in the Turda region" [36] and under men like Serafim Gónta in Cluj. Járai and Gónta were later condemned to death by the military tribunal of the Alba district, but their sentences, like those of the 34 men condemned along with them, were commuted to one-to-three years in prison by order of the emperor.[37]

Also fighting on the side of the rebels were many Magyars who worked in the state-owned mines of the Zlatna district. As early as 1770 miners of the Zarand and Hunedoară regions had refused to pay taxes to the mine administrators because they often demanded twice the lawful amount and because during the year the administrators withheld for themselves large parts of the workers' salaries. In 1784 the Magyar miners were quick to join the rebelling serfs; they "found themselves in close collaboration with them in their struggle." [38] The state archives of Cluj records the names of several of the miners—Ferenc Pál Szabó and Mathiás János, to name two.

On the other side of the dispute, we find that "the Romanian landowners took the side in 1784–85 of the Hungarian landowners against the Romanian peasants who rose up against their masters." [39] Since the majority of landed Romanian nobles had been Magyarized to a large extent and had converted to one of the "recognized" religions, this action on their part was hardly surprising. As the Hungarian serfs were treated equally with their Romanian counterparts in the "Hun-

[35] Alexandru Sterca-Suluțiu, *Istoria Horii și a Poporului Romîn din Munții Apuseni* [The history of Horia and the Romanian population of the Apuseni Mountains] (Bucharest, 1860), pp. 98–99, quoted in Al. Neamțu, "Situația Minerilor de pe Domeniul Slatnei și Participarea lor la Răscoala Populară de sub Conducerea lui Horia" [The situation of the miners of the Zlatna domain and their participation in the popular uprising under the leadership of Horia], *Studii: Revistă de Istorie,* IX (1956), 46.

[36] Daicoviciu *et al.,* p. 158. For the names of other Magyar participants in the rebellion see D. Prodan, *Răscoala lui Horia în Comitatele Cluj și Turda* [The Horia rebellion in Cluj and Turda counties] (Bucharest, 1938), p. 37.

[37] See Densușianu, p. 481. Gónta and Járai were identified by the tribunal as "of Magyar blood."

[38] On miners, see Neamțu, "Situația Minerilor," pp. 40–46.

[39] V.O. Dembo, *Horia, Cloșca, și Crișan* [Horia, Cloșca, and Crișan] (Balta, 1935), p. 7.

garian Lands," so the Romanian lords shared the fate of their Hungarian counterparts during the Horia Rebellion. On November 4, peasant brigades destroyed the castle of Antoniu Ioşica of Brănişca, a wealthy Romanian nobleman one of whose ancestors had been Chancellor of Transylvania during the disastrous reign of Prince Sigismond Báthory.[40]

An additional demonstration of the non-national character of the rebellion is provided by the fact that the first opposition by force to the rebel bands came from the Romanian soldiers of the Transylvanian Military Frontier. They were summoned by the largely Hungarian nobility of the city of Deva during the siege of that city on November 6 and 7, and they succeeded in routing the peasant army, killing nearly 100 of the rebels in the process.[41]

These bits of evidence about the forces drawn up on either side in the rebellion seem to disprove the allegations of historians like Densuşianu and Seton-Watson that the Horia Rebellion was basically a national rebellion. Densuşianu wrote:

the true purpose of the revolution was not a change of the social order, not the sweeping away of the burdens of feudalism . . . but a struggle of subjects against conquerors, a struggle for the reconquest of national liberty, for the revindication of the fatherland.[42]

Zoltán Tóth, taking into account the composition of the population of the disturbed areas, came much closer to the mark when he concludes:

This revolt was not directed against a nationality, but against feudalism in general, and this was represented by the great landed Hungarian nobility. . . . And just as the noble proprietor was the representative of oppressive feudalism, so the Romanian serf, of Orthodox religion, represented the other basic feudal class, the peasantry.[43]

The apparently religious or national character of the Horia Rebellion, it seems, can be attributed largely to the respective social positions

---

[40] Densuşianu, p. 172.   [41] *Ibid.*, pp. 181–82.

[42] *Ibid.*, p. 3. Marxist historians rather understate the case when they write that Densuşianu "accentuates in an exaggerated manner its [the rebellion's] national character"; see Ştefan Paşcu, "Răscoala Populară de la 1784" [The popular rebellion of 1784], *Lupta de Clasă*, XLIV, No. 12 (December, 1964), 30.

[43] Zoltán I. Tóth, *Mouvements paysans dans les Monts Apuseni jusqu'en 1848* (Bucharest, 1955), cited in Daicoviciu *et al.*, p. 160.

held in this region by the great mass of Orthodox Romanians and by a considerable number of Magyars.

Before moving on to the more positive social causes and characteristics of the rebellion, the question of foreign participation in the rebellion on the side of the peasants must be considered. In late 1784 Horia apparently did ask the reigning princes of Moldavia and Wallachia for help in his struggle. On October 10, 1785, Herbert Räthkael, the Austrian consul at Constantinople, wrote to Chancellor Kaunitz in Vienna: "Horia sent three of his men to Jassy to ask the reigning Prince of Moldavia Alexander Mavrocordato for Turkish help against the Hungarians." [44] However, there is no indication that any help was given. On the contrary, on March 3, 1785, Count Jankowitz wrote to the emperor:

I have interrogated with all care, attention, and precaution all of the captives and leaders of the rebellion to discover whether someone else, foreign or domestic, was the instigator of the rebellion, but I have found no trace of any foreign or domestic influence.[45]

A week later Joseph II sent a special letter of thanks to Mihai Suţu, Prince of Wallachia, "for the services of a good neighbor" [46] which he provided by not permitting the rebel leaders to take refuge in Wallachia.

In 1784 the condition of the feudal serfs of Transylvania was worse than that of the serfs of any other part of the Habsburg Empire (except Galicia), and their condition had deteriorated considerably since the early decades of the century. Király, for instance, writes:

The domination of the feudal lord over the peasant was far stronger than in Royal Hungary. In most parts of Transylvania urbarial obligations had risen by between 400 and 1000 percent since 1711.[47]

One reason for the deplorable state of the peasants was the fact that after 1714, when the Viennese Court forced the Transylvanian Diet to fix the robot obligations of the feudal serf at four days per week (three days for zséllerek, serfs with less than one-eighth of a session

[44] See Nicolae Iorga, *Documentele Familiei Callimachi* [The documents of the Callimachi family] (Bucharest, 1923), II, 513–14.

[45] Cited from the Jankowitz Archives in Cluj, in Densuşianu, p. 445.

[46] Cited *ibid.*, p. 481.   [47] Király, p. 217.

of land),[48] the Diet managed to veto or to obstruct the enforcement of every bit of Imperial urbarial legislation promulgated.[49] In 1747 Maria Theresa issued an ordinance setting the maximum weekly robot for a serf, with or without oxen, at three days, but the Transylvanian nobles refused to recognize its legality.[50] The Queen's 1769 *Certa Puncta* decree on serf-lord relations was rendered inoperative by the resistance of the landowners and the head of the Transylvanian Chancellery in Vienna, Samuel Brukenthal, who "did all in his power to cause the failure of the projected reform." [51] Faced with this stubborn opposition, Maria Theresa struck the item of Transylvanian reform from her agenda in 1779.[52]

As a result, right up until 1784 the legal robot obligation of the feudal serf to his lord in Transylvania was two hundred eight days per session per year, as opposed to one hundred four days (without animals) in Hungary and Styria and one hundred fifty-six days in Bohemia and Galicia.[53] While these legal maxima probably were not respected anywhere, they do provide some basis of comparison because we know definitely that they were abused in the Grand Principality. The landowners abused the two-hundred-eight-day limitation by requiring all of the members of the serf's family, rather than just the head of the family, to provide four days of labor service per week, by exacting the services due from the holder of a full session from serfs holding only a small fraction of a session, and by requiring that most of the robot be performed in the peak agricultural seasons.[54] In

[48] The land area of a full session varied according to the fertility of the soil. One session, according to Király, was "an area large enough to yield eight serfs enough produce to supply themselves and their families and to fulfill their obligations to lord, state, and church," p. 262.

[49] Prior to 1714 the robot was not legally limited. See Bujor Surdu, "Liniile Dezvoltării Social-Economic a Transilvaniei în Secolul al XVIII-lea pînă la Răscoala lui Horia" [The lines of socio-economic development of eighteenth-century Transylvania until the Horia Rebellion], *Anuarul Institutului de Istorie din Cluj*, III (1960), 116: "the lord could use the serf every day of the week. In addition, the serf had to give his master one-tenth of his produce. He was also obligated to a quitrent (cens) in kind or in money and to other gifts to the lord. . . . The feudal lord also enjoyed seigneurial monopolies. . . . The serf also had to bear all sorts of public duties."

[50] *Ibid.,* p. 117.   [51] Makkai, p. 279.   [52] *Ibid.,* p. 280.

[53] C. A. Macartney, *Hungary: A Short History* (Chicago, 1962), p. 115.

[54] For a long list of similar abuses see Domokos Teleki, *A Horatámadás Története* [History of the Horia Rebellion] (Pest, 1865); part of this list is

addition, while Maria Theresa's urbarial legislation for Royal Hungary had registered all peasant holdings for tax purposes and forbidden the further conversion of these holdings into dominical lands or the further enclosure of common lands, these practices continued unregulated and unabated in Transylvania.[55] Excesses of equal magnitude existed in the manner of collecting the tithe. Paul Bernard perhaps best summed up the pre-1784 situation when he wrote:

> In Transylvania not only was there no question of introducing the commutation of services (the so-called Raab system), but it turned out that the decree of 1781, putting an end to formal Leibeigenschaft, far from being carried out had not even been proclaimed to the population.[56]

On August 16, 1783, following his return to Vienna from Transylvania, Emperor Joseph II went so far as to issue a special Leibeigenschaftshebungspatent for Transylvania. This too was disregarded by the local authorities.[57]

Any comparison of the Transylvanian feudal serfs' burdens with those of the serfs of Moldavia and Wallachia is difficult because the boyars of the Romanian principalities had little dominical land and thus required little robot. While they collected the tithe on a slightly greater group of products—for instance, products of private gardens around the serfs' homes—than was collected in Transylvania, the robot was set at twenty-seven days per year in Moldavia in 1777, and at twelve days per year in Wallachia in 1780. In addition, "occasional" gifts to the lord (for Christmas, Easter, New Year's Day, etc.) were far fewer in the Romanian principalities than they were in Transylvania.[58] These factors, combined with the fact that as early as 1746 in Wallachia and 1749 in Moldavia Prince Constantin Mavrocordato had abolished Leibeigenschaft, might indicate a slightly more favorable living standard for the serfs of Moldavia and Walla-

---

cited in Gheorghe Baritiu, *Părti Alese din Istoria Transilvaniei* [Selected topics in Transylvanian history] (Sibiu, 1889), p. 474.

[55] *Ibid.*   [56] Paul P. Bernard, *Joseph II* (New York, 1968) p. 120.

[57] Seton-Watson, pp. 185–86.

[58] For a comparison of the situations in Moldavia, Wallachia, and Transylvania, see D. Prodan, *Les Migrations des Roumains au-delà des Carpathes au XVIII-ème Siècle* (Sibiu, 1945), pp. 80–133. While the interpretation of the respective situations in this monograph is heavily biased in favor of the Romanians, the documentation and statistical data, taken from both Hungarian and Romanian sources, seem to present a fairly objective picture.

chia than for those of Transylvania, but no positive judgment is possible on this question.

The deteriorating position of the feudal serfs of Transylvania was probably most widely felt in the "Hungarian Lands," [59] since the Romanian element among the peasants was strongest there and since even the Hungarian element of the peasantry in these regions enjoyed no special privileges. Hungarian and Romanian feudal serfs were treated equally by their masters, though the Romanians did bear the additional social stigma of belonging neither to a recognized nation nor to a recognized religion. The situation was considerably different in the Saxon and Székely lands, however. There a substantial portion of the peasantry came from these two nationalities, and all of the Székelys, though subjected to robot obligations in 1562, and many of the Saxons, including all of those living on crown lands, were constitutionally free men.[60] These factors explain why a greater proportion of the feudal serfs in the Hungarian Lands than that in the Székely or Saxon Lands were ready to take action against the nobility. In the course of the eighteenth century, as the nobles and state functionaries "sought to increase their revenues . . . by imposing increasingly heavy burdens on the serfs," [61] the situation of the *feudal serfs* was becoming increasingly ripe for rebellion.

Since 1715, when the Zlatna region was declared state domain for the purposes of more systematic tax collection and more efficient exploitation of the local mineral resources (especially gold and silver), the condition of the *state serfs,* the residents of these mountainous crown lands, had deteriorated steadily also. For over three centuries prior to 1715, the predominately Romanian inhabitants of these highland regions had enjoyed special customary rights and freedoms. After payment to the state of a small tax in cash, they had been in effect free from all feudal obligations and allowed the unhindered usufruct of the mountain forests and pastures.[62] After 1715, this tax in cash, collected by Imperial functionaries sent to Zlatna, was supplemented by specific labor obligations such as supplying wood to certain towns and transporting grain from the Hungarian border to various urban centers within the Transylvanian principality. As the century progressed cash taxes were increased

---

[59] See footnote 9.   [60] Surdu, p. 111.   [61] Makkai, p. 275.

[62] For a detailed review of the way in which the rights and obligations of these people developed beginning in 1500, see Densuşianu, pp. 82 ff.

to help finance Habsburg military operations, and, especially after the monarchy's loss of Silesia in 1746, compulsory labor services were increased as well in an attempt to compensate for the loss by intensifying the exploitation of the mineral deposits of the highland areas:

In the region of the Apuseni Mountains, the serfdom of the peasants was especially harsh, to permit the state to exploit the gold mines of the region . . . all serfs were required to do the work necessary for the construction of furnaces, the cutting and transporting of wood, the making of charcoal, and the transport and extraction of minerals.[63]

The cash tax due the Imperial treasury from the Zlatna district was increased from 5,859 florins in 1750 to 14,769 florins in 1775, and then to 21,555 florins in 1783.[64] This greatly increased fiscal burden was made even more difficult to bear by the Armenian and Jewish tax farmers who bought the revenue-collecting privileges of the region and did not spare the population in exercising their legally purchased rights.[65]

These bad and continually deteriorating conditions on the state domain and a specific incident arising from the farmed-out alcohol monopoly caused the state serfs of the region to send Horia to Vienna to plead their case in 1782 and again in 1783. The petitions which he took with him in 1782, as in 1778 and in 1780 were concerned exclusively with the complaints of state serfs.

In 1778, representatives of four Zlatna communes—Rîul-Mare, Vidra, Câmpeni, and Bistra—traveled to Sibiu to seek the aid of the Transylvanian Gubernium against the excesses of the Imperial functionaries of the district, but the supplicants were rebuffed by the newly promoted Governor Samuel Brukenthal, who claimed that he had no jurisdiction over crown lands.[66] When the delegation returned home,

---

[63] Daicoviciu *et al.*, p. 155.   [64] Densuşianu, p. 83.

[65] Iorga, *Histoire*, p. 169.

[66] Baron Samuel Brukenthal, a Saxon born in 1721, had a long and illustrious career in Transylvanian politics and was very highly thought of by Empress Maria Theresa. In 1757 he was appointed secretary of the Transylvanian Gubernium; in 1762 he became a member of the Transylvanian Chancellery at Vienna and was granted the title of Baron. In 1766 he became President of the Chancellery, in 1774 President of Gubernium at Sibiu, and finally, in 1777, Governor of the Grand Principality. Brukenthal sabotaged the Theresian urbarial reforms of 1769. In 1778 he refused to intervene on behalf

the Administrator of Zlatna, György Devai, ordered several of its members beaten and imprisoned. It was as a direct result of this maltreatment that the first delegation of state serfs, including Horia and Cloşca, traveled to Vienna. The delegation presented the following grievances to the Transylvanian Chancellery:

a) despite the low productivity of their land they were subjected to rapidly increasing tax and robot obligations, often pushed way above the legal limits by the tax-farmers and Zlatna functionaries

b) they were forced to supply the foundaries of Zlatna with 3,000 sagènes (1 sagène equals 2.1336 meters) of wood per year instead of the "customary" 800 sagènes

c) they were forced to buy wood for their personal use whereas in the past they had had free use of the resources of the forests

d) they were forced to work on road construction without compensation

e) they were forced to transport barley from Hungary to the beer factories of the "Saxon Lands," a twelve-day journey

f) the inheritance rights of serfs were being illegally restricted

g) the revenue farmers charged very high amounts for privileges which all highland serfs used to enjoy for nothing, such as the use of pasture lands and the right to sell alcoholic beverages

h) a number of serfs had been illegally imprisoned and beaten, and one even killed, for their entirely lawful participation in the delegation sent to Sibiu.[67]

When a second delegation repeated these complaints in 1780, the Aulic Chancellery forwarded the list of grievances to the Transylvanian government and ordered that it undertake a study to determine the real situation on the crown lands, that it recommend ways to correct the abuses found, and that it punish the parties responsible for the abuses. The Chancellery also ordered that no further arrests of deputation members be made until the completion of the government investigation. The Transylvanian government, however, the same one which had refused to help the serfs two years earlier pre-

---

of the serfs against the Imperial functionaries' excesses. His opposition to reform continued during his entire tenure as governor, and Joseph II finally felt obliged to remove him from the office.

[67] On these grievances see Daicoviciu *et al.*, pp. 155–56; and Densuşianu, p. 85.

sumably because any remedial action on the crown lands might spread to purely feudal regions, postponed the beginning of the investigation, and arrests continued.[68]

In May, 1782, violence erupted in the market of Câmpeni when Matiu Bosniac and Martin Petrubian, the Armenians who had leased the alcohol monopoly on the crown lands, tried to prevent some local peasants from selling their own liquors. When as a result of the outburst 23 peasants were imprisoned, 5 condemned to death, and a fine of 8,708 florins imposed on the inhabitants of the Rîul-Mare, Vidra, Câmpeni, and Bistra communes, a third deputation was sent to Vienna.[69] This time the Aulic Chancellery forwarded the serfs' petition to the Imperial State Council. The Imperial Council in turn ordered that the Transylvanian government hasten its investigation of the situation in the Apuseni regions and see to it that the 5 death sentences not be carried out. The sentences were commuted to prison terms of two to three years, but the general condition of the state serfs was in no way ameliorated, and there was more procrastination in regard to the investigation.

Horia's last trip to Vienna, the most important one, is unfortunately the one about which we know least. He left Transylvania in November, 1783, apparently unaccompanied by any of his former fellow travelers, and, having had to await the return of Joseph II from Rome, was finally granted an Imperial audience on April 1, 1784. While there is no official record of what transpired at the meeting, Horia presumably complained of the lack of improvement in the serf's condition and of the continuing harassment of the communes which had sent deputations to Vienna. He apparently learned for the first time that on August 16, 1783, as he had promised during his visit to Sibiu earlier in the year, Joseph had issued a rescript— still contested by the Aulic Chancellery in Vienna and as yet unan-

---

[68] The investigation was not completed until mid-1784 and all of its findings were unconditionally in favor of the landowners and functionaries; see Densuşianu, pp. 87, 114.

[69] On the Câmpeni incident and Horia's subsequent trip to Vienna see Densuşianu, pp. 88 ff.; and Daicoviciu *et al.*, p. 156. The 5 peasants condemned to death were Dumitru Todea Buta, Petru Manciu, Simeon Bostanu, Audrieş Paşcu, and Ursŭ Gomboş. Until 1778 anyone could purchase a license to sell alcoholic beverages for a very small fixed fee. In that year, however, a tax by volume sold was imposed. By 1781 an alcohol monoply had been purchased by these 2 Armenians for 12,000 florins per year.

nounced by the Transylvanian government—abolishing Leibeigen-schaft in Transylvania.[70] As a result of Horia's visit, Joseph once again ordered Brukenthal's government to expedite the investigation ordered in 1780, to protect the serfs from illegal harassment, and to release those imprisoned for participation in the various peasant delegations.[71]

Whatever actually transpired at his audience with the emperor, when Horia returned to Transylvania he took advantage of a situation already destabilized by the conscription controversy just coming into the open and began agitating for a general rebellion of both state and feudal serfs. Brandishing a gilded cross which he claimed was a gift from the emperor and a parchment upon which he claimed the emperor had written his instruction to the serfs,[72] Horia reported that Joseph II had promulgated many laws regarding the conditions of serfdom in Transylvania, but that the landowners and functionaries had disregarded them. To this point Horia was in fact telling the truth. But he further claimed that the emperor had ordered him to militar-ize the country and to persuade the serfs not to perform their obliga-tions to their lords but to despoil the landowners of their possessions, to expel the corrupt royal functionaries, and to divide all the land—both dominical (allodial) and rustical (urbarial)—among themselves. The emperor had promised him, he claimed, that Imperial troops would in no way oppose these actions by the peasants. They were no longer to be serfs, but Imperial soldiers, equal in rights and status to the peasant-soldiers of the Transylvanian Military Frontier.[73]

The peasants were prepared to believe Horia's allegations and to follow his orders for "militarization" for two reasons. First, because since Joseph's initial visit to Transylvania in 1773, the first time since the Monarchy's reacquisition of the principality in 1691 that any rul-ing Habsburg had been there, the serfs had come to look upon the emperor "almost as their patron saint." [74] Second, because a wide-spread conscription movement on the part of the peasants, opposed by their masters, began dramatically increasing tensions in the prov-ince just as Horia began making his revolutionary exhortations.

[70] See footnote 57.   [71] Densuşianu, pp. 107–8.

[72] *Ibid.*, p. 110. I have no evidence that Horia's claims were anything except fabrications. Densuşianu writes that Horia probably purchased the cross and parchment in the markets of Vienna.

[73] *Ibid.*, pp. 108 ff.   [74] Wright, p. 163.

In May, 1773, Joseph II visited Transylvania and accepted over 15,000 petitions from both state and feudal serfs complaining about the abuses to which they were subjected.[75] When he returned to Vienna, he reported to the State Council:

> I feel obliged to underline the fact that Transylvania is a very beautiful and good country, but one in need of urgent aid in the shape of radical reform, for simple improvements will not suffice because of the totally corrupt mentality of the nobles. . . . The Hungarian nobles fear nothing other than what might reduce their revenues or limit their privileges, which they increase by all means possible in order to exploit their subjects to the maximum. The serfs are like slaves to their masters, and having no means of defense they must work more or less according to the wishes of their masters.[76]

In 1784 he visited Transylvania again, and at Sibiu expressed his intention to suppress Leibeigenschaft "so that this servile humiliation of humanity may cease everwhere." [77] By 1784, the peasants clearly had some reason to believe that he was on their side.

Regarding the conscription, on January 31, 1784, Joseph, anxious over the plans of Catherine of Russia for war against the Ottoman Empire, ordered that the Transylvanian Military Frontier be expanded by the addition to it of a number of villages close to its original boundaries. The Transylvanian Military Frontier had been created in 1762–66 under the supervision of General Commander Baron Adolf Buccow.[78] In the regions incorporated by Maria Theresa into the frontier zone, serfdom was abolished and the lands of the feudal nobility expropriated.[79] "Unlike the Székelys, for whom military duty on the frontier meant a loss of former liberties, the Romanian peasants gained security and a higher standard of living by joining the border guards." [80] Thus while the Székely peasants revolted in 1763–64 rather than accept inclusion in the frontier zone, the Romanians accepted the creation of the region with enthusiasm. Fearing the loss of their land and also of their work force—initially by inclusion into the frontier areas and then by escape into them—the nobles protested, but Maria Theresa was intractable, and even went so far

---

[75] Densuşianu, p. 98 claims a figure of 19,000 petitions. I. Lupaş, "L'Empereur Joseph II et Horia," *Revue de Transylvanie,* I, No. 4 (January–March, 1935), 429, says 15,000.

[76] Daicoviciu *et al.,* p. 144.   [77] Makkai, p. 281.   [78] *Ibid.,* p. 277.

[79] Densuşianu, p. 116.   [80] Király, p. 217.

as to replace the then Governor Count Kemény, who opposed the measure, with General Buccow himself, in order to assure its execution. [81]

The nobles protested again in 1784, this time against the extension of the frontier area, and Joseph's conscription decree, like so many others in Transylvania, remained unpublished. In May, however, having learned of the conscription decree while in Vienna, Horia announced that the emperor had ordered that the *whole country* be militarized. The census announced by the Transylvanian government on May 1—ordered by Joseph for the purpose of improving the efficiency of the tax system—was seen by the peasants as verification of Horia's announcement: "The Transylvanian Romanians believed that the purpose of the census was the extension of the military frontier." [82] Starting in mid-July, whole villages flocked to the Imperial Military Offices at Alba-Iulia and Hațeg, asking to enlist in the military frontier zone. Military Commissioner Ortmayer at Alba-Iulia and Vice-Colonel Karp at Hațeg wrote to Sibiu for orders from Baron Preisz, the commander-general of Transylvania. Preisz advised that the enlistments could be accepted *subject to final approval by Vienna,* and ordered that the recruits continue to meet their feudal obligations until such approval arrived. By mid-August, the populations of 81 entire villages had enlisted at Alba-Iulia alone, and, despite Preisz's order, the peasants had begun to resist the fulfillment of their feudal and fiscal obligations. [83] When the landowners and royal functionaries tried to force them to perform their duties, tensions mounted tremendously. In September, to cite but one example, the serf Ion Lupaş of Săcămaş was recorded as saying,

After St. Michael's Day [September 29 and the day on which Ortmayer had told the enlisting peasants that he would be able to give them weapons] we will receive our weapons, and then for not a day longer will we perform our duties, but we will cut off the heads of the Hungarians like so many cabbages. [84]

In October, fearing that the situation was becoming critical and in order to prevent the arming of the peasants which had been delayed

[81] For more on the Székely Rebellion and on the 1762 conscription in general, see Makkai, pp. 277–78, and Király, p. 215.

[82] *Ibid.,* p. 16.   [83] Densuşianu, pp. 114–20.

[84] Entry for September 13, 1784, in the Jankowitz Archives of Cluj, cited in Densuşianu, p. 122.

only by the scarcity of arms at Alba-Iulia, Brukenthal declared that
the conscription was invalid, as indeed it was, since it was carried
out without the approval either of Vienna or of the Sibiu Gubernium.[85] Preisz, although he had accepted the mass enlistments only
on the condition that they be approved by Vienna, had considerably
exceeded his authority, as it is clear that the emperor had had no intention of militarizing the entire principality. The peasants, however,
refused to believe that the conscription had been invalid and, asserting that Preisz, Ortmayer, and Karp would have been punished had
they exceeded their authority, viewed Brukenthal's "invalidation" as
simply one more intrigue by the local authorities to deprive the
peasants of what was lawfully theirs, as one more attempt on the
part of the landowners and royal functionaries to maintain their
privileged positions.

"As the Romanians saw in military conscription the means of
freeing themselves from the yoke of serfdom, their exasperation
with their lords who opposed their departure grew daily." [86] Finally,
on November 2, 1784, a band of serfs traveling toward Alba-Iulia
to receive the weapons promised them actually began the rebellion
by killing two subprefects sent from Alba-Iulia to halt their advance.
During the same day the serfs attacked the estates of several landowners and killed 17 nobles.[87]

The rebellion spread unopposed through the counties of Zarand
and Hunedoară and all along the Mureş (Maros) River valley. When
Governor Brukenthal learned of the outbreak on November 4, he
asked Commander-General Preisz to put down the rebellion with
Imperial troops. However, "contradictory news about the attitude of
the Emperor stopped Baron Preisz from intervening." [88] Commander-
General since 1771, Preisz had a standing order not to intervene
militarily in the affairs of Transylvania without notifying the Council
of War in Vienna unless the situation was critical.[89] Moreover, he
saw no dynastic or state danger, but only a revolution directed against

[85] *Ibid.,* p. 124.   [86] Makkai, p. 281.
[87] Densuşianu, pp. 159 ff.   [88] Makkai, p. 282.
[89] Brukenthal to Joseph II, November 8, 1784, cited in J. G. Schaser,
Denkwürdigkeiten aus dem Leben des Freih. von Brukenthal (Hermannstadt,
1848), p. 67: "Weiter aber (das General Commando) eine Hofkriegsräthliche
Verordnung beigeräckt, nach welcher der Militärbestand ausser nur in dringen-
den Fällen ohne Vorwissen des Hofkriegsraths nicht eingestanden werden
dürfte."

a class "which always opposed the Emperor's orders and did not even recognize Joseph as King of Hungary"; [90] he did not order his troops into action. However, unwilling to see the unbridled destruction and killing continue to spread as the peasants took courage from the strict passivity of the Imperial forces, Preisz decided to see whether he could arrange an armistice with the rebels. By November 12 he had succeeded in negotiating one.

The Armistice of Tibru provides us with the clearest exposition of the concessions which the peasants were seeking. The day before the armistice was signed, Horia, through the intermediary Carol Brünek, sent an ultimatum to the nobles of Hunedoară County who had taken refuge in the fortress of Deva. In return for their safety he demanded that the nobles make 5 concessions:

1. all the nobles swear loyalty "to the cross"
2. there be no more noble class, but that each noble should live by his own work
3. the landowners give up forever *all* of their lands
4. the nobles pay taxes just as the peasants had to
5. *all* the lands of the nobles be divided among the peasants [91]

By the next day, however, the religous notion expressed in the first point had disappeared and the peasants' demands had been simplified into the tripartite Tibru formula which was to be the basis of all further negotiations. The Armistice of Tibru was to last eight days. During that period Preisz was to set before the Transylvanian government and the Imperial functionaries in the principality the following demands: *a*) serfdom be abolished and the lands of the lords divided among the peasants, *b*) the peasants be permitted to become soldiers, and *c*) the prisoners held in the Gelda prison be liberated.[92] It would seem that the rebels could have had little doubt about how the civil authorities would react to these demands. It was perhaps because Preisz was considered the emperor's representative that the revolutionary captains agreed temporarily to abandon the offensive.

On November 20 the armistice expired, and, having received from Brukenthal only the response that he did not have the authority to accept their first two demands, that he could not free the Gelda

---

[90] Densuşianu, p. 241.

[91] *Ibid.*, p. 197. This document from the Hunedoară Archive is quoted here in its entirety.

[92] *Ibid.*, pp. 257–65. The report from Colonel Anton Schultz von Leichtenthal, who actually negotiated the armistice, to Preisz is found on these pages.

prisoners since they had been legally tried, and that, in any case, he would refuse to deal with armed insurgents,[93] the peasants, who had returned to their homes, began to gather once again. By this time, however, Preisz had received the emperor's order of November 15 to crush the rebellion:

> I have no doubt that you, though far away, have taken the most exten-sive measures to end the rebellion . . . and if not, that you will do this with all seriousness . . . I have ordered the Commander-General of Hungary that once peace is re-established there [the peasants had also rebelled in several border regions of Hungary] he send you General Koppenzollern with two infantry regiments . . . and General Sturm with swordsmen . . . so that you . . . will have the rebels "between two fires. . . ." And if the rebels cannot be convinced to surrender their leaders to the authorities then of necessity you will use force, but only until the peasant troops agree to disperse and withdraw.[94]

On November 27 Preisz began military operations against the ma-rauding peasants. By December 7 the last battle, the Battle of Miha-leni, had taken place, and on December 14, Horia disbanded his troops. Horia and Cloşca were captured on December 27, 1784, and Crişan on January 30, 1785. On February 14 Crişan committed suicide in his prison cell; on February 28 Horia and Cloşca were broken on the wheel and disemboweled in public, and their limbs were placed on spikes and carried through the regions which had participated in the rebellion.[95] With this, the violent stage of the rebellion ended.

The real position of Joseph II in what transpired in Transylvania in 1784–85 must be considered. There is no doubt that he ordered the suppression of the rebellion by Imperial troops. He had certainly wanted to increase the military frontier zones. In view of his reformist tendencies, he was probably sympathetic toward the peasants and anxious to act against nobles and functionaries he knew were corrupt. However, "as a ruler he could not openly favor rebellion." [96] It was not part of enlightened despotism to tolerate reforms not promulgated

[93] Daicoviciu *et al,* p. 159.
[94] Densuşianu, p. 302. Letter from Joseph II to Preisz, November 15, 1784.
[95] Lupaş, "L'Empereur," p. 438.
[96] Saul K. Padover, *The Revolutionary Emperor: Joseph II of Austria* (Hamden, Conn., 1967), p. 54.

by oneself but achieved by force. Joseph was concerned at this time about the possibility of war with Holland and could ill afford any internal disorders. Thus, as Király concludes about a similar situation in Bohemia in 1790, even if the emperor had wanted to incite a peasant rebellion, "the Habsburg Empire was in much too volatile a state to risk such a policy." [97]

Joseph's resolve to use Imperial troops to quash the rebellion was strengthened by the additional fact that on November 11 Governor Brukenthal, unable to get Preisz's military support and as willing to overstep his authority as Preisz had been in the conscription affair, authorized the nobles to prepare for an *insurrectio* (*posse comitatus*).[98] On November 13, he wrote to the emperor:

> The governor proposed on November 9 to the commander-general that if the army is not ready to suppress the revolution in all parts of the country, then he would use the only other means in his power and order an *insurrectio* of the nobles and free communities in the interest of their own protection.[99]

Immediately after the arrival of this message in Vienna, Count Mihály Sztárai of the county of Szabolcs proposed to the Hungarian-Transylvanian Chancellery [100] that an *insurrectio* of the whole nobility of Hungary be called out against the rebellion.[101] Joseph's anxieties over the dangers of any such action are well reflected in his scathing letter of November 22, 1784, to Governor Brukenthal. He first rebukes Brukenthal's authorization of the condemnation of prisoners to death by noble *ad hoc* tribunals in various counties and then continues:

> But the worst offense is that you wanted to provoke a general *insurrectio* of the nobles. . . . If you have not done this then we believe that you have come to the healthiest solution. You have no right to provoke such an *insurrectio* without our order and desire, and thus we consider this intention as an example of the greatest impudence, which could

[97] Király, p. 221.

[98] The *insurrectio* was the obligation of nobles to go to war if the land was in danger and the king called them to arms.

[99] Densuşianu, p. 306. Letter from Brukenthal to Joseph II, November 13, 1784.

[100] Joseph II combined the Hungarian and Transylvanian chancelleries early in his reign. They were separated again after his death.

[101] Densuşianu, p. 292.

have the saddest results in the future; only we have the right and means to establish quiet; while the method of *insurrectio* . . . would surely be able to provoke an internal national and religious war, the conclusion of which cannot be foreseen.[102]

Joseph could not condone a peasant rebellion, but it is clear that he also felt unable to risk *insurrectio*.

There is ample proof that the emperor recognized the corruption of the Transylvania landowners and Imperial functionaries. In December, 1784, prior to the demise of the Horia Rebellion, he wrote to his brother Leopold:

All sorts of excesses. perpetrated for many years by the landholders, have caused general complaints on the part of all the inhabitants of Transylvania, and especially the Romanian nation. But never has it been possible to put an end to these excesses or to introduce an urbarial code. . . . I ordered the government and the Chancellery to reduce them, but nothing has yet been done. The functionaries of the Zlatna domain, who are under the direction of the Department of Mines, have distinguished themselves with all kinds of extortion. . . . The peasants sent deputies here, and they received from the Hungarian Chancellery the assurance in writing that they could go home and await a decision without any fear. But they had hardly arrived at Zlatna when they were arrested and maltreated again.[103]

In mid-November, 1784, Joseph appointed Count Antonin Jankowitz of the Banat to undertake an objective investigation of the causes of the rebellion and urged him specifically to make recommendations for the suppression of the excesses of the local functionaries.[104] Despite the objections of Count Brukenthal, Transylvanian government officials were not allowed to witness any of Jankowitz's interrogations. In response to one of Brukenthal's complaints, Joseph wrote:

All of the petitions, letters, requests, and acts of the government boards and assemblies of nobles demonstrate that they have lost all sense of equilibrium, and that they believe that they will find security only by

[102] *Ibid.,* p. 304. Rescript from Joseph II to the government of Transylvania, November 22, 1784.

[103] A. Arneth, ed., *Ioseph II und Leopold von Toscana: Ihr Briefwechsel* (Vienna, 1872), I, 240–43. Joseph II to Leopold of Tuscany, December 3, 1784.

[104] Densuşianu, p. 309. Letter from Joseph II to Count Jankowitz, November 27, 1784.

impaling men and breaking men on the wheel, regardless of whom and how many.[105]

Contrary to these intentions of the privileged classes, Joseph forced the government to issue a general amnesty for all except the major leaders of the rebellion,[106] and after the rebellion was suppressed, only Horia, Cloşca, and Crişan were placed on trial. When the Transylvanian authorities tried to exile participants in the rebellion to the Banat, Joseph ordered that the policy be abandoned and that the peasants be left alone.[107]

In addition to all of these demonstrations of where his sympathies lay, Joseph's feelings can also be gauged by the nature of the reforms which he instituted after the rebellion. In mid-1785, Michael Brukenthal, entrusted by Joseph with the investigation of the situation in the crown lands administered from Zlatna, confirmed that the pre-rebellion complaints of the state serfs had been well founded—that the functionaries were small tyrants supported by the Transylvanian authorities, that they had illegally deprived the serfs of their belongings and of their customary "old rights," that they had imposed illegal taxes, and that they had exacted unwarranted punishments. In response to Brukenthal's report, Joseph returned the free use of forests and pastures to the serfs on the royal domain, excused them and their families from domestic services for their lords or for royal representatives, and excused them from wood-and hay-cutting and transporting duties and from work in or related to the mines. All these former robota were to become contractual salaried work. He ordered the granting of liquor licenses on easy terms and rectified the inheritance laws. He replaced Baron János Bornemisza as assessor on the royal domain with the reform-minded Michael Brukenthal and instructed Brukenthal to replace any functionaries who had engaged in illegal practices.[108]

When Count Jankowitz reported on July 6, 1785, that the three primary causes of the Horia Rebellion were: *a*) oppression of the serfs by the nobles, *b*) the confusion which permeated the military conscription affair, and *c*) the failure of the Transylvanian government to try to alleviate peasant discontent,[109] Joseph responded with

[105] *Ibid.*, p. 366. Letter from Joseph II to Samuel Brukenthal, December 13, 1784.

[106] *Ibid.*, p. 370.   [107] *Ibid.*, p. 505.

[108] *Ibid.*, pp. 508 ff.   [109] Lupaş "L'Empereur," p. 442.

a comparable spate of reforms for the areas not included in the royal domain. On August 22, 1785, he issued another patent abolishing personal serfdom (Leibeigenschaft) in Transylvania. He excluded from all public office Count János Csaky of Cluj and several other nobles who had been very anxious to instigate a noble *insurrectio*.[110] In January, 1787, Joseph also ousted Samuel Brukenthal from office, replacing him with "two enlightened magnates, Count György Bánffy as governor and Count Samuel Teleki as chancellor." [111] With these changes the final repercussions of the Horia Rebellion subsided.

The Horia Rebellion began as the protest of the state serfs of a few small communes on the royal domain around Zlatna and Abrud, quickly spread to encompass most of the serfs, state and feudal, Romanian and Hungarian, of southwestern Transylvania, and, at the cost of the lives of several hundred peasants, resulted in the destruction of some 230 castles and the death of over 100 nobles.[112] It was typical of peasant rebellions in the Habsburg Hausmacht only in the sense that it grew out of peasant discontent and combined in a new way some of the characteristics of numerous previous rebellions—an appeal to and faith in the emperor, military weakness when ultimately faced with a standing army, demands for the easing of feudal and fiscal burdens, and a yearning for "old rights." While it spread quickly to purely feudal areas, it began as a revolution not against the feudal nobility of Transylvania, but against the corruption of Imperial administrators, and one wonders whether the rebellion would have taken place at all had Horia and his fellow state serfs not felt that they had the right to appeal directly to their immediate feudal lord, Emperor Joseph II. It was certainly during his trip to Vienna that Horia decided to raise the standard of rebellion, and it was because he could raise that standard credibly (for the peasants at least) in the name of the emperor that he was followed.

[110] Densuşianu, pp. 494–95.   [111] Makkai, p. 273.

[112] These figures are from Seton-Watson, p. 187. Densuşianu set the number of nobles killed at 133, mostly in Zarand County and somewhat fewer in Hunedoară, as those of Hunedoară and of other counties had advanced warning that an attack was coming and took refuge in strongly fortified places. While no one gave a total figure for the number of peasants killed, Densuşianu writes of approximately 400 peasants killed in the battles which he describes in detail.

The Horia Rebellion was essentially what I term a *social rebellion,* one caused by the deterioration, during the eighteenth century, of the living conditions of both state and feudal serfs, in Transylvania. The rebellion's religious and national aspects were secondary, due more to the social positions of national and religious groups in the principality than to actual religious or national hatred. Though this hatred no doubt did exist to some extent, it was not a motive force of the rebellion and it played only a minor part in its initial successes and ultimate failure.

There can be no doubt that Emperor Joseph II recognized the "social nature" of the rebellion and the validity of the complaints lodged against the Transylvanian nobles and state functionaries. While he could not openly condone the rebellion, he demonstrated his sympathy with its purposes by granting an amnesty to all participants with the exceptions of Horia, Cloşca, and Crişan, and by promulgating numerous fiscal and urbarial reform measures once peace was reestablished.

Sweden's View of the Non-Proliferation Treaty

GERTRUD SVALA

The Treaty on the Non-Proliferation of Nuclear Weapons was hailed by former President Johnson as "the most important international agreement limiting nuclear arms since the nuclear age began." [1] Yet, Sweden, an ardent advocate of measures to promote peace, has only reluctantly given its support to the Treaty: although the Swedish government has now ratified the Treaty, Sweden accompanied its signature on August 19, 1968, with a list of "further expected arms control measures" [2] and has remained a staunch critic of many of the Treaty's provisions.

To understand the controversy surrounding the Treaty and, particularly, Sweden's criticism, let us examine: first, briefly, the background, the negotiations, and the main provisions of the Treaty; second, Sweden's specific objections to the Treaty; third, the arms-control measures that Sweden has proposed as an alternative to the present Non-Proliferation Treaty (NPT); and, finally, Sweden's concern with the Treaty in terms of its foreign and defense policies.

---

[1] United States Arms Control and Disarmament Agency, *International Negotiations on the Treaty on the Non-proliferation of Nuclear Weapons,* January, 1969, p. 181.

[2] The arms control measures that Sweden "expected" would follow the NPT were: (1) an agreement on defensive and offensive strategic nuclear missile systems; (2) maintenance of the Moscow Treaty of 1963; (3) supplementation of the above with a complete test ban; (4) regulation, under an international regime, of the exemptions from these prohibitions, which, in special cases, may be desirable for peaceful purposes. From UN Doc. ENDC/Pv391, August 20, 1968.

The Non-Proliferation Treaty

The underlying argument for a non-proliferation agreement is that the probability of nuclear weapons being used becomes greater as the number of fingers on the trigger increases. This probability "theorem" is based on the view that "in a world of many nuclear powers, there may well be some who unlike the United States and the Soviet Union have relatively little to lose if nuclear weapons are used." [3] In other words, the United States and the Soviet Union are today mature nations that are aware of the cataclysmic consequences of a nuclear conflict and, hence, can be trusted with a large nuclear arsenal, while some of the potential nuclear-weapon states are less rational and must not be given the responsibility that is connected with the possession of nuclear weapons. [4]

The urgency of the non-proliferation issue is attributed to what has been called the Plutonium Loophole. [5] Only a few years ago, nuclear power was not thought of as commercially profitable. Today, projections are made for a tremendous rise in the use of nuclear power as a substitute for hydroelectric power and oil. For example, it has been estimated that by 1985, 50 percent of Sweden's power needs will be supplied by nuclear energy. [6] The problem is that every uranium-feuled power plant produces as a by-product plutonium, which can subsequently be used for weapon production. To illustrate, it is expected that by 1980, the Federal Republic of Germany and Japan would each be able to manufacture annually 800 nuclear bombs from its plutonium by-product. In ten years, even Sweden could possibly produce 300 nuclear weapons annually. [7]

The argument that nuclear-weapons manufacture is becoming cheaper and more accessible has also inspired the NPT. [8] It is held that since a large part of the initial cost of nuclear weapons came

[3] ACDA Director Foster, "New Direction in Arms Control and Disarmament, July 1965", reprinted from *Foreign Affairs* in *Documents on Disarmament 1965*, pp. 269–70.

[4] See *Documents on Disarmament 1966*, p. 52.

[5] St. Louis (Mo.) *Post-Dispatch*, July 7, 1967.

[6] AB Atomenergi 1967, *Summary of Annual Report 1967*.

[7] For calculations, see Bruce Smith, "The Non-Proliferation Treaty and East-West Detente," *Journal of International Affairs*, XXII, No. 1 (1968), 98.

[8] Foster, p. 269.

from the expense of research and development, weapons can be manufactured at greatly reduced costs today. Furthermore, the technology
involved in building nuclear weapons is supposedly no longer a
well-kept secret. The fact that a detailed description of how to test
weapons underground can be found in the transcript of a hearing of
the United States Joint Congressional Committee on Atomic Energy
is used as evidence of the ease with which one can acquire highly
technical knowledge.[9] The preceding argument is misleading.
Weapon production might be less costly today for the United States
and the other nuclear powers, but not necessarily for the non-nuclear
weapon states. Underground testing directions might be free and
public, but the actual designs for the bombs are very much "classified." Hence, if a non-nuclear weapon state decided to go nuclear, it
would still have to bear much of the initial cost of research and development.[10]

A second major factor for explaining the emphasis that the Soviet
Union and the United States have come to place on the NPT is the
failure to reach an agreement on general and complete disarmament.[11] Both the United States and the Soviet Union presented such
plans in 1962, but the differences over the inspection system were
too great to hope for any accommodation. Consequently, both the
United States and the Soviet Union turned to partial measures with
the aim of regulating and limiting the arms race. What followed—the
partial test ban, the outer-space and Antarctic pacts, the hot-line
agreement, and finally the NPT—were arms control or nonarmament
measures rather than disarmament agreements.

Although resolutions to prevent nuclear proliferation were presented at the United Nations as early as 1958 and at the Geneva Disarmament Conference starting in 1962, the United States did not
give full support to a non-proliferation agreement until 1965.[12] The
United States had opposed both the 1958 and 1960 Irish Resolutions
on non-proliferation and a Swedish Resolution in 1961, the so-called
Undén Plan, for examining the possibility of a formation by the
non-nuclear states of a "non-nuclear club." [13] To explain the Ameri-

[9] William Bader, *The United States and the Spread of Nuclear Weapons,* p.
57.

[10] The preceding statements are based on information obtained at an interview with a member of the Disarmament Agency of the United Nations.

[11] Foster, p. 266.   [12] Bader, p. 23.

[13] United States Arms Control and Disarmament Agency, p. 4.

can vote on the 1960 Irish Resolution, the American delegate contended that

the nuclear Powers cannot expect other nations indefinitely to deny to themselves such weapons as they may believe are required for their self-defense if they—the nuclear Powers—refuse to accept the responsibility of halting their own build-up of nuclear weapons and refuse to begin the process of their destruction. One of our concerns with this draft resolution, therefore, is that it does not recognize the central responsibility of the nuclear Powers.[14]

The preceding sentiment is very similar to the arguments that the nonaligned nations have set forth against the Soviet-American sponsored NPT.

What probably gave the Americans the final impetus for pressing for a non-proliferation agreement was the Chinese Lob Nor nuclear explosion in 1964 and the realization that the only ally Congress was willing to give nuclear support to was Great Britain.[15] In 1965, the United States and the Soviet Union submitted separate drafts for such a treaty. Because the United States was torn between support for NATO and for the Geneva Disarmament Conference, one observer quipped that the American draft treaty "could only have been written by a ball point pen mounted on a cork screw." [16] Not until 1967 were the super powers able to agree on a draft. The main obstacles had been the Atlantic multilateral force and a possible future European nuclear force. The United States maintained that neither the MLF nor a European force would imply proliferation, while the Soviet Union held that it would. Although it is still unclear whether the treaty precludes a MLF or a European force, the issue lost its relevance with the abandonment of the MLF campaign. Since the non-nuclear weapon states had not participated in the drafting of the 1967 treaty, their support could be engendered only in return for substantial additions and revisions of the text. The influence of the non-nuclear weapon states on the final draft is particularly noticeable in regard to the articles on the peaceful uses of nuclear energy. Moreover, the article on safeguards had been left blank in the original draft and the discussion on the control system occupied most of the negotiations during 1967–68. On July 1, 1968, the Treaty was signed by Britain, the United States, and the Soviet Union as well as 56 other states. However, many of the so-called threshold states did

---

[14] Bader, p. 42.   [15] *Ibid.*, p. 40.   [16] *Ibid.*, p. 60.

not sign it at that time—Argentina, Brazil, the Federal Republic of Germany, India, Israel, Japan, Sweden, Switzerland, and the United Arab Republic.[17]

What the signatory states finally agreed to was the following:

1. The nuclear weapon states undertake not to transfer nuclear weapons or nuclear explosives to any state. The reason for including nuclear explosives, even if they were for peaceful purposes, is that these devices are virtually indistinguishable from nuclear weapons.

2. Each non-nuclear weapon state undertakes neither to receive such devices from any state nor to manufacture any such weapon or device.

3. Each non-nuclear weapon state has to submit to inspection by the International Atomic Energy Agency in order to assure that no nuclear energy is diverted for weapon purposes.

4. All parties undertake to cooperate in the development of peaceful applications of nuclear energy.

5. Assurance is made by the nuclear powers that they will supply the non-nuclear states with a nuclear explosive service. Since the non-nuclear states will not be permitted to acquire nuclear explosive devices, the nuclear states will make available the benefits from peaceful explosions, allegedly on a non-discriminatory basis and at a low cost.

6. The nuclear weapon states undertake to resume disarmament talks at an early date.

7. The Treaty is not to interfere with the setting up of nuclear free zones.

Finally, there are separate articles regarding the amendment process, review conferences, specifications on how the Treaty shall come into force, and the provision for withdrawal from the Treaty.[18]

Sweden's Objections to the Treaty

It should be remembered that Sweden's attitude toward the Treaty is not the same as, for example, West Germany's. Sweden is a non-aligned nation that does not have the fears or goals that the Federal Republic has. Nor is the Swedish situation similar to India's or Israel's, as their reasons for opposing the Treaty are based mainly on regional considerations. Nevertheless, many of the reservations that

[17] For the list of signatory states, see U.S. ACDA, p. 168. As of 1970, the Federal Republic of Germany, Sweden, and the United Arab Republic have been added to the list.

[18] For the text of the Treaty, see *ibid.*, pp. 168–73.

Sweden has voiced have been supported by the other non-nuclear states, in particular by the other nonaligned nations in the Eighteen Nation Disarmament Committee at Geneva.

Sweden's objections to the Treaty can be divided into two main categories. The first refers to the economic and commercial implications of the Treaty; the second, to the Treaty's effectiveness in preventing nuclear proliferation and in furthering negotiations toward disarmament. Despite the fact that Sweden has not focused on the military-security aspect of the Treaty, the NPT's effect on the non-nuclear nations' security has been of such great concern for many of the other nonaligned nations that it would be fitting to introduce this section with an account of the question of security guarantees.

The fear of nuclear attack or of nuclear blackmail has especially been expressed by India, but also by the representatives of Nigeria, Brazil, the UAR, and Mexico in Geneva.[19] As early as 1964, former President Johnson, in response to the Communist Chinese test, stated that if the non-nuclear nations "need our strong support against some threat of nuclear blackmail, then they will have it." [20] This pledge was also reaffirmed [21] by the former President on January 27, 1966.[22] Premier Kosygin, in a message to the Eighteen Nation Committee on Disarmament in 1966, declared his willingness "to include in the draft treaty a clause on the prohibition of the use of nuclear weapons against non-nuclear parties to the treaty which have no nuclear weapons in their territory." [23] The United States was unwilling to support Kosygin's proposal, allegedly because of the difficulty of verifying in which nations nuclear weapons were stationed. Such verification, it was argued, would require extensive controls of weapon deployment and would further delay the completion of the NPT.[24] One can also speculate that the United States felt that Kosygin's proposal would discriminate against West Germany, which, by virtue of its NATO membership, has nuclear weapons stationed on its soil.

[19] For a brief summary, see *ibid.*, pp. 73–74.

[20] *Documents on Disarmament 1964*, p. 468.

[21] *Documents on Disarmament 1966*, p. 6.

[22] However, at the Twenty-third Session of the General Assembly, the United States representative declared that "no responsible government could obligate itself to take military action automatically in a wide and unspecified variety of contingencies." Carnegie Endowment for International Peace, *International Conciliation: Issues before the Twenty-fourth General Assembly*, September 1969/No. 574, p. 31.

[23] *Ibid.*, p. 11.   [24] See *Documents on Disarmament 1966*, pp. 698, 727.

The result was that no security guarantees were incorporated into the Treaty. The preamble does contain a reminder of the United Nations principles regarding the threat or use of force in international relations. The larger question of security guarantees was delegated to the Security Council, where a resolution was passed June 19, 1968, affirming the Council's duty to "act immediately in accordance with their obligations under the United Nations Charter," if a non-nuclear weapon state were threatened with nuclear weapons.[25]

The insertion of the UN principles in the preamble and the Security Council Resolution could hardly be seen as steps forward in stemming war or aggression. The discrepancy between "paper" pledges and Realpolitik was clearly illustrated by the Soviet invasion of Czechoslovakia less than two months after the Soviet Union had signed the Treaty. If the United Nations could not protect Czechoslovakia against non-nuclear aggression, it is highly unlikely that the United Nations would act in the case of a nuclear attack. In response to the Johnson message and the Kosygin offer, the Swedish representative, Mrs. Myrdal, emphasized the difficulty of formulating a universal security guarantee.[26] Indeed, the security needs of allied nations do not correspond to the needs of the nonaligned. In connection with the Undén Plan in 1961, Sweden had suggested that the nuclear powers might pledge not to attack with nuclear weapons any of the members of the "nonatomic club." [27] The absence of a similar Swedish proposal during the non-proliferation negotiations probably stems from skepticism of the credibility of such a guarantee as well as reluctance to conclude any type of security arrangement with either of the two super powers.

The general lack of concern that Sweden has shown for pressing for a security pledge is perhaps also a reflection of its military-strategic position: at least at the present time, there is no imminent threat to Sweden's territory. Yet, it should not be concluded that Sweden neglects its defense. Its defense budget for 1969/70 is about $1.2 billion, or approximately 4.6 percent of its estimated 1969 GNP.[28] Its air force is one of the largest in Europe and is equipped with modern weapons of the highest standard. There are also indications that the Swedish government, or at least the Swedish military,

---

[25] U.S. ACDA, p. 155.   [26] *Documents of Disarmament 1966,* pp. 57–58.
[27] U.S. ACDA, p. 8.
[28] *The Swedish Budget 1969/70,* a summary published by the Minister of Finance (Stockholm, 1969), p. 49.

does not completely rule out an attack on its territory. First, the acquisition of tactical nuclear weapons has been advocated on several occasions by the military, although a parliamentary decision was made in 1968 not to obtain nuclear weapons. Second, Sweden has constructed an extensive civil-defense system and a network of underground and "tunnel shelters" for warships and coast-guard artillery and is continuing its research on the means of protection against nuclear war. Since Sweden's defense policy is intimately connected with its foreign policy and its view of international relations, the last section elaborates on Sweden's military-strategic policies.

Sweden has been more concerned with the possible adverse economic and commercial effects of the Treaty. Sweden fears that the technological gap, between the United States and Western Europe, on the one hand, and between the nuclear powers and the developing nations, on the other, will only widen after the Treaty comes into effect.[29]

Regarding industrial espionage and the spin-off effect, Sweden has actually showed little anxiety. It appears that industrial espionage has been more of an issue in such nations as the Federal Republic and Italy, where East European inspectors would not be greeted warmly.[30] *Spin-off* is the term used to describe the benefits that might accrue to civil nuclear activities from military nuclear programs. It is difficult to state how important these benefits have been or could be. Sweden feels that the loss in relation to the spin-off for the non-nuclear nations will be negligible, as nuclear technology has become so widely disseminated. What Sweden has been more worried about is a different kind of spin-off—the unrestricted military advantages that the nuclear powers can gain from their civilian nuclear programs.[31]

Of greater economic significance, at least for Sweden, is the issue of commercial nuclear discrimination. The charge that the nuclear powers could form an atomic commercial super-monopoly [32] cannot be dismissed easily. There is a very real possibility that the nuclear

[29] See Statement by Mrs. Myrdal on May 9, 1968, in the First Committee on agenda item 28 (mimeographed), pp. 8–9.

[30] Smith, p. 101. However, according to a member of the United Nations Disarmament Division, it is not the East Europeans but the Americans that the West Europeans fear. The reason is that while the East European nuclear industry would not present a commercial threat, the American industry would.

[31] UN Doc. ENDC/PV 364, February 13, 1968.   [32] U.S. ACDA, p. 68.

powers will acquire a monopoly over the export of atomic energy and equipment. The IAEA safeguard measures that will be applied to all civilian nuclear programs of the non-nuclear signatory states can have a negative effect on these countries' nuclear exports. Not only will the price of a safeguarded nuclear reactor be somewhat higher (as there are inspection fees), but inspection could also interfere with deliveries. The result might be that a buyer would turn to a nuclear-weapon state for his purchases.[33]

Although nuclear exports from a non-nuclear to a nuclear state may not currently be significant, it could in the future assume important proportions. There are already indications of them becoming significant. Swedish industry has announced that it is interested in expanding its exports of fuel and components for nuclear power plants. Sweden in the first six months of 1969 exported nuclear materials and equipment at a value of $260,000—a relatively small sum but a large increase when compared to the *annual* figures for the middle Sixties, which ranged from $90,000 to $160,000.[34]

Sweden is also skeptical regarding the nuclear explosive services, which the nuclear powers have promised to provide on a nondiscriminatory basis and at a cost that would be as low as possible and that would exclude the charge of research and development. Mrs. Myrdal has intimated that the creation of the international company Nobelpaso Geonuclear, as a follow-up to Project Gasbuggy, with American, French, and some Belgian and West German capital, does not give the impression of a nonprofit organization.[35] There is also some doubt regarding the nondiscriminatory element of the service. According to the Treaty, non-nuclear states can obtain the benefits of peaceful nuclear explosions following "special international agreement or agreements, through an appropriate international body with adequate representation of non-nuclear weapon states." But the service can also be provided "pursuant to bilateral agreements."[36] The picture is complicated by the fact that some nations, such as Canada and the Soviet Union, have fewer and less strict controls than the

[33] See Arnold Kramish, "The Watched and the Unwatched: Inspection in the Non-Proliferation Treaty," in *Adelphi Papers*, No. 36 (June, 1967), p. 5; and Smith, p. 101.

[34] See *Utrikeshandel, Sveriges Officiella Statistik*, Statistika Centralbyran 1965 through 1969 (first half).

[35] UN Doc. ENDC/PV 373, March 5, 1968, para. 16.

[36] Article V of the NPT.

IAEA has. If the service were provided through bilateral agreements, one could expect circumvention of IAEA controls—a situation that would not be conducive to the development of uniform safeguard measures. Since allies also tend to be favored in bilateral arrangements, the Swedish representative questioned whether equal opportunities could be ensured if agreements were negotiated on a bilateral basis.[37]

Sweden's second general objection centers on the Treaty's effectiveness as a measure for stopping proliferation and limiting nuclear armaments. What is meant by nuclear' proliferation? Do the provisions of the Treaty, in fact, prevent the spread of nuclear weapons? Are there loopholes through which nuclear bombs could steal? Is the NPT a step toward a relaxation of international tensions and a reduction of the arms race's momentum? These are some of the questions that have greatly disturbed Sweden as well as many of the other non-nuclear states.

What is the purpose of a non-proliferation agreement? Allegedly, the present Treaty is directed to two problems: the dissemination and proliferation of nuclear weapons. The former denotes the actual transfer of nuclear weapons from one country to another; the latter has the more restricted meaning of a weapon-manufacturing program that a former non-nuclear nation has undertaken on its own.[38] Proliferation can also be interpreted as the quantitative and qualitative increase of nuclear weapons in the world. One of Sweden's main criticisms of the Treaty is that it does not cope with the latter and more general type of nuclear proliferation.[39]

How effective is the Treaty in stopping the spread of nuclear weapons? In terms of the narrower interpretation of proliferation, the Treaty has overlooked two potential problems. First, plutonium can still be stockpiled in the non-nuclear country. If a non-nuclear state were to decide that "extraordinary events," referred to in Article X of the NPT, "have jeopardized the supreme interests of its country," the state could easily withdraw,[40] use its plutonium stock-

[37] UN Doc. ENDC/PV 373, March 5, 1968, para. 10.

[38] Alva Myrdal, "Political Aspects of Non-Proliferation," *Adelphi Papers,* No. 29, p. 10.

[39] *Documents of Disarmament 1966,* p. 54.

[40] Obviously, the political consequences of such an act might be considerable. Yet as the Soviet invasion of Czechoslovakia, the American intervention in the Dominican Republic, and the North Korean shooting down in 1969 of

pile for weapons production, and initiate underground testing. As plutonium is the main fuel and component in the fast-breeder reactors, a prohibition on plutonium stockpiling would not be a fair and balanced solution. Instead, Sweden has suggested that a test ban would be a more appropriate and effective measure for preventing nuclear proliferation.[41]

The second loophole refers to the safeguard system for the non-nuclear states. The Swedish representative has observed that the control applies only to the peaceful activities and not to certain types of military activities, for example, the propulsion of submarines and the production of fissionable materials for export to nuclear weapon states.[42] It would be difficult for even the best legal and technical experts to draft a watertight treaty. However, it is difficult to dispute the contention that a non-proliferation treaty in conjunction with a comprehensive test ban would be more effective in counteracting the initiation and growth of nuclear arsenals.

In reference to the broader meaning of nuclear proliferation, Sweden has brought up the fact that there is no control on the *transfers* of nuclear materials from non-nuclear weapon states to nuclear weapon states. In other words, any non-nuclear state could build up the stockpiles of any of the nuclear-weapon states without violating the Treaty. Again, any measures to prohibit or restrict the non-nuclear states' exports would only abet charges of economic discrimination and super-power monopoly. Sweden's proposal to apply the safeguards to all transfers of nuclear materials would be a more equitable arms-control measure, but would still not remove the commercial inequity of the control system. The solution, however, is not to relax the control system. On the contrary, Sweden argues that the most balanced and reasonable course would be to expand the safeguards to cover not only the transfers but also the civilian nuclear industries of *all* nations.[43]

The transfer loophole is also an illustration of a more basic objec-

---

an unarmed American military plane show, violations, that have been committed by both large and small nations, are not necessarily followed by retaliatory action on the part of the world community.

[41] *Documents on Disarmament 1966*, p. 508.

[42] Kungliga Majestatets proposition nr. 164, 1969 from *Bihang till Riksdagens Protokoll 1969*, p. 11.

[43] For Sweden's view of the safeguard system, see particularly *Documents on Disarmament 1967*, pp. 242–45.

tion to the Treaty. All nonaligned nations in the ENDC have attacked the Treaty on the grounds that it does not contain a balance of mutual obligations and responsibilities.[44] Under the NPT the main obligations will be borne by the non-nuclear states. While the peaceful nuclear installations in the non-nuclear states are to be inspected, there will be no restrictions on the civilian nuclear activities of the nuclear-weapon states. The discriminatory element of the inspection system is even evident in the title of an article by Arnold Kramish. He calls the inspection system in the NPT, "The Watched and The Unwatched." Although Sweden supports the IAEA's safeguard system, the Swedish representative feels, to repeat, that the system should have been extended to the peaceful nuclear activities of all parties—nuclear and non-nuclear.

The mutual obligation argument has not only been used in regard to the peaceful nuclear programs. The criticism has also been launched against the nuclear powers' military programs. Although the Treaty contains an article urging the nuclear powers to continue negotiations for the reductions of armaments, the NPT could be interpreted as an institutionalization of the nuclear *status quo* in that no restrictions are placed on the atomic powers' nuclear arsenals or programs.

This leads to the final question. Is the Treaty a step toward nuclear disarmament? One could very well argue that the dangers of nuclear proliferation have been exaggerated and that other measures would have contributed more to disarmament than the present Treaty. It has been pointed out that there is nothing inevitable about the spread of nuclear weapons.[45] Even if certain nations are capable of producing nuclear weapons, it does not mean that they have the corresponding will. The argument that since France, Great Britain, and Communist China went nuclear, the Federal Republic of Germany, Sweden, or Switzerland automatically will take the same course, is based more on capability than on intentions. The inevitability of the spread of nuclear weapons has too many parallels to other ill-fated domino theories. Despite (or perhaps because of) the preoccupation with the "Nth country problem," there has been a tendency to confuse the possession of fissionable materials with a nuclear capability. Even a few atomic weapons does not constitute a nuclear capability. A reliable striking force must include delivery,

---

[44] U.S. ACDA, pp. 81–82, 101–3.   [45] Bader, pp. 63–66.

control, and command systems, which are not only complex but costly.

Although the above arguments indicate that a non-proliferation measure was not so urgent as the super powers have pronounced, Sweden has not relied on these arguments in criticizing the Treaty. Sweden has never doubted the intrinsic value of a non-proliferation measure. The purpose of its criticism was to improve the form of the Treaty and not to dispute the potential dangers of nuclear dissemination. What Sweden has disputed, however, is the tendency to regard the NPT as having priority over other arms-control measures; [46] in this sense, Sweden would respond that nuclear proliferation is less of a danger than the super-powers' arms race. In other words, Sweden feels that the Treaty is deficient because it does not focus on the perils of the super-powers' arms race. The Indian representative to the ENDC summed up the nonaligned states' position when he compared the Treaty's provisions to a seventeenth-century Indian emperor, who was a drunkard himself, but who prohibited drinking throughout his empire. [47]

Sweden's Proposed Alternative: "The Package Deal"

To ensure that a non-proliferation agreement would indeed be a meaningful step on the road to nuclear disarmament, Sweden has continually stressed that one must not ignore other arms-control measures. Specifically, Sweden proposed that the NPT be accompanied by a comprehensive test-ban treaty and a cut-off in the production of fissionable material. [48] The Swedish representative has contended that a comprehensive test ban would by itself be an effective non-proliferation measure, as it would be very difficult to acquire an adequate weapons system without testing. It is true that nuclear weapons can be developed without testing, but it is probably impossible to develop a reliable striking force without a testing program.

Furthermore, one indication of the acceleration of the arms race is the rate of nuclear-weapon testing. A recent study found that nuclear testing has increased in the world since the Moscow 1963 Treaty. [49]

[46] *Documents on Disarmament 1966*, p. 551.   [47] *Ibid.*, p. 18.

[48] For a good summary of Sweden's "package deal," see *Documents on Disarmament 1967*, p. 246.

[49] For a summary of the report published by Stockholm International Peace Research Institute, see New York *Times*, November 20, 1969.

While the Soviet annual testing has decreased, the United States has stepped up its testing considerably. The gravest implication of these tests is the development of more destructive weapons. For example, the MIRV could not be credibly deployed without the testing of its hydrogen warheads. A second result of the testing actually constitutes a violation of the Moscow Treaty: the leakage of radioactive gases outside the testing nation's territory. Hence, the continuation of underground nuclear-weapon explosions poses an immediate health danger and the even greater danger of an uncontrollable arms race.

In April, 1969, Sweden submitted a working paper on a Treaty Banning Underground Nuclear Weapon Tests.[50] It would ban all underground tests with one exception—nuclear explosions for peaceful purposes. To avoid violations of the use of peaceful nuclear explosions, the Swedish representative suggested that two separate agreements be reached. The first would embody a general prohibition of all underground explosions. The second would set up an international organ or grant power to the IAEA to license and survey peaceful explosions. The stocks of explosives would remain with the nuclear powers, to prevent dissemination, but their use would be subject to approval by an international organ.

The reason for drawing up a separate agreement for the use of nuclear explosions for peaceful purposes is the need for an equitable access to peaceful nuclear explosions. It is true that there is no consensus on how commercially important peaceful nuclear explosives will be. However, the United States has already started a Plowshare Program to investigate the possibility of extracting oil from oil shale by nuclear explosions. It is also widely recognized that if methods could be devised to ensure against radioactive contamination of the environment and seismic effects (earthquakes), nuclear explosives would be invaluable for building harbors, canals, and clearing mountain passes.[51]

The major obstacle, at least officially, to a comprehensive test ban has been the inspection system. The United States has insisted on on-site inspection, while the Soviet Union maintains that national verification is sufficient.[52] Over the last couple of years, there has been a significant progress in the use of seismological methods for detecting underground explosions. In 1968, scientists from various

[50] ENDC/242, April 1969.   [51] Bader, pp. 24–25.

[52] To compare the positions of the two governments, see the Soviet and American statements quoted in Statement by Mrs. Myrdal, in the Conference of the ENDC on April 1, 1969, p. 5.

nations, including 4 nuclear powers, met in Stockholm to study detection and identification of underground explosions by seismological
means only. The report that was subsequently published concluded
that it was possible to separate clearly the waves from explosions in
granite with yields down to 20-60 kilotons from those generated by
earthquakes.[53] The fact that one cannot separate earthquakes from
nuclear explosions at a lower range means that a seismologically ver-
ified test ban would not be a foolproof one—Swedish scientists have
estimated, for example, that there would be one ambiguous event in
the Soviet Union every ten to fifteen years.

The Swedish representative maintains that through further im-
provements in seismological monitoring methods and by the use of a
"verification by challenge" method, a comprehensive test-ban treaty
could be concluded without on-site inspection. The verification by
challenge is essentially a psychological method that is expected to operate at the time of an "ambiguous event." [54] It is felt that the pressure on the possible violator would be so great that the party would
invite inspection in order to prove his innocence. Obviously, a test-
ban treaty without an international inspection system has, to a large
extent, to be based on a belief in the weight and influence of world
opinion. On the other hand, one can question the effectiveness of an
inspection system in deterring a violator, since the problem of sanc-
tions exists regardless of whether there are inspections or not.

Finally, Sweden has proposed the formation of a detection club—
an international network of seismological stations that would exchange data and cooperate in monitoring the test ban.[55] Although the
United States does not believe that a detection club would solve the
verification problem, the United States has announced that it plans to
build a monitoring station in Norway, which would be linked to the
station in Montana for the purpose of improving the methods of
identifying underground explosions.[56]

In addition to a non-proliferation agreement and a comprehensive
test ban, the Swedish representative has advocated a fissionable material production cut-off.[57] The cut-off agreement would comprise the
cessation of all current production of nuclear materials for weapons
purposes in all signatory states. The cut-off, in contrast to an under-

[53] For a summary of the report, see UN Doc. ENDC/230, July 29, 1968.
[54] Statement by Mrs. Myrdal, April 1, 1969, p. 4.   [55] *Ibid.*, p. 7.
[56] Washington *Post,* August 9, 1967.
[57] *Documents on Disarmament 1966,* p. 547.

ground test ban, could for obvious reasons not be dependent on a national verification system. The safeguards system of the IAEA could, however, be extended to include inspection of the production of fissionable material. The following general timetable for the control system has been proposed:

1. There would be controls on all transfers of atomic materials.
2. The control system would be expanded to include all new nuclear facilities producing fissionable materials.
3. The controls would be extended to cover all already existing production facilities.[58]

The central importance of a cut-off lies in that it is directed against the growth of nuclear arsenals. Such a cut-off would not only prevent the production of new explosives in the signatory states but probably also in the nonsignatory nations, as there would be control on all transfers.

Although Sweden has now signed and ratified the NPT, the Swedish delegation continues to argue that the above two arms-control measures are essential steps toward disarmament. Since the super powers defended the NPT on the grounds that it would open the way for further agreements,[59] the non-nuclear nations' impatience with the lack of progress in the negotiations is understandable. One could even go further and state that the lack of progress indicates that the non-nuclear nations' skepticism of the super powers' motivations in regard to the NPT was warranted.

The inertia in the field of nuclear disarmament [60] is especially frustrating for those nations that have forgone nuclear weapons, in light of the number of resolutions in the United Nations and the pledges by the super powers to halt the arms race. The following is a short history of the proposals for a comprehensive test ban and a cut-off of the production of fissionable material: [61]

The Soviet Union had first proposed the discontinuation of weapon tests on May 10, 1955. The Western position at that time was that the prohibition of weapon tests should be part of a compre-

[58] *Ibid.*, pp. 548–49.   [59] U.S. ACDA, p. 183.

[60] Mention should be made of the preliminary strategic arms limitation talks, which were held in Helsinki late 1969. Although the "atmosphere" was friendly, there are no indications of speedy agreements.

[61] For the history of these proposals, see *The United Nations and Disarmament 1945–1965:* for the test ban, especially, pp. 135–82 and on the cut-off, pp. 115–16, 202, 252, 267.

hensive disarmament program. In October, 1958, the Soviet Union, the United Kingdom, and the United States had agreed to begin negotiations on a treaty banning nuclear-weapon tests in all environments. Although the result, after five years of negotiations, was the treaty banning tests in the atmosphere, outer space, and under water, the parties to the Treaty declared their intention to "achieve the discontinuance of all test explosions of nuclear weapons for all time (and) . . . to continue negotiations to this end." [62] What followed were joint memoranda by the 8 nonaligned nations in the ENDC and numerous General Assembly resolutions on a comprehensive test ban but no formal agreement by the Soviet Union and the United States to prohibit nuclear weapon tests. [63]

Similarly, there has been no effective action on the proposals to cease the production of fissionable material. In both the Soviet and the American draft on General and Complete Disarmament in 1962, there were provisions for halting the production of fissionable material for weapons purposes. The super powers' positions on the American cut-off proposal in January, 1964, were reversed, if compared to their stands in 1955 on a comprehensive test ban: the Soviet Union stressed the need to link the cut-off to other measures, while the United States emphasized the importance of partial and initial steps. [64] It should be added that a cut-off has received less attention than the comprehensive test ban. Although the non-nuclear states have generally upheld a cut-off, it is primarily Sweden that has advanced the proposal. [65]

Although the inspection system remains an obstacle in achieving a comprehensive test ban and a cut-off, the Swedish representative asserts that it does not represent an insurmountable problem. According to Mrs. Myrdal, "the technical control issue cannot be regarded as the decisive problem. The crux is political." [66] The contention that it is the will to disarm that is lacking was further dramatized by the recent development of ABMs, FOBS, and MIRVs. Furthermore, Sweden is by no means the only nation expressing concern over the

[62] *Ibid.*, p. 176.

[63] There was a voluntary suspension of testing by the United States, the U.K., and the Soviet Union from 1958 to 1961.

[64] The United States, the Soviet Union, and the U.K. announced unilateral decisions to curtail the production of fissile material in 1964.

[65] *Documents on Disarmament 1966*, pp. 547–53.

[66] Statement by Mrs. Alva Myrdal, April 1, 1969, p. 2.

build-up of nuclear arsenals. The United Nations Conference of Non-Nuclear Weapon States, attended by 96 countries, was convened for the purpose of discussing the non-nuclear nations' apprehensions.[67] In addition to the issues of security guarantees and the peaceful uses of atomic energy, the Conference focused on nuclear disarmament. In particular, the non-nuclear nations felt that their submission to the nuclear hegemony of the United States and the Soviet Union was not being met by any concessions on the part of the super powers. Hence, Sweden's hesitant approval of the NPT cannot be written off as inconsequential criticism by a small, neutral nation. On the contrary, the NPT negotiations have revealed the non-nuclear nations' increasing insecurity and frustration with an arms race that they can neither stop nor counteract.

Sweden's Foreign and Defense Policies

Sweden's concern with the NPT must also be viewed against the background of its general foreign policy. The characteristic mark of Sweden's policy is its freedom from alliances. Although the main purpose of its nonalignment is to preserve neutrality in the event of war, other arguments in support of its nonalignment have also been promoted. In fact, the government's foreign policy has been described as comprising three strands of thought.[68] The first is that of traditional neutrality, based not only on an aversion to war but on a feeling of futility in affecting the great powers' policies. The second attitude is more inspired by a freedom of action principle. Nonalignment in this sense stems from a desire to determine Sweden's course of action on a case-by-case basis. Because of Liberal and Conservative influence on this argument, those supporting this view have tended to adopt an anticommunist stance and to advocate closer ties with the West. A final strand is described as a "third-force" tendency, as it is marked by the argument that Sweden's role should be that of a mediator and arbitrator between the East and the West. Since third-force attitudes allegedly arose as a reaction against McCarthyism in the United States, supporters of these attitudes have often displayed a more positive view toward Communism than toward the freedom of action adherents. Nevertheless, the central idea

[67] Carnegie Endowment, pp. 28–37.
[68] Special Study Group of the Swedish Institute of International Affairs, *Sweden and the United Nations*, pp. 157–63.

of this trend is to avoid involvement in a great-power conflict and at the same time promote peaceful coexistence between the two "camps."

It is difficult to determine which view has been predominant within the Swedish government. Since the liberty of action argument has often been attributed to the Liberals and the Conservatives, Swedish foreign policy has probably been mainly a mixture of classical neutrality and "third forcism." The term *neutrality* must be used with care, however. First, neutrality is interpreted in Sweden as a concept that applies only in time of war.[69] Second, *neutrality* often has the connotation of abstention from judgments of world problems. Sweden's vociferous attacks on the Soviet invasion of Czechoslovakia in 1968 and the American involvement in Viet Nam cannot be called attitudinal neutrality. At the same time, the present government maintains that such criticism is consistent with Sweden's policy of neutrality. To contrast current policy with the isolationist and passive trends of traditional neutrality, Prime Minister Palme has preferred "active neutrality" or "nonalignment" in describing his government's policy.

Sweden's championing of peace is directed to two ends: the protection of the Swedish people from involvement in war and the promotion of international security and peace. Although the two goals are highly interdependent, they demand different methods and approaches. To safeguard Sweden's peace and to protect its independence, the government maintains a strong defense. To further world peace, Sweden actively supports United Nations peace-keeping operations and disarmament measures. And because of the inability of the United Nations forces to maintain peace, Sweden has increasingly turned to disarmament as a long-term contribution to peace.

Although advocacy for a strong defense *might* appear inconsistent with demands for world disarmament, the Swedish military asserts that the geographic position of Sweden warrants a "total defense," that is, an extensive military and civil-defense program, including preparations against a limited nuclear attack.[70] It is felt that in a

---

[69] Nils Andrén, *Svensk Utrikespolitik Efter 1945,* p. 110.

[70] For information regarding Sweden's defense, see *Fact Sheets on Sweden,* Swedish Institute for Cultural Relations with Foreign Countries, August, 1968; *The Total Defense of Sweden,* Press Department of the Swedish Defense Staff 1963; Andrén, pp. 32–38; Svenska Dagbladet, Friday, November 21, 1969, "Den Vapnade Neutraliteten."

great-power conflict, Sweden would be an attractive target on account of its transportation network [71] and its position between the Eastern and Western sphere of influence. These views are put forth mainly by the military and seem less persuasive than the following statements, that summarize, albeit simplistically, Sweden's political and strategic situation. First, Sweden as a nonaligned nation can not count on military support from any other nation and hence must provide for its own defense. Second, a strong defense is desired to guard against the development of a "vacuum." [72] In other words, a strong defense is needed to deter rather than to defend against an invasion.

As nuclear weapons are generally promoted on the grounds of deterrence, it is not so surprising that the question of equipping the Swedish defense with tactical nuclear weapons has been raised. However, the question of Swedish atomic weapons has been settled, at least for the present. In May, 1968, it was decided by the government, with the support of the defense department, that "nuclear weapons should not be acquired for the time being." [73] Although the resolution was worded so as not to prejudice Sweden's freedom of action at a future date, it was mainly at the insistence of some Conservative parliamentary members. Their argument is as follows: Sweden's foreign policy should be characterized by complete freedom of action to enable Sweden, if the world situation in ten or twenty years appears to threaten its sovereignty, to defend itself, if need be by nuclear weapons.[74] This view is not held by the Social Democratic Party, which has been in office since the early 1930s. The Socialists assert that in regard to nuclear weapons there is no reason for Sweden to retain its freedom of action.[75] As former Prime Minister Erlander summed up Swedish policy: "We shall make our stands on the different world problems not on the basis of our selfish interest but with the idea in mind that our position possibly can come to influence the peace." [76]

In December, 1969, the Swedish Parliament voted to ratify the

[71] As a transportation network would probably have little significance in a nuclear war, the preceding would seem to apply mainly to conventional warfare.

[72] The "vacuum" explanation was derived from an interview with a member of the Disarmament Division of the United Nations.

[73] Parliamentary proposal nr. 110, *Riksdagens Protokoll 1969,* Forsta Kammaren, No. 27, p. 51.

[74] See Andrén, pp. 78–79.

[75] Forsta Kammaren, No. 26, p. 51.   [76] *Ibid.,* No. 13, p. 49.

Treaty and in January, 1970, the instruments of ratification were deposited. Despite the fact that Sweden was not wholly satisfied with the final form of the Non-Proliferation Treaty, Sweden's delay might appear unwarranted or selfish, especially if compared to the early ratifications by the other Scandinavian countries. Sweden could certainly not expect to change the Treaty after it had been signed and ratified by a number of countries. Nevertheless, a major reason for the delay is that Sweden wanted to wait until after decisions had been made by some of the other potential nuclear-weapon nations in Europe, for example, the Federal Republic of Germany or Switzerland.[77] If West Germany had decided that it could not deny itself the acquisition of nuclear weapons, Sweden might not have committed itself to the Treaty. Sweden might possibly have felt threatened by a nuclear West Germany.

What is more important than the delay is the criticism that Sweden has launched against the Treaty. Hopefully, the above has shown that Sweden's criticism does not reflect a desire to "get the bomb." What it does reflect is a desire to ease international tensions and release the financial resources and the scientific brainpower that have been poured into the production of weapons of mass destruction.

Nor has the criticism been unheeded. The final draft treaty showed substantial improvement over the earlier Soviet and American sponsored drafts. Although the Swedish delegation's proposals for controls on all transfers of nuclear materials and for a special international agreement on peaceful nuclear explosions were not met with success, Sweden's support for IAEA safeguards and its stress on the importance of peaceful applications of nuclear energy was recognized in the final text. The Swedish delegation was also responsible for the provision of a review conference and, in cooperation with Mexico, for the separate article on the nuclear powers' pledge to pursue disarmament negotiations.[78]

Sweden's questioning of the NPT also illustrates the present trend of small-power rebellion—a rebellion that is directed against the super powers' attempts to freeze the power configuration of today's world for posterity. Unless one is willing to resign oneself to a world of inequality and "nuclear haves" and "nuclear have-nots," one should not view the small powers' attempts to influence international

[77] Riksdagens Protokoll, No. 27, p. 50.
[78] See Kungliga Majestatets propositon nr 164, pp. 5, 7, 13, 14.

events and policies as futile or irrelevant. When Mrs. Myrdal stated that "if there is something of an eleventh commandment 'Thou shalt not carry nuclear weapons'—why should it be valid only for some?" [79] she did not express a desire by Sweden to obtain nuclear weapons. Instead, she expressed the hope that international relations could be based on something other than military power. Perhaps the equality of all nations?

[79] *Documents of Disarmament 1966*, p. 52.

The EEC and the Maghreb

GLENDA ROSENTHAL

Upon signing the Treaty of Rome in March, 1957, the six member states of the European Community declared their readiness to propose to the independent countries of the franc area "the opening of negotiations with a view to concluding conventions for economic association with the Community." [1] Twelve years later, in March, 1969, the Community signed conventions of partial association with Morocco and Tunisia. What does this belated and partial implementation of the 1957 Declaration portend for the Maghreb? For the wider Mediterranean area? For the European Community?

The Maghreb countries form an integral part of the wider Mediterranean geographic and economic area. Any change in the relationships of one or more of these countries with the EEC will have far-reaching effects on the other countries of the Mediterranean basin as well as on their relationships with the EEC. Moves toward closer Maghreb-Common Market ties have been accompanied by requests for "parallel" treatment from Israel, Egypt, Lebanon, Yugoslavia, Spain, Malta, and Cyprus. Greece and Turkey are already linked with the EEC by association agreements. Spokesmen for the EEC have repeatedly emphasized the Community's desire to play an active part in promoting the development of the countries bordering on the Mediterranean, as a contribution to peace, stability, and progress in the area. The EEC policy toward the Maghreb must therefore be examined in the light of its broader implications for the Community's Mediterranean policy.

Parallel with this growing interest in EEC-Maghreb relations, serious doubts have been voiced, particularly by the United States, about the validity, under GATT rules, of additional preferential trade arrangements, negotiated or proposed, between the Common Market

[1] *Treaty Establishing the European Economic Community and Connected Documents* (Luxembourg, 1962), p. 348 (hereafter cited as *Rome Treaty*).

and the countries in the Mediterranean region. The proliferation of such special arrangements, it is claimed, not only ignores vital American interests but threatens to undermine GATT. The accusation has been advanced more and more frequently that EEC policy in this area is insensitive to the economic problems and military burdens of the United States. Thus, not only world trade questions but also over-all political issues have become involved; these are examined briefly in this study.

Troubled Course of
EEC-Maghreb Negotiations

Some twelve years after the signing of the Rome Treaty, and five years after the beginning of negotiations, the European Community took the first step toward full association with Tunisia and Morocco: partial association agreements were signed with Tunisia on March 28, 1969, and with Morocco on March 31, 1969. As late as mid-1970 Algeria, the largest of the Maghreb states, and likewise independent country of the franc area, had not entered into any special agreement with the EEC. Although on an equal political footing with Morocco and Tunisia since it achieved independence in July, 1962, Algeria enjoys a different status under the Rome Treaty. When the Rome Treaty was signed, Algeria, as an integral part of the French Republic, was included in the provisions under Article 227.[2] Since 1962, the policies of the individual EEC countries toward Algeria have steadily diverged, despite attempts at various times by both Algeria and the EEC to regularize them in some way. It seems appropriate, therefore, to deal with Algeria separately from Morocco and Tunisia.

The original applications for association by Morocco and Tunisia date from 1963.[3] The Tunisia government had in fact put out a number of feelers as early as 1959, expressing its desire to avail itself of the opportunity offered by the EEC Declaration of Intention of

[2] *Rome Treaty*, p. 159. Article 227, 2 reads: "With regard to Algeria and the French overseas departments, the general and special provisions of this Treaty . . . shall apply as from the date of the entry into force of this Treaty."

[3] Commission of the European Communities, Spokesman's Group, *Information Memo* P / 16 (Brussels, March, 1969), p. 1.

1957. For both political and economic reasons, no concrete steps were taken by Tunisia or Morocco at that time. Politically, it was widely felt that the Algerian questions should be settled first. Economically, there was no pressing need to come to terms with the Common Market since both countries continued to enjoy preferential access to the French market on the basis of bilateral agreements. Direct association agreements with the Community, in which the bilateral preferences would be incorporated, would of course provide greater security by removing the possibility of French unilateral decisions or political pressure. Algerian independence opened the way to a shift in policy, and on October 3, 1963 Tunisia and, on December 14 of the same year, Morocco submitted applications to Brussels for the opening of negotiations.

Exploratory talks took place in 1964. Tunisia and Morocco asked for the widest possible preferential arrangements, within a free-trade area, but also urged that allowances should be made for the less-developed state of their economies. In addition, they sought financial aid, technical assistance, and freer movement of their workers to the Community. Actual negotiations, begun in July, 1965, made little progress, largely because of the severe limitations placed by the Council of Ministers on the EEC Commission, the negotiating body for the Six. The mandate was restricted to commercial issues and did not cover a number of export products important for the Maghreb countries, particularly fruit and vegetables.

New and more flexible terms of reference were adopted only in October, 1967, mainly because of political difficulties within the Community. The French refusal to participate in ministerial meetings from July, 1965, to February, 1966, completely blocked any new initiatives in EEC external relations during this period. Even after normal activity was resumed, consideration of the Tunisian and Moroccan applications was held up by pressure from other EEC quarters, particularly from Italian agricultural interests, which held that the Community must first settle those parts of the common agricultural policy that concerned fruit and vegetables and oils and fats. A political coloration was also injected into the discussions by Dutch threats to hold up negotiations until a satisfactory position had been adopted on the Israeli request for association. By the time most of the differences had been ironed out and the EEC was prepared to resume negotiations, in November, 1967, on the basis of a broadened Commission mandate, it quickly became apparent that the Maghreb countries had decided to lose no further time. They asked for the rapid conclusion of agreements with immediate applicability, even if they were limited to those items that the EEC had already listed, and with the stated assumption that these limited arrangements would be only a first step toward a comprehensive association agreement. For this reason, the two agreements that emerged after a further ten months of discussion were limited to trade and did not contain provisions for financial aid, technical assistance, or free movement of labor.

The two agreements, though strictly commercial, are based on Article 238 of the Rome Treaty.[4] Consequently, even though they do not exhaust the full potential of the 1957 Declaration of Intention, they constitute an important step toward its full application. They are likely to have far-reaching effects on relationships between the contracting parties, on the economies of the two Maghreb countries involved, and to some degree on the economies of the Six.

Under the commercial arrangements, free-trade areas are established between the Community and Tunisia and between the Community and Morocco. All industrial products, except cork and iron and steel products, enter the Common Market duty free. For agricultural products, the concessions offered by the EEC vary. According to the Commission spokesman, the arrangements were designed to maintain the protection and preferences enjoyed by Community producers, while maintaining the existing balance between competing Mediterranean producers. The special advantages which exports of the two associated countries continue to enjoy in the French market also had to be taken into account.[5] For Morocco, the most important single preference is that on citrus fruit, for which the EEC's common external tariff is reduced by 80 percent, provided a minimum import price is observed. For Tunisia, the most important concession concerns crude olive oil. Other concessions cover fish, some processed foods, and some canned fruits and vegetables. In return, Morocco and Tunisia grant the EEC certain advantages as *quid pro quo*. Morocco is, of course, bound by the 1906 Act of Algeciras,[6] which is based on the principle that Morocco must refrain

---

[4] *Ibid.* Article 238, I of the *Rome Treaty* reads: "The Community may conclude with a third country, a union or an international organisation agreements creating an association embodying reciprocal rights and obligations, joint actions and special procedures."

[5] *Ibid.*, p. 3.

[6] "Morocco and Tunisia Sign with the Community," *European Community,*

from granting preferences. The kingdom therefore grants a 25-percent tariff reduction on imports irrespective of their origin. Thus, the treaty with Morocco gives to the EEC, as previously to France, no preferential privileges with respect to imports into Morocco, although more substantial concessions are made with respect to quantitative restrictions. Tunisia grants the Community a preference representing 70 percent of that accorded to France, and this preferential tariff is to be introduced over a thirty-six-month period to lessen the impact on Tunisian industry. In other words, imports into Tunisia are subject to a tariff which remains lower for French goods than for those of other EEC members.

The EEC is the chief market of both Tunisia and Morocco. In 1968, the Common Market accounted for 60 percent of Tunisia's exports and 69 percent of those of Morocco. It was the source of 60 percent of Tunisia's imports and of 48 percent of Morocco's. Since the bulk of Maghreb export earnings derive from agricultural products, the immediate interest of the association for them lies in this area. The preferences granted under the association to citrus fruit, which represents approximately one-third of Morocco's exports to the EEC, and olive oil, which accounts for a similar percentage of Tunisia's exports, will clearly provide a stimulus to production in these two sectors. But the preferences do not cover the entire range of agricultural exports of the two countries. The exclusion of products such as wine, tomatoes, and most canned fruit and vegetables, all of which appear prominently on Morocco's and Tunisia's export lists, has given rise to sharp criticism in certain quarters, particularly in Morocco.[7] This criticism is not well founded, however, since products not covered by the agreements still come under the Protocol annexed to the Treaty of Rome, under which France grants preferential arrangements to imports from Morocco and Tunisia.[8] The Protocol is

---

May, 1969, p. *17n:* "The Act, signed by the Great Powers, reaffirmed the independence and integrity of Morocco following the 'first Moroccan crisis' of 1905–1906 and in effect established the Open Door in that country."

[7] *Le Monde,* April 1, 1969, refers to a highly critical statement made by the spokesman of the progressists, Mr. Abderrahim Bouabib, former minister of the National Economy, in an interview with the review *Lamalif. L'Echo de la Bourse,* April 6–8, 1969, also refers to criticism by the Istiqual party.

[8] Protocol relating to "Goods Originating In and Coming From Certain Countries" and enjoying special treatment on importation into one of the member states, *Rome Treaty,* pp. 259–62. Continuation of the Protocol is referred to in exchanges of letters annexed to the association agreements.

merely suspended for those products to which a Community preference applies. The preferential arrangements for citrus fruit and olive oil have also encountered some criticism from Community circles. This was to some extent inevitable, since both southern France and southern Italy are fairly important producers of the two commodities. Italian anxiety was particularly pronounced throughout the negotiations.[9] Probably the only substantive measures that may compensate EEC farm interests for the increased competition lie in the area of structural reform of agriculture and the implementation of the much-heralded over-all policy for the entire Mediterranean area.

Morocco and Tunisia are relatively small exporters of manufactured goods. However, the new right of duty-free entry into the Community, and the absence of quantitative restrictions and fiscal barriers will probably provide a strong impetus to their future industrial development. Investment will be stimulated since both Community and non-Community firms, once established in Tunisia and Morocco, will have assured access to markets of almost 200 million consumers. This stimulus to the development of industry will be reinforced by the investment codes adopted by Morocco and Tunisia for the purpose of encouraging private investment; new investors are provided with various tax, customs, and other benefits, as well as guarantees for the repatriation of profits and capital. On the EEC side, advantages will be derived from the possibilities opened up for increased exports to two rapidly expanding markets, despite the existence of fairly tight currency controls.

Special Features of the Association Agreements

From a procedural and institutional standpoint, the two agreements contain a number of noteworthy innovations. The agreements are valid for five years from September 1, 1969, the date on which they came into effect. They provide for the opening, after three years, of new negotiations for more comprehensive terms of association. The Six have thus given assurances, but no binding commitment, that they will offer some noncommercial concessions after three years, as well as filling in certain gaps in the existing commer-

[9] *Parlement Européen, Documents de Séance 1969–1970*. Document 48, May 28, 1969 (Luxembourg), pp. 11–12, 17–18, 20, 23 (hereafter cited as *European Parliament Document 48*).

cial arrangements. It is clearly in the interest of Morocco and Tunisia to enlist EEC financial and technical assistance as quickly as possible, for both countries are heavily dependent on foreign aid and also shoulder large foreign debt burdens. In addition, they are both implementing ambitious development plans (Morocco, a five-year plan, 1968–72; Tunisia, a four-year plan, 1969–72) aimed at increasing gross investment and building up scarce foreign exchange reserves.[10] EEC assistance under broadened association arrangements would do much to further their economic expansion.

The association agreements contain two procedural innovations. The sole contracting party to the agreements on the Community side is the Council of Ministers. The EEC thus broke with a tradition followed in all previous association agreements (Convention with the African and Malagasy states, agreements with Greece, Turkey, Nigeria, and the three East African countries) in which the governments of the six member states participated alongside the Council of Ministers. The change would seem to indicate some inclination toward accepting a reduction in the separate roles of the national states in the affairs of the Community. As a corollary to this break with tradition, the two association agreements omitted the previous requirement for separate parliamentary ratification. The Rabat and Tunis agreements were the first association agreements to come into force without lengthy and difficult parliamentary ratification in the six member states.[11] The sole limitation on the authority of the Council was the requirement that it consult with the European Parliament in accordance with Article 238 of the Rome Treaty.

Two aspects of the institutional arrangements also constitute departures from the precedents established in previous association agreements. The only administrative body provided for under each agreement is the Council of Association; no joint agencies on the parliamentary level and no joint cooperation committees were created. This may be attributed largely to the absence of parliamentary

[10] *International Commerce,* January 19, 1970, p. 64; New York *Times,* January 30, 1970.

[11] The association agreement signed with Nigeria on July 16, 1966, expired before it could be ratified by all the contracting parties. The first Arusha Agreement signed with Kenya, Uganda, and Tanzania on July 26, 1968, expired on May 31, 1969, before it could be ratified. The second agreement was signed on September 24, 1969, and is currently in the process of ratification.

institutions in Morocco since King Hassan II dissolved the National Assembly in 1965 and declared a "state of exception." Each Association Council consists of all members of the Council and some members of the Commission of the European Communities, on one side, and representatives of the associated state, on the other. The Association Council has power to recommend any steps needed to ensure implementation of the agreement. A second institutional innovation derives from the provision for reciprocal consultation and information. In all previous association agreements, the items on which the two parties were expected to consult were individually specified. The absence of such specifications in the Tunis and Rabat agreements suggests that consultations may be held without restriction as to subject matter and whenever they are deemed necessary by either side. The possibilities for discussing a broad range of subjects are thus much wider.

Over the long range, the two association agreements cannot fail to have profound economic and political effects. They provide an important stimulus to the modernization and industrialization of the two associated countries, which must still be classified among the less-developed nations of the world. Their populations are for the most part agricultural, and, despite vigorous efforts, the expansion in gross national product has exceeded population growth (3.2 percent a year in Morocco; 2.8 percent in Tunisia) by a narrow margin; their annual per capita income only barely tops the $200 mark. A combination of national efforts, increased facilities afforded by the EEC and international aid may enable the two countries to overcome many of their problems. On the negative side, however, the inclusion of additional countries within the EEC preferential trade regime heightens discriminatory effects for the countries that remain outside. By the opposite token, the benefits derived from a preferential system by the countries within it are correspondingly reduced. It is for this reason that the EEC has frequently iterated its belief in the need for a more comprehensive Community approach to economic development problems in the entire Mediterranean area.

The political issues may be seen from two standpoints. It is possible to argue on the one side that the EEC is capitalizing on the strong powers of attraction exerted by its commercial success to extend its sphere of influence. It could then really turn the Mediterranean into its favored *mare nostrum*. In time, it has been speculated, the Maghreb, with its untapped natural resources, would become the Community's "new frontier" or its "California." [12] The attitude is somewhat different in EEC quarters. The countries of the Maghreb, in particular, and the Mediterranean, as a whole, it is claimed, have long maintained cultural ties with one or more countries of the Community. "The over-all grand design of the EEC," one committee of the European Parliament asserts, "will have to be that of a comprehensive policy aimed at consolidating peace in this region [the Mediterranean basin] and contributing to its development." [13] Whether it is the result of European self-interest, or genuine altruism, there can be little doubt that the development of modern, prosperous, and stable economies in Morocco and Tunisia can make a contribution to reducing political, economic, and social conflict in the Mediterranean area.

The Uncertain Relationship: Algeria and the EEC

The history of Algerian relationships with the EEC continues to be punctuated by even more problems than those of the other two Maghreb countries. From 1958, the Algerian Departments, as integral parts of France, complied with duty-lowering operations within the EEC under the Rome Treaty until the formation of the Algerian Republic in July, 1962. Shortly after independence, the Ben Bella government requested time to become established and the temporary continuation of Algeria's EEC trade privileges. It was not until February and May, 1964, therefore, that the first meetings were held with the EEC Commission in order to discuss future arrangements. Before any real progress could be made, however, the Algerian case fell victim to political disputes within the EEC similar to those that plagued the negotiations with Tunisia and Morocco.[14] In response to French opposition to the negotiation of a preferential trade arrangement with Israel, the Netherlands persistently blocked any negotiation with Algeria. Finally, after two unsuccessful approaches by the Algerian government in 1968, the deadlock was broken at the Octo-

[12] Geoffrey Parker, *An Economic Geography of the Common Market* (New York, 1969), p. 156.

[13] *European Parliament Document 48*, p. 11 (my translation from the French).

[14] *Le Monde Economique et Financier*, November 22–23, 1964.

ber 17, 1969, meeting of the EEC Council of Ministers. When the French recalled the need for rapid consideration of the Algerian situation, no reservation of principle was raised by any other delegation. Apparently, the Dutch responded to the French go-ahead on negotiations with Israel (in return for negotiations with Egypt and Lebanon) and are now prepared to allow the EEC to pursue the negotiations with Algeria.[15]

Five years of delays and uncertainties have thus resulted in the EEC's failure to adopt any coherent or unified trading policy toward Algeria. Although the EEC Commission submitted to the Council of Ministers, in May, 1968, a comprehensive proposal for harmonizing the status of Algerian imports into the EEC member countries, only two decisions on the subject had been taken by the Community up to mid-1970. On July 30, 1968, the Council approved the adoption of tariff quotas at reduced rates for imports of Algerian wines into Germany and the Benelux countries;[16] and a Commission decision on August 28, 1969, authorized Germany to defer duty increases on certain Algerian wines.[17] For all other products the Six have maintained the *status quo* of July 1, 1968. Italy thus considers Algeria a nonmember country for commercial purposes; France continues to apply a preferential tariff; and the other four members apply systems that fall somewhere in-between and vary from product to product. Obviously, this rather chaotic situation can lead to serious trade distortions, especially since France takes more than three-quarters of Algerian exports to the Community as a whole. In addition, both the wine and petroleum sectors, the two most important foreign-exchange earners, raise special problems.[18] The EEC, which has been working on common policies for the two sectors for a long time but has final-

[15] Bulletin Quotidien, *EUROPE,* Agence Internationale d'Information pour la Presse, October 20, 1969 (hereafter cited as *EUROPE Bulletin*).

[16] European Coal and Steel Community, European Economic Community, European Atomic Energy Community, *Commission, Second General Report* on the Activities of the Communities, 1968 (Brussels-Luxembourg, 1969), Section 492, p. 355.

[17] CECA, CEE, CEEA, *Commission, Troisième Rapport Général* sur l'Activité des Communautés, 1969 (Brussels-Luxembourg, 1970), Section 390, p. 371.

[18] *Commerce Extérieur, Tableaux Analytiques, CST, Importations 1968* (Brussels-Luxembourg, 1969). In 1968, out of total Algerian exports to the EEC valued at $771 million, wine accounted for $63 million and crude oil $612 million.

ized nothing, will have to see that arrangements for imports of Algerian wine and petroleum fit in well with the proposed common policies.

If the Algerians have their way, the current abnormal trade situation will not persist much longer. In an announcement in Brussels on March 17, 1970, the Minister of Trade expressed Algeria's hope for the rapid conclusion of an economic cooperation agreement with the EEC,[19] to include economic and financial cooperation and technical and social aid as well as the expected trade preferences. The agreement sought by Algeria is thus very similar to those originally requested by Morocco and Tunisia, but it goes considerably further than the agreements actually obtained by the other two Maghreb countries. The Algerian minister claimed that a broader agreement is necessary since Algeria's total trade is much larger than that of either Morocco or Tunisia and three-quarters of it is with the EEC.[20] In addition, there are about 650,000 Algerian workers in Common Market countries at present, mainly in France. The Algerian announcement coincided with a marked improvement in member country attitudes toward Algeria.[21]

On April 16, 1970, the EEC Commission approved a communication to the Council on the opening of negotiations with Algeria.[22] The agreement outlined by the Commission in the communication does not make provision for technical and economic cooperation or free movement of workers. The Commission merely asked that studies be conducted on these subjects, for possible inclusion in a subsequent stage of the association. In effect, the Commission has suggested extending to Algeria the preferential system granted to Morocco and Tunisia, with special provisions for Algeria's wine exports. Between 80 percent and 90 percent of Algeria's dutiable exports to the Community would be covered under the proposed agreement. In certain respects Algeria would be in a less advantageous position than it is now. For example, its exports of refined petroleum products would be subject to a tariff quota, and its preferences for fruit and vegetables would be lower than at present. On the Algerian side, higher preferences on EEC imports are proposed, to match

[19] *EUROPE Bulletin,* March 17, 1970.

[20] *Department of State Background Notes,* Democratic and Popular Republic of Algeria (Washington, D.C., December, 1968). More than 70 percent of Algeria's exports go to France alone.

[21] *EUROPE Bulletin,* March 17, 1970.   [22] *Ibid.,* April 16, 1970.

EEC concessions on Algerian wine. The EEC Commission claims that the proposed agreement with Algeria would help increase EEC exports of industrial equipment and of food products, particularly of wheat and dairy products.[23]

Even without a special agreement with the EEC, the Algerian economy appears to be doing well according to news reports.[24] In 1969 Algeria earned $250 million in foreign exchange through its petroleum exports, and its production of crude oil and natural gas has been going up steadily. On the agricultural side, a seven-year trade agreement with the Soviet Union has brought about a considerable improvement in its wine exports. In 1969 Algeria was able to meet its commitment of 132 million gallons to the Soviet Union and increase its exports to France to 145 million gallons. According to recent estimates, trade with the Soviet Union will account for 10 percent of Algeria's foreign trade by the mid-1970s. Although France continues to be Algeria's main trading partner, taking more than 70 percent of its exports and providing 80 percent of its imports, its share is gradually being decreased as the result of a deliberate policy choice by the Algerians. Algeria's relations with the United States have also improved, despite its breaking off of diplomatic relations upon the outbreak of the Arab-Israeli war, in June, 1967. The El Paso Natural Gas Company has recently concluded a large long-term contract with the state oil concern for the sale abroad of liquified Saharan natural gas. Apparently, there is a general mood of optimism and self-confidence among Algerian leaders. This sense of progress, coupled with the Boumedienne regime's determination to avoid subjection to any outside influence, to improve relations with its Maghreb neighbors,[25] and to leave open as many development possibilities as it can, is likely to produce some hard bargaining when negotiations with the EEC eventually begin.

The years 1969 and 1970 offered some indications of improved relations among the Maghreb countries and even of the establishment of a Maghreb economic union. In September, 1969, a new protocol to Morocco's trade treaty with Algeria provided for doubling trade between the two countries in 1970.[26] In January, 1970, after several years of strained relations between Algeria and Tunisia, a treaty of

[23] *Ibid.,* April 22, 1970.   [24] New York *Times,* January 30, 1970.

[25] Algeria extended its trade ties with Morocco in September, 1969, and concluded a treaty of friendship with Tunisia in January, 1970.

[26] *International Commerce,* March 2, 1970, p. 31.

friendship was concluded between them.[27] Finally, in pursuit of the
various efforts since 1963 to integrate the economies of the three
Maghreb countries and also to extend the process of integration to
include Libya, a conference of economic ministers had been scheduled for the second week of March, 1970.[28] The four countries already participate in a Permanent Maghreb Consultative Committee,
which has submitted a proposal for an initial 50-percent cut in tariffs
on industrial goods, reductions in quantitative trade restrictions, and
the harmonization of industrial and monetary policies. The association agreements provide that an exception will be made to the "most
favored nation treatment" of EEC imports in case Tunisia or Morocco enters into agreements leading to the establishment of a free-
trade area or a customs union. The conference, which was to have
discussed a five-year experimental agreement, was, however, indefinitely postponed, largely as a result of the refusal of the new Libyan
government to participate. Apparently, the Algerians objected to
holding the conference without the Libyans, who have adopted an increasingly pro-Cairo stance since the military coup that unseated
King Idris in September, 1969. The Boumedienne government is
clearly anxious to avoid any action or gesture that might strengthen
or confirm the pro-Cairo orientation of the new Libyan regime. Unlike the Maghreb countries, Libya, which is the subject of an almost
identical Declaration of Intention annexed to the Rome Treaty, has
never availed itself of the opportunity or requested any form of special arrangement with the EEC. In view of its changed political situation, it seems unlikely that Libya will make any effort to promote
North African unity in the near future.

The Mediterranean Policy of the EEC

The signing of the Rabat and Tunis agreements brought to a current total of four the association arrangements concluded by the EEC
with Mediterranean countries. In 1961 it signed an agreement with
Greece providing for the establishment of an association, designed
ultimately to lead to full membership under Article 237 of the Rome
Treaty.[29] In 1963 Turkey followed suit. Anxious not to be left out,

[27] New York *Times,* January 30, 1970.   [28] *Ibid.,* March 11, 1970.
[29] *Rome Treaty,* pp. 162–63. According to Article 237, "any European State
may apply to become a member of the Community."

Israel, Yugoslavia, and Spain intensified their efforts to establish closer economic ties with the Common Market. The Six, unwilling to be accused of discrimination, and not wishing to upset economic and trade relationships in the Mediterranean area, in early 1970 concluded negotiations with each of the three countries. A three-year trade agreement with Yugoslavia was signed in Brussels on March 19 and came into effect on May 1, 1970, and the agreements with Spain and Israel will be signed as soon as the formalities have been concluded. France, concerned that an agreement with Israel might jeopardize the EEC's neutrality in the Middle East, has demanded that similar privileges be accorded Israel's Arab neighbors. Both Egypt and Lebanon, therefore, embarked in 1970 on talks with the EEC on the possibility for some form of preferential trade arrangements. Malta and Cyprus have also requested a special relationship with the Community. The first round of talks was held with Malta in early April, 1970, and it is believed that the negotiations can be concluded in June. Following in Malta's footsteps, Cyprus requested, in March, 1970, that its 1962 application for a special arrangement be revived.

A complex web of relationships is thus being woven between the EEC and most of the countries of the Mediterranean area. Although EEC circles claim that there has been no coherent pattern in this development and urge the need for a comprehensive Mediterranean policy, there is no denying the economic and political "billiard-ball" effect that has occurred since mid-1969. The intensification of EEC activity in the Mediterranean, whether deliberate or fortuitous, creates delicate problems of balance.

The prospective agreement with Israel raises the question of equitable concessions to the Arab countries and the need to avoid adding fuel to the fire of Arab-Israeli hostility. The arrangements concluded with Yugoslavia bring up the issue of trade with other Communist countries, which have until quite recently refused to recognize the existence of the Common Market. By adopting a radically different attitude, Yugoslavia may give rise to new developments in the policies of the other state-trading countries; liberal arrangements with the EEC may also permit Yugoslavia to consolidate its independent line toward the Soviet Union.

The question of EEC relations with nondemocratic Western governments has come up in connection with the proposed agreement with Spain and with the maintenance of the association with Greece. For many years some political and most labor circles within the EEC have opposed any agreement with Spain. This opposition was only circumvented by writing careful checks into the agreement, for example, by providing for two stages of association with no automatic transition to the second stage. Thus the EEC can always veto the broadening of the association if it wishes. In the case of Greece, pressure has been building up steadily in favor of terminating the association, so long as Greece is ruled by the military junta. The Council of Ministers has issued a strong statement of disapproval of the Greek regime, the Commission has announced its intention of reconsidering the agreement, and the functioning of the joint political institutions has been suspended; nevertheless, in mid-1970 the trade arrangements continued to operate. Finally, the applications of Malta and Cyprus to a certain extent involve the question of Britain's future membership in the EEC. Both island states are members of the Commonwealth and the sterling area; both are oriented toward Great Britain. Should Britain join the EEC, their relationships with both Britain and the EEC will be affected. Malta and Cyprus occupy positions of some strategic importance in the Mediterranean, and in Cyprus an extremely delicate balance is maintained between the interests of Greece, with which the EEC's relations are in a state of near-paralysis, and Turkey, which is forging ahead toward its goal of full membership in the Common Market. The complexity of all these interlocking, yet frequently antagonistic, relationships will require careful handling by EEC authorities if they are not to add to the antagonisms.

The Mediterranean Agreements and GATT

The association agreements with Morocco and Tunisia, and the preferential arrangements negotiated by the EEC with other Mediterranean countries, have caused a rising crescendo of protest by international trade circles, particularly by the United States, in GATT. The first sign of hostility came in November, 1969, when the U.S. delegation to GATT requested the withdrawal of a special 40-percent preference on citrus fruit which the EEC had granted Spain and Israel in September, 1969. The preference was in fact condemned by the contracting parties and later abandoned by the EEC, but the intensified negotiations of the EEC with Israel, Spain, Yugoslavia, Egypt, and Lebanon, in December, 1969 and January, 1970, prompted a second American move in GATT in February, 1970. This time, a clear challenge was issued to what has been described as "the Common Market's free-wheeling propensity to develop special trade relations in Africa and Europe, to the potential disadvantage of the U.S. and other 'outsiders'." [30] The United States has claimed that it is specifically concerned about the loss of its citrus-fruit sales to the Common Market; this claim can, in all probability, be discounted since the United States supplied less than 1 percent of EEC imports of oranges in 1968. On a broader level of policy, however, it is clear that the United States is interested in forestalling what it regards as a fragmentation of international trade into special arrangements which are neither *bona fide* trade areas nor customs unions. It has therefore challenged these special arrangements as violations of Article XXIV of the General Agreement on Tariffs and Trade, which authorizes preferences only in the event of the immediate or projected creation of a customs union or a free-trade area which includes a precise schedule for the elimination of barriers on most items traded. By mid-February, 1970, it had become clear that the United States had decided to go beyond *pro forma* protests. In a widely noted speech at Bonn on February 12, 1970, J. Robert Schaetzel, U.S. Ambassador to the European Communities, asserted that the EEC was running the risk of fatally undermining the GATT system and, more ominously, went on to issue a warning that American troop commitments to NATO were bound to be affected by the growing system of EEC discrimination against U.S. exports.[31] This outspoken attack was bound to carry special weight since Schaetzel has long been known as a vigorous advocate of European integration.

The Bonn speech was not an isolated incident. A week later, Henry Brodie, the U.S. delegate to GATT, renewed the attack on the EEC's Maghreb and Mediterranean policy, denouncing the danger posed by what he called the "growing proliferation of special trade arrangements of a discriminatory character." [32] At the end of February, 1970, the EEC responded in a Commission position paper, a news conference given by Commission President Jean Rey, and a statement to the GATT Contracting Parties by the Commission member responsible for trade questions, Jean-François Deniau. The EEC claimed that a special situation, more the result of circum-

[30] *Journal of Commerce,* January 8, 1970.
[31] New York *Times,* February 14, 1970.   [32] *Ibid.,* February 19, 1970.

stances than of explicit policy, exists in the Mediterranean. The Moroccan and Tunisian agreements, provided for in the Rome Treaty, merely replace on a multilateral level the special relations that had long existed between these countries and France. So long as some Mediterranean countries are linked to the EEC, they went on, comparable arrangements with other countries in the area cannot be refused; it would be discriminatory toward them to deny them equivalent preferences. In addition, both Rey and Deniau stressed the political necessity of accepting applications from all Mediterranean countries in order to avoid increasing the factors making for instability in the area. It was also stressed that the EEC had no intention of extending its preferential policy beyond the countries of the Mediterranean seaboard.[33]

Although American criticism continued undiminished into March, 1970,[34] further attempts were made to assuage them. The German and Dutch representatives to the Council of Ministers stressed the need to reply adequately to criticism of EEC policy by strictly defining and respecting the geographical limits and contents of its preferential arrangements. German Foreign Minister Walter Scheel also suggested setting up a joint EEC-U.S. committee to study the problems affecting their mutual relations.[35] Although the Scheel suggestion met with a favorable reception in some U.S. governmental circles,[36] the United States adopted a hard-line attitude at a meeting of the GATT Council in late April, 1970, and denounced the Maghreb agreements as violating GATT rules. In addition, a group of important trading countries, led by Canada, and including Japan, Australia, Chile, and Argentina, suggested giving the GATT Council the right to supervise the agreements and allowing the other contracting parties to open negotiations with the Community, Morocco and Tunisia if they should conclude that their commercial interests were

[33] *EUROPE Bulletin,* February 27, 1970; Commission of the European Communities, Spokesman's Group, *Information Memo* P-8 (Brussels, February, 1970).

[34] According to the New York *Times,* March 10, 1970, Assistant Secretary of Commerce Kenneth N. Davis, Jr., stated that the United States viewed with "grave concern" the trade agreements recently concluded by the Common Market.

[35] *EUROPE Bulletin,* March 10, 1970.

[36] *Ibid.,* April 3, 1970. Special Representative Carl Gilbert, speaking before the Anglo-American Chamber of Commerce in New York, came out in favor of the Scheel suggestion.

being hurt. As a result of the dispute, the Council was unable to reach any decision on the compatibility of the Rabat and Tunis agreements with GATT and agreed only to take up this subject again in July, 1970.[37]

This war of words, which may prelude a trade war, must be viewed in the context of the continued large imbalance of U.S. foreign payments, the increasing congressional restiveness over U.S. military expenditures in Europe, and U.S. objections that the European are not doing enough for their own defense. It may be a symptom of a shift in U.S. policy away from State Department circles, which, for political reasons, have traditionally advocated a benevolently "hands off" policy toward the Common Market, to a more militant defense of commercial interests against Europe's growing economic strength. This new uncertainty in U.S.-EEC relations raises several fundamental questions of policy. Is it, for example, in the long-range U.S. interest to see the Mediterranean role of the EEC strengthened, even at the cost of accepting some measure of immediate discrimination against U.S. imports? Or will the EEC stimulus to economic development in the Mediterranean area eventually offset these temporary U.S. losses by providing larger markets for U.S. industrial exports and greater opportunities for investment? Or will the recent growth of discriminatory preferences be offset in part by the adoption by the industrialized countries of generalized preferences for manufactured goods of all less-developed countries?

Thus, the association of the Mediterranean countries with EEC must be viewed in the light of the broader problems of maintaining an open system of world trade, and, at the same time, overcoming the otherwise ever-widening gap between the developed and the less-developed nations of the world.

[37] *EUROPE Bulletin,* April 29, 1970.

Italy and NATO: The Policy of the Italian Communist Party

KEITH J. SOURS

The Warsaw Pact countries' invasion of Czechoslovakia had drastic domestic consequences for the Italian Communist Party (PCI); both for the character of the reforms which were thereby crushed and for the Brezhnev doctrine which the Soviet Union promulgated to justify its destruction of Czechoslovakia's independence. These factors impinge directly upon the political strategy of the Party and have profound implications for its attitude toward the Atlantic Alliance.

The domestic goal of the PCI is to govern Italy. Having accepted the power realities of the Italian political scene, the Party has opted for the "democratic" road to power. Its strategy has been simultaneously to increase its share of the vote and to work toward building a coalition of the Left in order to keep from being politically isolated in a posture of permanent opposition. This potential unity of the Left must be sought in a coincidence of interests on particular domestic issues. One of the principal issues upon which the Communists have been able to capitalize has been Italy's membership in the North Atlantic Treaty Organization.

The Italian Communists have been able to profit from their traditional anti-NATO stance because much of the Left in Italy is basically neutralist, especially in military matters, and is in some way uncomfortable with Italian membership in the Atlantic Alliance. Even among some Christian Democrats, the Treaty has simply been accepted as a fact of life, on the grounds that Italy has no alternative to membership. Thus, a major part of the PCI's strategy has been to present an alternative which would appeal to broader segments of the Italian Left. In every case, if the PCI comes to share in responsibility for governing Italy, it would be obliged to formulate a policy toward NATO.

A great deal of the difficulty the Communists have encountered with this strategy is that anti-NATO or neutralist sentiment has often been accompanied by equally strong anti-Soviet feelings. As with all nonruling communist parties, the PCI has had to operate both as a domestic political party and as a member of the international communist movement. Unlike the French Communist Party, the Italian party has been more successful in combining these two roles by placing emphasis more on its domestic role than on its international position. This is precisely the reason why the PCI requires "unity in diversity" within the international movement so that it will be left alone to pursue its own domestic goals free from interference from abroad.

Yet maintaining these two roles has not been at all easy. The Italian Communist leaders have striven to keep them as separate and distinct as possible in order to convince their potential domestic allies that they are in fact "free agents." Difficulty appears at any time that one role impinges upon the other, as illustrated in the PCI reaction to the Soviet invasion of Hungary in 1956. The most recent example of this clash of roles has been the PCI response to the Czechoslovakian events of 1968.

The Dubček Program and the Italian Road to Socialism

When the Czechoslovakian government began the series of reforms which set off an intense debate within the "Communist Commonwealth," the Italian Communists immediately declared themselves on the side of the Dubček Action Plan. The support they offered was at first cautious. The Italians had generally been reluctant to tie themselves to any development within the movement, since the failure of the development would endanger their own position. They have, in fact, developed their own idea of "unity in diversity" which would allow for different "roads to socialism."

Simultaneous with the unveiling of the reform plans in Prague, the PCI was opening its campaign for the nation-wide elections to be held in May, 1968. It quickly became apparent that one of the issues of the campaign was going to be the Action Plan. The Socialists were looking for an issue with which to stave off the strong offensive by the Communists. They had, for the previous four years, participated in the Center-Left government and had reunited with the Social

Democrats in 1966. Unable, as they were, to campaign on the doubtful "successes" of the Center-Left experiment, they could best rally
their supporters by evoking the fear of Communism. They began to
attack the PCI for not fully supporting the Action Plan while describing it as a repudiation of Communism, but not of socialism.

Luigi Longo began the campaign with a statement that the PCI
recognized the importance of these attempts to "create conditions of
a full development of socialist democracy, capable of liberating and
setting in motion all the forces of society." [1] But as the campaign
proceeded, the Party felt compelled by the Socialist attack to make
stronger and stronger statements. It began to place the importance of
the reforms within the ideological framework of "different roads to
socialism." It reproduced both the interview in *Nuovi Argomenti*
with Togliatti in 1956 (before the Hungarian invasion) in which he
first used the word *polycentrism* to describe the post-Stalin character
of the international movement; and Togliatti's Yalta Memorial of
1964 which essentially criticizes the Soviet Union's conduct of the
movement. This led them to tie their entire electoral campaign and
the success of their idea of "unity in diversity" to the Czechoslovak
reforms. By April they were saying that

> The events in Czechoslovakia help us to lend more force of persuasion to
> our argument in favor of the Italian road to socialism which we intend to
> pursue in full liberty and autonomy, together with all forces of the laic
> and Catholic left.[2]

Thus the campaign slogan of "è possible cambiare" assumed broader
dimensions.

Fortunately for the PCI, the elections took place before any overt
move was made against the reforms which they had come to support
so enthusiastically. They were, thus, able to play the two roles successfully without endangering either. Their electoral successes may
have actually convinced them of the correctness of their position; in
any case, they postponed any necessity for opting immediately for
one or the other of the two roles. Nevertheless, their conduct during
the election campaign provided increasing indications that the Italian
Communists, if forced to choose, were inclined to regard their national role as more important than their international role.

The post-election period was characterized by continued support
for the Czechoslovak reforms, but caution in open discussions. The

[1] *Unità*, March 29, 1968, p. 1.   [2] *Rinascita*, April 12, 1968, p. 4.

press retreated to the policy of publishing facts and reprinting articles from the European Communist press. The continuing debate between Prague and Moscow over such critical questions as the danger of counterrevolution and the ability of the CCP to control the situation was handled with a great deal of uneasiness. The PCI tended, for example, to reprint articles from *Rudé Pravo* and *Pravda,* which referred to the Warsaw Pact letter to Prague criticizing the reforms and to the answer by the CCP, rather than reprinting the documents themselves.[3] The PCI's uneasiness was also shown by the considerable relief with which they greeted the Bratislava agreements of August 3. The Politburo expressed "profound satisfaction" which could easily be interpreted as profound relief.[4] They were aware that they were out on a limb and needed to assure themselves of the soundness of that limb.

Additional evidence that the Italian Communists did not believe that military intervention in Czechoslovakia was likely, at least in the short run, is found not only in the considerable warmth with which they greeted the Bratislava agreements but in the absence of many PCI leaders from Rome in August. Further, Longo was on vacation in the Soviet Union when the invasion took place (he heard about it only through a phone call from Rome). The PCI Politburo, meeting without Longo and many others, promptly expressed its "grave dissent" in a communique.[5] This was accompanied once again by the Togliatti Memorial of 1964. The noncommunist press swung into attack immediately for the ambiguity and softness of the PCI stand.

On August 23, the Direction met under the chairmanship of Longo and issued a sharp rejection of the attacks, accusing them of fake sympathy for Czechoslovakia and speculation for their own purposes. But once again the Party was forced to respond to such attacks from their potential allies of the Left. They reaffirmed their dissent and "reproof" of the Soviet military intervention "because in no case can a violation of the independence of a State be permitted." [6] In this, and in other documents, the Italian Communists denied that the leading role of the CCP was ever in danger.

The August 23 meeting laid the preliminary groundwork for the PCI rejection of the so-called "right of intervention." The important things to note are the character of the Italian dissent over the specific

[3] See *ibid.,* July 19, 1968, pp. 15–17, and July 26, 1968, pp. 29–30.

[4] *Ibid.,* April 12, 1968, p. 1. [5] Communiqué, *Rinascita,* August 23, 1968.

[6] Luigi Longo, *Sui Fatti Cecoslovacchi* (Rome, 1968), pp. 120–24.

events in Czechoslovakia and the wording of their objections to the
"Brezhnev Doctrine." On the first point, the PCI refused to condemn
the invasion by repudiating the Soviet political system; it thus rejected the demand of the noncommunist Left, which wanted a condemnation on the grounds that the Russian system was "undemocratic." The PCI preferred to attribute the military intervention to
the "logic" of the two military blocs, rather than to the logic of an
undemocratic system.

This interpretation was a result of the PCI's own internal logic.
The noncommunist elements were either trying to prod the PCI into
repudiating the "totalitarian" model of the Soviet Union, thus forcing
it to break off its special ties to Moscow or else forcing it to identify
itself with the Soviet leadership to such a degree so as to make it an
unacceptable partner for a Left coalition within Italian politics. The
PCI, at the same time, was trying to hold onto an anti-NATO position while resisting these pressures from its potential political allies
and trying to contain dissensions within the Party itself.

The adversaries of the PCI were prompt to leap into the breach
that had been opened by the vision of the Soviet tanks in the streets
of Prague. *Corriere della Sera* stated on August 22 that

Communism of the Soviet type, to which the Italian Communists have
been the most faithful and zealous servants for many years, the crimes of
Stalin included, is irreconcilable with any form of liberty and must in
fact violently oppose any contact with liberty.

Inevitably, the *Corriere* assumed that its readers would overlook the
fact that the PCI had ceased being Moscow's "faithful servant" and
that it had long since rejected the Soviet experience as a model for
Italy.

Nevertheless, the editorial correctly analyzed the difficulties within
the PCI over the stand it had taken on the invasion. While the PCI
has nearly always rejected any model as being antithetical to the idea
of "national roads to socialism," in its propaganda among the rank-
and-file it has consistently referred to the Soviet Union as the "first
nation of Socialism." After decades of this and similar propaganda,
the Party militants could not easily accept any condemnation of Russian actions or much less, a repudiation of the Soviet system. It is
partially for this reason that the Italian Communists have resorted to
historical documents left by Togliatti in order to legitimize their
stand on Czechoslovakia. The continual reaffirmation and references

to the past was an effort to minimize the confusion and bewilderment of the rank-and-file and to head off criticism from militants.

This was not the only reason for establishing the historical legitimacy of the Party's policy as strongly as possible. It was essential to reassure its potential allies and its membership, many of whom were dismayed and alarmed at Moscow's resort to military intervention in order to force a drastic change of policy upon a "fraternal" socialist government. The PCI had cited the program of the Dubcek government on many occasions as an example, though not a model, of its own domestic strategy and as proof of the feasibility of "unity in diversity" within the international movement. In a single stroke, both assertions had been thrown into jeopardy. What were they to say to the leftist elements of the Catholic and Socialist movements with which they sought to ally themselves? How were they to convince them that the Soviet Union would not also intervene in an Italy where the Communists, alone or in coalition, were following a line which displeased Moscow? These questions over the meaning of the Brezhnev Doctrine grew in force as reports of Yugoslavia and Rumanian mobilization came in. If Socialist Yugoslavia was genuinely afraid, then what of a "Socialist" Italy? In other words, would letting the Communists into government open Italy to the "right of intervention"?

If the PCI were to continue to oppose Italy's adherence to the North Atlantic Treaty, it would have to convince its potential allies on the Left that the Brezhnev Doctrine did not apply in all cases. It was not enough simply to oppose it since the Italians had no control over how the Soviet leadership might interpret or apply its own doctrines. It had also to convince its friends that there was no real danger to Rumania or, especially, to Yugoslavia.

The PCI leadership had first to convince itself and its followers of the theoretical soundness of its rejection of the right of intervention. In his speech to the Central Committee on August 27, Luigi Longo stated twice that the frontiers of Socialism "do not coincide with the frontiers of the Socialist states, but are wider than that and include all the forces which in the whole world are fighting against capitalism and imperialism." [7] This interpretation means that the tasks of Communist parties cannot be confined to the defense of frontiers and cannot mean that the future of the communist world revolution is to be left in the hands of the Socialist states alone. The domestic situation

[7] *Ibid.*, pp. 33, 37.

of any one country is therefore a matter of international concern and cannot be left to individual judgment or to action of any one of the Socialist states in particular or to the collective judgment or action of the Communists of all Socialist states. It is simply a matter of concern for the Communists of every country.

In an interview granted to *Astrolabio* on September 8 (and reprinted in *Unità*), Longo rejected, in all cases, resorting to military intervention as inappropriate to the character of the struggle. He said that the threat of imperialism to Socialist states is no longer a military threat but derives from the policy of infiltration and concluded:

The ideological and philosophical confrontation which exists should be conducted with ideological and philosophical weapons, with ideological and philosophical initiatives and counteroffensives; not with administrative measures which lead to the extreme, to military intervention such as that conducted in Czechoslovakia.

If this interpretation of the right of intervention were accepted by the Soviet leadership, the Italian Communists would be free to pursue their own line, free of fear of military intervention. They would also be free to continue their attacks against NATO, having turned the Brezhnev Doctrine into an isolated example of the "logic" of military blocs.

Yet this interpretation could not be accepted by the PCI's potential allies as long as Yugoslavia and Rumania seemed to be in danger. It was difficult for the PCI even to minimize Italian fears of a general Soviet threat to Western Europe; this mood, if it continued to spread, could even result in an increased Italian commitment to NATO.

The second element of the PCI strategy, therefore, was to play down the post-Prague mobilizations in Yugoslavia and Rumania. In the days following the invasion, the Communist press watched events in Belgrade and Bucharest with nervous interest. While playing down frantic preparations for military resistance within both countries, the PCI journals reprinted Yugloslav and Rumanian articles which accused the West of exploiting the Czechoslovak events for its own purposes, just as the Italian Communists accused the conservative press in Italy. On September 5, for example, *Unità* reported on an article from *Politika* (Belgrade):

According to the Yugoslav correspondent, the United States is trying to profit politically from the feeling of crisis in Western Europe for its own internal and NATO designs without doing anything which could endanger American-Soviet relations, especially the forthcoming talks on nuclear arms limitations.

A further element of the strategy was to undercut as strongly as possible the idea that Yugoslavia might be turning to the West for its help in case of a Soviet invasion. For example, *Unità* reported on September 6 that

After having underlined that the military intervention on Czechoslovak soil has contributed to making international tension more acute, Tito confirmed that "the nonaligned nations must harmonize even more their positions and must ultimately take action to prevent a return to the cold war and to the politics of military blocs."

Thus, the PCI endeavored to persuade both followers and potential allies that reports of military preparations in Yugoslavia were merely being played up by the Americans for their own reasons and that in reality Tito had no intention of turning to NATO for help; if the PCI could make this view stick, it would be in a better position to work toward unity of the Left with rejection of NATO as one of its main pillars. This maneuver was, however, undercut by the fact that the PCI was thus forced to echo much more strongly the traditional Socialist argument for dismantling of *both* military blocs. The PCI could hardly resist this argument, in view of its shift to describe the Soviet military intervention as a consequence of the logic of the system of military blocs.

The PCI fears of a strengthened Italian commitment seemed about to be confirmed. On September 7, *Unità* headlined a report that the Italian Foreign Affairs Ministry had proposed an extension of the Atlantic Pact by five or ten years and that the U.S. Department of State had officially declared it was "studying" the Italian proposal. The same issue published denials of the reports by the Ministry and the State Department. Whether or not such a proposal had been made is less important than the evidence of PCI fears of a strengthening of NATO and a reinforced Italian commitment to it.

Provoked by these reports and by a statement of the Republican Party chief, Ugo La Malfa, that the West should now accept the division of the world into two opposing blocs, each lead by a "leader state," an editorial in *Unità* retorted by reaffirming PCI rejection of NATO.

142   *Keith J. Sours*

Nor can we be brought to say that the only way to guarantee the "equilibrium" of Europe would be to maintain the blocs and to favor understanding between the two powers, the United States and the Soviet Union, which stand at their head. This "argument" was false yesterday and is false today, and this must be recognized by all who wish to escape from a "logic" which is not only sterile but terribly dangerous.[8]

Thus the PCI made clear once again its unchanging opposition to Italy's membership in NATO and its support for a European security conference which would be the first step toward dismantling both blocs.

At home, the PCI continued its bid for allies on the basis of a shared anti-NATO stance. They reported statements made by noncommunist leftists which supported its own attitude in an effort to convince potential allies, and perhaps themselves, that the invasion had not destroyed its credibility. *Unità* reported, for example, a statement by the leader of the Left faction in the Socialist Party, De Martino, that

it is beyond present reality to ask for the withdrawal of Italy from the Atlantic Pact, it would be an error to ask for a reenforcement of NATO and to renounce possible agreements such as the nuclear nonproliferation treaty.[9]

In the same issue of *Unità,* the leaders of two principal and rival factions within the PCI, Pietro Ingrao and Giorgio Amendola, both reaffirmed the Party's efforts to build bridges outside the Party. Amendola concentrated his remarks on a political party level:

Here is the basis for a new unity of the laic and Catholic left: a policy of peace and independence, of democratic planning founded on reforms, increased participation of workers in the administration of democratic institutions. It is necessary, therefore, that the legitimate emotion provoked by the Czechoslovak events should not distract us from our duty: the realization of unity against the imperialism which is present in Italy and against the class enemy: capitalism.

Ingrao, concentrating on his thesis of unity of the Left based on unity among the trade unions, said:

Thus, we are not limited to "pronouncing" our stand on Czechoslovakia: we draw from the facts a position of struggle over the issues which are and will be expounded in the next weeks by the workers, students and peasants in our country. The capacity of the forces of the Italian left to

[8] *Unità,* September 7, 1968, p. 1.   [9] *Ibid.,* September 9, 1968, p. 2.

draw the necessary lesson from the dramatic developments which we have observed, will be seen from the conclusions that they know how to draw for their immediate and concrete political efforts.

Though the differences in tactics still remained, the effort to build a unity of the Left had not been abandoned in the face of difficulties the Party faced after Czechoslovakia. In fact, referring to the La Malfa statement on NATO and the Warsaw Pact, Ingrao said; "We cannot accept this line because it would mean accepting the *status quo* in the capitalistic West and we, instead, struggle for the democratic transformation of Italy."

The fact that the PCI continued its efforts to expand its influence is not surprising. It would have been illogical to abandon at this point all the years they had devoted to building a "unity of the Left." To do this it had to urge a two-front battle: defense of its own stand on Czechoslovakia against attacks by militants inside the party and by Warsaw Pact governments; continued denunciation of the Atlantic Alliance and an intensified struggle against both military blocs.

The PCI continued to observe events in Yugoslavia with great interest. Its precarious position both within the international movement and in the political struggle at home would have been completely destroyed by any overt move by Moscow and the Warsaw Pact against Yugoslavia. Not only is Yugoslavia not a member of the Warsaw Pact; it is also a "neutralist" state, a position which the PCI would like Italy to adopt. A move against Tito would negate even more the Italian doctrine of "national" roads to socialism. It was with great relief that *Unità* headlined on September 19 Belgrade's decision to demobilize reserves, as a sign that the threat of intervention had passed. The Party once again reported an article in *Politika* condemning NATO maneuvers in West Germany as "the most senseless maneuvers carried on by West Germany since the end of the war." In addition, it quoted *Vjesnik* (Zagreb) which accused NATO of attempting to profit from the situation to accelerate plans for the military partition of the Mediterranean and, above all, for its objective of maintaining a NATO fleet permanently in that area.

On October 16, 1968, Washington announced that it was sending Under Secretary of State Nicholas Katzenbach to Belgrade for talks with Tito. The reported goal of this journey was to express American "concern" over implied Soviet threats to Yugoslavia.[10] After speculations as to what Tito would ask from the U.S. or from NATO

[10] New York *Times,* October 16, 1968, p. 1.

in terms of a defense commitment and how much the Americans were willing to provide, the New York *Times* reported that Tito had asked for no specific commitments and that Katzenbach had given none.[11] The Italian Communists took no note of Tito's alleged concern for enlisting Western support or sympathy. On October 19, *Unità,* in a 4-line item reported that "According to Western sources, the theme of the discussions was the current situation in Europe in light of the Czechoslovak events." The fact that Tito met with Katzenbach at that time was alarming enough to the PCI because it meant that Tito did not consider the situation fully "normalized" as the Italians had reported. Yet, since no concrete results of the meeting were announced in Belgrade, the PCI was content to let this diplomatic by-play pass without comment.

Discussions still raged within the Party. At a meeting of the Central Committee in mid-October, 1968, two of the hard-line Stalinist leaders, Pietro Secchia and Edoardo d'Onofrio, spoke out against the Party's stand. Furthermore, *Unità* continued to print an occasional letter from rank-and-file comrades protesting the Party's criticisms of the Soviet Union and asking the Party to pause and take a second look at anything that endangered "proletarian unity." The fact that *Unità* continued to publish these and similar letters showed that the confusion still prevailed within the Party and that the Directorate was not prepared to force the "doubters" to toe a single line.

Once the most intense shock and revulsion had passed and once it seemed clear that the Soviet leaders were not going to turn their military might against Yugoslavia or Rumania, the PCI returned to its attacks on NATO, a theme best suited to rally its followers. It pressed the militants into service to disseminate the party's official policy among the membership, and, by the beginning of February, 1969, *Rinascita* was able to report that the theme of the 109 provincial congresses of the party had been "the liquidation of the blocs and Italy's withdrawal from NATO." [12] These provincial congresses in turn set the tone and the theme of the Twelfth Party Congress which met in early February, 1969, at Bologna and which endorsed the leadership's policies.

President Nixon's visit to Eastern Europe in February, 1969, also gave the PCI an opportunity to placate the desire of its militants to abandon a defensive posture and return to the offensive. The visit served as a catalyst not only for violent demonstrations in Rome on

[11] *Ibid.,* October 19, 1968, p. 6.   [12] *Rinascita,* February 7, 1969, pp. 5–6.

February 27 and 28 but also for vehement denunciations by *Unità* and *Rinascita*. On February 27, *Unità* published an editorial asserting that Europe could not continue as an appendage of the U.S. and that the time had come for the European masses to discuss European problems saying that "With or without the United States, the discussion and the negotiations on security, without making them depend upon the success or failure of eventual and open negotiations between the United States and the Soviet Union" must begin immediately.

Following the visit, Carlo Galuzzi wrote an article for the March 7 edition of *Rinascita* entitled "An Occasion Missed" saying:

> The timidity and the impulsiveness of these justifications demonstrate that once again Italy has assumed a fully subordinate position in front of the most powerful ally, declaring its agreement, without understanding the real underlying intentions and objectives of the policies expounded by this ally.
>
> In effect, any ideal of autonomy can only be realized by overcoming old schemes and by looking for a new coalition, capable of initiating a constructive dialogue between the two Europes. This is the line that we have proposed at our Twelfth Congress, when we asked that Italy recover freedom of initiative and movement, impossible today if the problem of the withdrawal of our nation from NATO is not posed.

Amendola, speaking at Strasbourg on March 12, at the first meeting of the Council of Europe attended by the Italian Communists, stated:

> The Communists held a conference in Karlovy Vary in 1967 of all European Communist Parties with the goal of studying the possibility of working together to overcome the military blocs and to create European denuclearized zones. This idea was not made any easier, unfortunately, by the events of last year, and it is precisely for this reason that the Italian Communists have criticized the intervention of the Warsaw Pact troops in Czechoslovakia, for the measure in which this intervention provided the pretext to the Atlanticists to reenforce the blocs. On the occasion of the twentieth anniversary of the foundation of the Atlantic Alliance, the word for the day of the Italian Communists is and remains: Italy out of NATO; NATO out of Italy.[13]

The campaign against NATO continued on all levels. The Party organized regular street demonstrations all over Italy against the Atlantic Pact, and they combined with the PSIUP (left Socialist break-

[13] *Unità*, March 13, 1969, p. 10.

away faction) and the Left Independents to present a motion in Parliament to study the strategy and future of the Atlantic Pact in
Italy.[14] The Communist press followed closely the various NATO
meetings, reporting all efforts to increase Italy's commitment and
protesting all NATO moves as provocative and endangering the possibilities of an East-West European conference.

The Warsaw Pact proposal for the European security conference
brought an immediate warm response from the PCI. An editorial in
Rinascita on March 28 entitled "The European Dilemma" said:

For our part, we certainly do not relax with the Warsaw Pact document;
we know very well that it is not enough by itself, neither for its authors
nor for its readers, to create a new equilibrium. But in this document, we
read the confirmation of the line pursued by the PCI. . . . It is the line
which we maintained in spite of the events in Czechoslovakia; and that
we tenaciously continue to propose as an alternative to the chasms and
dangers of the old, time-worn equilibrium.

Subsequently, the PCI expressed its extreme disappointment in the
Washington NATO meeting, for failing to respond to the Budapest
document and especially its disappointment in Pietro Nenni who attended the meeting as Foreign Minister:

Europe was presented with a great opportunity to open new discussions
on prospects for the continent; that is, the discussions approved and promoted by the Budapest appeal. We do not wish at all to mythicize this
appeal. We do not believe that appeals alone are enough, and we are convinced that they must be founded upon concrete facts and come from
precise political initiatives. We do not try to hide in any way the difficulties which the Czechoslovakian story impressed on the current European
situation. Given all of this, the fact remains that the Western powers—
and the Socialist Foreign Minister of the Italian government—have refused definitely to open a political pan-European discussion.[15]

The PCI was also preparing for the International Conference of
Communist Parties to be held in Moscow in early June; a meeting
which it had fought to postpone indefinitely. On May 28, *Unità* published Longo's speech to the Central Committee in which he outlined
the positions that the Party would assume on various issues which
would come up at the Conference. This document is a very complete
statement of the Party's ideas on a wide range of subjects beginning
with their stand on the Conference itself and including Czechoslova-

[14] *Ibid.,* March 15, 1969, p. 1.   [15] *Rinascita,* April 18, 1969, p. 14.

kia, the Sino-Soviet dispute, and European security. Basically, Longo asked for an open discussion of all the problems which divide the Communist world, without any view toward settling on one "correct" point of view which would then be imposed upon all parties:

Today the frontiers of socialism no longer coincide with those of the Socialist states, for which reason a unitary plan of international action cannot but take account of the needs, the possibilities and the forms of action unique to each country. Furthermore, in the preparatory material elaborated, there is a view of socialism which does not correspond to the type of socialism which we ask the democratic and workers' movement to fight for in Italy; and a totally positive picture of the Socialist states is painted which cannot be accepted without benefit of study.

After saying that a true situation of detente and understanding cannot take place until "peace, independence, and liberty" come to Viet Nam, Longo repeated his Party's formulation for peace in Europe: the overcoming of the logic of opposing military and political blocs.

All of which indicates that the Italian Communists have not given up their fight against the Atlantic Alliance in spite of the intensity of the months which followed the invasion of Czechoslovakia. It is obvious that the struggle against NATO is an integral part of the PCI's ideology and is an issue which they can manipulate for domestic ends. But it is also apparent that the stand they have taken has set them in direct confrontation with their Soviet and East European allies. Yet, it would be a mistake to interpret the tenacity that the Italian Communists have shown in resisting pressures to abandon the battle against NATO in view of the Brezhnev Doctrine and the growing unpopularity of the Soviet Union as a sign that they would not be unwilling at some other time to compromise this position for a more immediate goal. The Italian Communists are not dogmatic when it comes to political tactics.

The same reasoning which explains, in large part, the Party's insistence on an anti-NATO stance can also explain why and in what situation they might be willing to abandon temporarily such a stance. The PCI wishes to govern Italy, and to do this they must form a coalition of the Left which must include elements of the Christian Democratic Left. If such a coalition demands playing down their anti-NATO stance (as it did with the Socialists and the Center-Left coalition), the PCI will do so.

There are signs that they might temporarily tone down the struggle against Italy's membership in NATO if this would ease the way into government. In an article which appeared in *Rinascita* on April 11, such signs were in evidence. Most of this article, entitled "Long Struggle of the Masses against the Atlantic Pact," is devoted to an analysis of the function of NATO as an arm of American imperialism in Europe and a tool of the Americans in the continuation of the cold war. The author, Romano Ledda, expresses what perhaps are the real fears of the PCI; the fact that right-wing elements in Italy have arrayed themselves around the NATO issue in such a way that they hope to be able to count on NATO to intervene in their favor if the Communists should attain power in Italy.

But the lead part of the article tells the most interesting story:

The campaign against the Atlantic Pact . . . does not . . . have the characteristics of a confrontation that peaks and dies within a few months and then adjourns with another appointment for many years in the future. It is, rather, an important factor in the longer and more important struggle to change the current direction of Italian foreign policy and to determine a different arrangement for Italy upon her withdrawal from the Atlantic Pact.

Obviously, we do not call to mind the scope of the objective to obscure clarity or decision. On the contrary; we do it to underline the fact that the struggle against the Atlantic Pact, precisely because of its importance, cannot die out even in a vigorous campaign of agitation and propaganda which denounces it for what it has represented and represents in Italy, Europe and the world; nor can it be the work of a courageous, passionate, but restricted avant garde. As with every large national problem . . . such a struggle requires the strength of a robust and extensive popular movement and the diligence of a coalition of political forces. It requires, in other words, a permanent and concrete effort for a mass political initiative and the marshaling of forces which would make foreign policy one of the battlefields of action in the nation and would bring about a real process of reversal in our current international position.

The author seems to be asking the militants to have patience since the struggle against NATO will take a long time and require a unity of the Left to bring about the final demise of NATO in Italy. He also seems to be warning the reader that the Party is willing to negotiate with these other forces over the procedure:

The Atlantic forces (the Atlantic Party, as it is called) are stronger than we are. But the forces which are already fighting to bring Italy out of the Pact are considerable. . . . We fight for the withdrawal of Italy from the

Atlantic Pact, and we mean by this to promote in this country a real movement which will bring about this result. We are ready to discuss (as we have often repeated) the means and measures to realize this end; to consider seriously stages and timetables; to encourage and support initiatives (even partial) which aim in this direction.

Thus, the PCI is moving along a path once traveled by the PSI. They have already accepted the Common Market and are now represented in the Council of Europe. It is obvious that they do not enjoy being isolated on the Left. They have confidence that they are pursuing the right course since they have steadily increased their share of the popular vote, even in the by-elections immediately following the Czechoslovakian crisis.

If negotiations should ever begin over a new Left coalition, it is unlikely that the PCI will make Italy's withdrawal from NATO one of its conditions for participation. This conclusion may seem antithetical to the evidence of dedication to the demise of NATO presented above. But the evidence indicating that the Italian Communist leadership increasingly regards its domestic role as more important than its position within the international communist movement explains this conclusion. It is quite simply a matter of political "trade-off."

The PCI is perfectly capable of maintaining a militant anti-NATO stance in its propaganda, without doing anything concrete in the short run to bring about its end in Italy. The Party can continue to stage demonstrations and propose studies; while, at the same time, explaining to the militants and activists (as the article quoted above suggests) that the road is a long and difficult one. This is not to say that the PCI is not genuinely interested in getting Italy out of NATO; they very much are. But above everything else, the Italian Communist Party is aware of what is meant by *political realism*.

The second part of the PCI's domestic strategy is by far the more important one. This strategy takes into account the more pressing domestic issues in Italy today. Since September of 1969, the tremendous strikes mounted against the government and against the industrial organization *Confindustria* have cost the nation a great deal. Nominally, the reason for these strikes has been the fact that over 4 million workers had contracts coming up for renegotiation in this period. But the extent of the unrest has gone far beyond discussions of wages and does not appear to be over.

The unrest in Italy goes deeper into complicated social issues which the *lentocrazia* has simply not been able to solve. Most pressing for the workers is the acute housing problem created by the mass migration from the countryside into the cities creating tremendous ghetto problems around the major cities of Milan, Turin, and Rome. The people quickly find that even if they have a job and find housing, rent alone will cost from 40 percent to 50 percent of their salaries. Even then, the housing is often inadequate and unhealthy. Furthermore, there are the problems of the universities, of the newly constituted health insurance, transportation, central city decay, divorce, crime, and the like—all of which could add up to chaos.

If the reconstituted Center-Left coalition is unable to bring about concrete results and if the Italian Communists can promise and deliver some real and substantial reforms, they can afford to overlook such issues as NATO without causing unrest among Party militants. If the present government again fails to reconcile its own internal differences and does not begin to solve Italy's pressing domestic problems, a renewed governmental crisis would once again raise the possibility of Communist participation in government. In such an event, we can look for it to make demands on such issues as housing which affects the workers' movement much more directly than that of NATO. Meanwhile, the PCI will continue its propaganda campaign against the Alliance. After all, this flexibility is what "the Italian road to socialism" has been all about.

Problems of Political Equilibrium in the Soviet Proposals for a European Security Conference

JANUSZ A. WISNIOWSKI

The basic concept of this article is *system*. System is not a thing; rather, it is a list of variables that are to be taken into account in the analysis of the behavior of a system.[1] This list is not invariant. Differing analytical approaches may stress different sets of explanatory variables. New variables are introduced to secure *singleness,* or predictability. This singleness, also called determinateness, means that we can predict, given the state of the variables, the behavior of the system once a disturbance is introduced into it. The inclusion of new variables is especially important as a system evolves through time.

One of the most important characteristics of a system is that it can be coupled with another system. Out of two isolated systems comes a larger system comprised of two subsystems. Of course, "the defining of the component parts does not determine the way of coupling." [2]

The Pure Model of Spheres of Influence

This somewhat theoretical introduction requires an example. Let us consider a *pure* model of spheres of influence. In 1947 Secretary of State James Byrnes noted "the Soviet preference for the simpler task of dividing the world into two spheres of influence." [3] This is

---

[1] W. Ross Ashby, *An Introduction to Cybernetics* (New York, 1966), p. 40.

[2] *Ibid.,* p. 53.

[3] James F. Byrnes in *Speaking Frankly,* p. 105, cited in Adam B. Ulam, *Expansion and Coexistence: The History of Soviet Foreign Policy 1917–1967* (New York, 1968), p. 407.

opposed to the American desire for collective security. Applied to present-day Europe, the Russian plan, if interpreted statically, would have Eastern Europe dominated by the Soviet Union while Western Europe would be under the direct influence of the United States.[4] We would have two totally isolated systems as shown in Figure 1.

FIGURE 1

A description of Europe corresponding to Figure 1 would be totally unsatisfactory, since the behavior of neither the Eastern part nor the Western part in postwar Europe could thereby be explained with any degree of realism or logical consistency. We shall see below why the concept of isolated systems is not valid. If we want to retain the idea of spheres of influence, still understood as a static concept, we must first relax the assumption of total isolation.

First of all, we know that the United States and the Soviet Union interact with each other outside Europe and that results of this interaction are disseminated over both parts of Europe. This is explicit in a statement made by Molotov: "One cannot decide now any serious problem of international relations without the U.S.S.R. or without listening to the voice of our Fatherland." [5]

We can carry the argument still further. If we postulate the possibility, however remote, of coupling the two systems, there would always exist the need for introducing new variables which would se-

---

[4] In fact in the late 1940s the Soviet Union was not satisfied with the concept of two isolated systems. On the contrary, their foreign policy was outward oriented and based on the presumption of two competing and interacting systems. The formulation given in the text more closely follows *revisionistic* writings on the history of the cold war and helps to bring into much sharper relief the concept of pure spheres of influence. For a revisionistic view, see especially Walter Lafeber, *America, Russia, and the Cold War, 1945–1966* (New York, 1967).

[5] V. M. Molotov in *Problems of Foreign Policy*, p. 24, cited in Ulam, p. 405.

cure continuing isolation.[6] The state of these new variables would depend directly on the behavior of the super powers within their spheres of influence. Because the U.S. and USSR both operate in Europe, this establishes a direct link between the Eastern part and its Western counterpart and, thus, by definition destroys total isolation. Russian decisions about Eastern Europe will influence the American stand vis-à-vis its Western European allies.

The importance of this link is further enhanced by the fact that what would appear as purely intra-bloc decisions are extrapolated by the other powers as carrying an inter-bloc message. There are numerous examples to support this thesis. Classic ones are NATO's reaction to the application of the Brezhnev doctrine in Czechoslovakia [7] and Russia's response to the admission of Western Germany into NATO as a full member.

It emerges from the argument that some of the new variables are of the military form. This is so because preservation of the spheres of influence in the modern world relies basically on the military deterrent; conversely, the influence of the super powers on their respective allies stems from their ability to provide credible deterrence on their behalf against another super power.[8]

This brings us to the second objection to the pure model of spheres of influence. So far we have assumed that the interests of the European countries are transmitted between blocs by the super powers. We thus excluded the possibility of European countries conducting a dialogue outside the boundaries of their blocs. This assumption was partially valid at the peak of the cold war.[9] The imminent threat

[6] War, nuclear or conventional, is not the only possible coupling.

[7] We obviously are not subscribing here to the thesis that the Soviet intervention was prompted by the meddling of Western powers into the internal affairs of Czechoslovakia or that Czechoslovakia was leaving the Soviet sphere of influence.

[8] It may be impossible to use a common denominator for the American alignment with Western Europe and Russia's relations with the countries of Eastern Europe. Working from a general grasp of the concept "sphere of influence" derived from eighteenth- and nineteenth-century history, we may find it necessary to call Western Europe a true sphere of influence and Eastern Europe a collection of colonies. The experience of China, and Africa after the Berlin Conference of 1884–85, leads us to describe *sphere of influence* in terms of commercial exploitation and political suasion based on military and administrative occupation of at least a portion of the *sphere*. Colonies are the next step, with complete foreign domination of all state functions.

[9] In the future, a model of a sphere of influence would be as presented in

of war forced upon the nonsuper-power members of the alliances a reduction in their freedom of action in international political and military matters. In Eastern Europe the situation was further accentuated by the colonial status to which Stalin had assigned the communist countries of Europe. Since then, the assessment of the Russian threat by the Western Europeans has undergone important changes.

The main direction of these changes was toward a reduced belief in the probability of Russian aggression in Western Europe, which resulted in a mounting unwillingness to contribute to the military requirements of security.[10] On the other hand, there was an increasing desire for direct rapprochement between Western Europe and the Soviet Union and especially the countries of Eastern Europe, which had regained a still severely limited degree of freedom in their foreign policy.[11] This led to a situation in which "the [Western] Europeans are spending a much smaller fraction of their GNP on defence than is the United States and this fraction continues to grow smaller." [12]

Out of this reassessment of the political situation with regard to the Russian threat emerged two main types of foreign policy. One, which we may term *maximal,* was introduced by France and approximated, within the existing constraints, by Rumania. Another, *minimal,* was developed by Germany and is approximated by Hungary and most recently, Poland. Preintervention Czechoslovakia falls in this category.[13]

At the root of maximal policy lies the assumption that restructuring Europe should begin with at least weakening, if not dissolving, the two military alignments, NATO and WTO. This, in turn, would make the escape from the orbits of the super powers much easier. The United States would withdraw its troops from Europe, with the

---

Alastair Buchan, ed., *Europe's Future, Europe's Choices* (New York, 1969), Chapter 2. "In Atlanticized Europe, they [European states] have renounced the aspiration of developing an independent system; they see their interests irrevocably linked to the United States and accept American leadership, though without enthusiasm." *Ibid.,* p. 38.

[10] Marshall Shulman, "Europe versus Detente," *Foreign Affairs* (April, 1967), pp. 390–91.

[11] These political links and attitudes can easily be identified as new variables.

[12] Alain Enthoven and K. Wayne Smith, "What Forces from NATO? From Whom?" *Foreign Affairs* (October, 1969), p. 90.

[13] Pierre Hassner, *Change and Security in Europe, Part II,* Adelphi Papers No. 49, I.S.S. (London, 1968), p. 6.

exception perhaps of the Berlin contingent, and would rely, on "strategic vigilance" in order to secure its interests and provide "Western Europe's self-confidence vis-à-vis Soviet Russia." [14]

Freed from its Atlantic ballast, Western Europe could then proceed with its plans for developing the detente with the Soviet Union and Eastern Europe, since in the opinion of the Soviet Union, limitation of Atlantization of Western Europe is a primary requirement for the possibility of rapprochement.[15]

The Soviets, on the other hand, would disband the WTO in accordance with the statements made in the Declaration on Strengthening Peace and Security in Europe and, later iterated, in the Karlovy Vary Declaration. At the same time, "any Soviet argument for strengthening or further centralizing the machinery of COMECON for political purposes" would be weakened.[16] There is, however, one flaw in this idealized model—the Soviet Union would not accept any degree of "political divorce" between itself and its satellites.

The minimal approach rests on the assumption that the bipolar solution has merits, at least in the nearest future. It envisages consolidation within each of the two military alignments, accompanied by increasing contacts between WTO and NATO countries. These contacts would perhaps lead to a solution of political problems, especially in Central Europe, and finally to a dismantling of the Atlantic and Warsaw pacts in favor of a collective security scheme. The best example of this type of thinking is West Germany's Ostpolitik. The main goal of this policy is to reach some sort of agreement with East Germany and perhaps Poland without at the same time diminishing its security, by, say, withdrawing from NATO and agreeing to some sort of demilitarization plan. Both moves would be conducive to the solution of the German problem, but not on the terms which the government in Bonn would find acceptable. The German plan involves, in Willy Brandt's words, "patient experimentation" in the East and a furthering of federal and confederal tendencies in the West, aiming at the coupling in the future of East and West subsystems, and thus resolving the problem of frontiers by making it irrelevant.[17]

[14] George Liska, *Imperial America: The International Politics of Primacy* (Baltimore, 1967), p. 61.

[15] Yuri Zhukov, "Nato: What Now?" *International Affairs* (Moscow), No. 7 (1969), pp. 88–89.

[16] Buchan, p. 65.

[17] For an excellent survey of German foreign policy, see "Willy Brandt's Germany: a Survey," *The Economist*, January 10, 1970, pp. xiv–xxvii.

This discussion of policy patterns takes us outside the realm of static analysis. I introduced it specifically, first, to show that there are direct links between European countries which further reduce the applicability of the concept of pure spheres of influence and, second, to point out the dynamic forces operating in Europe, the main purpose of which is to invalidate the concept of spheres of influence.

In the light of analysis, the concept of spheres of influence retains its validity, but loses its sharpness. Its validity is based upon the strong tendency for smaller countries to be aligned with one of the super powers, whether this alignment is based on military coercion, as in the case of Eastern Europe and the Soviet Union, or based on mutual consent, as in the case of the United States and its Western allies. The loss of its sharpness is due to the multiplicity of direct and indirect links among all bloc countries, producing a maze of constantly changing relations. In the context of the cybernetic model, these relations are in the form of feedbacks; that is, action, reaction, reaction to the reaction, and so on.

It is often overlooked that feedbacks are not always stabilizing in the sense that they may not bring the system, with some time lag, back to its starting point after a disturbance has occurred. The obvious example, of course, is the arms race, in which the level of mutual deterrence is constantly pushed to higher levels in response to increases (i.e., disturbances) in the level of deterrence of the other side.[18]

At the same time Marshal Shulman turns our attention to the idea that the mere increase in contact between East and West, often assumed almost by definition as leading toward greater stability in Europe, may produce quite contrary results.[19] Shulman forcefully argues that a stabilizing result can be achieved only if the proper machinery for such contact is available. Establishing this machinery may entail the rearrangement of links between Western European countries, that is, a rearrangement of feedback relations.[20]

Patterns of feedback in present-day Europe are stabilizing if the disturbance is such that it may lead to the annihilation of the system itself. Bundy points out that

[18] McGeorge Bundy, "To Cap the Volcano," *Foreign Affairs* (October, 1969), pp. 2–3.
[19] Shulman, p. 369.
[20] Norbert Wiener, *Cybernetics* (Cambridge, Mass., 1965), pp. 105–7.

it was never the American superiority in nuclear weapons that was decisive in protecting Europe; it was simply the high probability that any large scale use of force against a NATO country would set loose a chain of events that could lead to nuclear war.[21]

The feedback to focus upon is the *anticipatory* feedback; instead of stabilizing the system after the disturbance has occurred, it tries to prevent the disturbance from reaching the essential variables of the system. An important feature of this type of feedback as it operates in Western Europe is that it stabilizes the system before the ultimate disturbance occurs, that is, nuclear attack. The anticipatory feedback, however, may produce a different response, for example, the preemptive nuclear attack.

The operation of anticipatory feedback was made very plain during the recurring Berlin crises.[22] The system "Europe" possesses homeostatic characteristics: it tries to preserve its existence. However, if homeostasis depends upon the anticipatory feedback and regulation of the level of security, we have to make sure that the components which perform this function are reliable. In other words, they must *always* prevent the ultimate disturbance. This seems to be the first requirement for any form of security system.

Simple Dynamic Behavior

Let us now turn to a simplified model which will allow us to study the dynamic properties of systems.

We assume only two countries, the Soviet Union and the United States. We differentiate between their "governments" and their "armies," and we also postulate a particular map of connections between these four elements of the system. Assume now that for some unspecified reason the Russians want to generate a new Berlin crisis. The type of command does not need to be specified here; we need to know only that the Soviet "government" sends a message in the form of a command to their "army," in Berlin. This message reaches the United States "government" as a diplomatic-type message, as well as through military intelligence. When the Russian "army" obeys the command, there is an absolute increase in the "energy" in the system, which we may measure by some appropriate index, say of "preparedness."

[21] Bundy, "To Cap the Volcano," pp. 17–18.
[22] Ulam, pp. 619–20, 631, 655–56.

Next, the increase in energy is transmitted to the U.S. "government," which in turn responds with a command message to its "army" for a new increase in energy. This command, as well as a diplomatic-type message to the Russian "government" (an ultimatum, say), is transmitted to the Russians at about the same time as the information from their own "army" that the energy has been increased. This is a classic example of feedback.

The Soviet government has several policy options. But since we assumed earlier that the system possesses homeostatic properties, the second and subsequent rounds of this process will lead to a non-nuclear settlement. The new equilibrium, however, may mean that the total energy of the system is increased due to the strengthening of the forces around Berlin. The schematic diagram (Figure 2), though

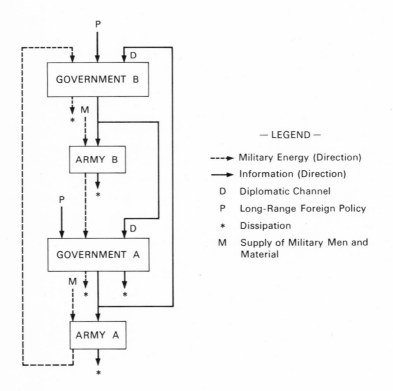

— LEGEND —

- - -▶ Military Energy (Direction)
───▶ Information (Direction)
D   Diplomatic Channel
P   Long-Range Foreign Policy
*   Dissipation
M   Supply of Military Men and Material

FIGURE 2

somewhat simplified, describes the system. We should just note that
P, long-range foreign policy, comes from outside the system and does
not participate directly in the responses once the disturbance has
been initiated.[23]

What are the major points emerging from this analysis? First of
all, we can distinguish in most systems between flows of information
and flows of supply (or energy, as here).[24]

Second, each part of the system can be classified as either a transformer of energy (*army*) or a transformer of information (*government*). This dichotomy is crucial, since transformers of energy can be
regulated by transformers of information, while the opposite is not
true. This provides a formal basis for the conjecture, often made,
that military problems within Central Europe cannot be solved unless
there is agreement on the political issues first.

All schemes advocating the military neutralization of West Germany are
politically unrealistic. The Central European problem cannot be solved
by drastic changes in the existing security structure—faulty and tense
though it may be—for the problem is basically a political one. The military situation is its consequence.[25]

Third, it becomes obvious that the existence of transformers of energy is essential for the working of the system. Any message of the
type considered in the model will have essentially no information
content if it cannot be transformed into an energy flow. In the model
each government watches or observes the realization of the other
government's policies by the other government's army before it decides on its own response. The second government will not activate
its transformers of energy (army) if the first government's transformer of energy (army) is not activated. Putting it less formally:
governments react to deeds rather than words.

Finally, in order to make the system determinate, that is, predictable, we must assume that the governments possess memory. We know
that the workings of one government are only partially observable by
the other government: spies provide only limited information and in-

[23] This simplification follows from our short-run analysis. The long-run
model should explain the formation of long-run policies.

[24] Henryk Greniewski and Maria Kempisty, *Cybernetyka z Lotu Ptaka* [*Cybernetics, the Bird's Eye View*] (Warsaw, 1963), pp. 51–66.

[25] Zbigniew Brzezinski, *Peaceful Engagement in Europe's Future,* School of
International Affairs, Columbia University Occasional Papers (New York,
1965), p. 25.

sight. This makes the behavior of the observed government unpredictable. But when we assume that the observer has in its possession the whole history of past behavior of the observed system, we see that the observer can deduce the responses of the observed system from the basis of past values revealed. The general rule is stated:

If a determinant system is only partially observable, and thereby becomes (for that observer) not predictable, that observer may be able to restore predictability by taking the system's past history into account, i.e., by assuming the existence within it of some form of "memory." [26]

Closely related to this last point is the situation in which the observer induces a disturbance to which the observed has never before been exposed. This may produce highy undesirable results by posing "a serious threat to security," since the observer may have been taking security "too easily for granted." [27] Putting if differently, the observer may have had in mind some probabilistic distribution of responses, with each particular response having an assigned subjective probability of occurrence. Subjective probabilities assigned to undesirable outcomes may have been unjustifiably low, and the "calculated risk" higher than the observer had expected.[28]

Three Concepts of Status Quo

Let us examine the problems surrounding the concept of status quo and try to use some of the results derived in the sections above. Every system, including the one considered above, can be characterized by three main variables. Each one is instrumental in focusing on different aspects of status quo.

1. the state of its transformers of energy and information
2. the net of links between the elements of the system
3. the result (*output*) the system produces when a given disturbance is introduced.

[26] Ashby, p. 115; see also Wiener, Chapter IX.

[27] Pierre Hassner, *Change and Security in Europe, Part I,* Adelphi Papers No. 45, I.S.S. (London, 1968), p. 4.

[28] It is interesting to note that we can calculate the gain in information possessed by the observer after the experiment by comparing his subjective probabilities and the probabilities of the actual outcome. The techniques are given in Henry Thiel, *Economics and Information Theory* (Amsterdam, North Holland, 1967).

TRANSFORMERS OF ENERGY AND INFORMATION

To begin with the first variable, status quo would mean the invariance over time of political and military postures. This can occur in either of two cases. First, the starting point of the system is the position toward which the system will always return after a disturbance which could be introduced from inside or outside the system. In this case, we would call the system *metastable* around its starting point. Second, there may be a freeze of activity of unspecified duration. This is a rather unlikely situation, although it was approximated in the statement made by the signatories of the Budapest Declaration, in which it was vowed to "refrain from any action that may poison the atmosphere in relations between states." [29] In light of this definition, status quo becomes a rather useless concept: it is a mere photographic description of the system as viewed at any given moment.

LINKS BETWEEN THE ELEMENTS OF THE SYSTEM

Variable 2 gives the basis for a much more useful definition of status quo. Now status quo allows for change in either political postures or military postures or both simultaneously. The last is the most probable. There is, however, no change in the method of joining the component elements.

If we hold political postures constant and allow for changes in the military component, we are dealing with the *maximization problem:* we try to maximize the effectiveness of deterrence and military stability within the bounds of existing political realities. This is to a large extent the problem discussed by MacGuire in his book on the arms race.[30] It is almost universally believed in the West that present military arrangements are stable. There are two aspects of stability. One is the optimality of existing military structure based on two alliances; the other is the optimality of the level of deterrence. At the moment let us concentrate only on the latter.

There are two main methods for lowering the level of deterrence in Europe. One would be an agreement on an all-European arms control scheme, the main stress lying on the reduction of the nuclear arsenal of both super powers located in Europe. This could be a di-

[29] "Budapest Meeting Communique," *Survival,* XI (May, 1969), 161.
[30] Martin MacGuire, *Secrecy and the Arms Race* (Cambridge, Mass., 1965), pp. 167–73.

rect result of a global nuclear-arms limitation agreement reached by the Soviet Union and the United States. A reduction in the American nuclear deterrent in Europe would necessarily be accompanied by similar cuts in the number of Soviet medium-range ballistic missiles.[31] This could alleviate European fears about the American capability of defending Europe. It is difficult to foresee a possibility of reduction in the level of conventional troops in Europe.

A proposal for such a reduction was sketched in the Bucharest Declaration, emphasizing troop reductions in both Germanies.[32] This proposal was and still is unfeasible from the Western point of view, since it reduces the level of the conventional deterrent of the NATO countries and does not, in fact, impair the military power of the WTO countries. The acceptability of this proposal is reduced further because it was part of a "package deal" including

the withdrawal of all foreign forces from alien territories . . . discontinuance of flights by foreign planes carrying atom or hydrogen bombs over the territories of the European states and the entry of foreign submarines and surface ships with nuclear arms on board into the ports of such states.[33]

Another method for reduction in troop levels in Europe derives from the concept of demilitarized and denuclearized zones, specifically in Central Europe. One positive aspect of this solution is that it would tend to lead to the withdrawal of Soviet troops from Central Europe and at the same time dispel Eastern European fears of the "revanchistic" West German military machinery. The major drawback is that all the gains accrue to the Soviet Union with NATO at the same time incapacitated.

At present there is very little room for maneuver in the military arrangements. From the Soviet point of view the present strategic situation is highly favorable and the long-range trend points toward even further improvement. Thus the West could agree to the "legitimization of the strategic status quo" only in exchange for a "modification in the political one, designed to make it more acceptable to

[31] At the present the Soviet Union is reducing its arsenal of MRBMs in favor of ICBMs.

[32] "Bucharest Conference: Declaration on Strengthening Peace and Security in Europe," Embassy of the U.S.S.R. (Washington, D.C., July, 1966), p. 6; see also "Karlovy Vary Conference"—Communique, *Survival*, IX (1967), 211–12.

[33] "Bucharest Conference," p. 6.

Germany." [34] Legitimization would specifically involve the signing of the nonaggression and nonproliferation treaties. This, however, would have to be accompanied by "normalization [i.e., formal recognition] of relations between all states and the German Democratic Republic." [35] This is understandably more than the Western countries would agree to. It is significant that in the same breath the Russians stress the need for "consistent defence and development of democracy in the German Federal Republic." [36] "Defence of democracy" means the right to intervene in the internal affairs of West Germany if internal developments seem, in the Soviet view, to threaten the peace. As long as the Soviet Union still regards Articles 53 and 107 of the United Nations Charter as valid, a bilateral treaty renouncing the use of force as a policy measure between the Soviet Union and West Germany may be of little value to Germany.

It is also highly improbable that the Russians would abandon the Brezhnev doctrine, which at the moment provides the best, if not the only, method for securing Russian dominance in Eastern Europe. There seem to be no visible gains to the West which could accrue from signing the pledges of nonintervention and renunciation of the use of force. Russia would still be in a position to produce false charges of Western intervention, as it did during the Czechoslovakian crisis, to cover its "counterintervention." The West would be at the same time severely impaired in its ability to intervene in a future Berlin crisis, especially if the Russians persist in their treatment of West Berlin as a separate political entity.[37]

Adjustments in military arrangements have been treated as a problem of maximization of military security within the political constraint. A dual problem is the *minimization of political instability* within the constraints of the existing military solution to the problems of security, in our case the NATO and WTO alignments. In post-World War II Europe the problem of minimization can be viewed as a resolution of the German problem. Hassner says:

the European problem and the German problem are seen from the security viewpoint as two aspects of the same question—what kind of Ger-

[34] Hassner, Part II, p. 14. For a review of the possibilities of the reversal of this trend, see Enthoven and Smith.

[35] "Karlovy Vary Conference," p. 211.

[36] *Ibid.*

[37] "European Security," from *Information* (G.D.R.), reprinted in *Survival,* XI (1969), 357; see also "Karlovy Vary Conference," p. 160.

many would fit into what kind of Europe so as to be neither too strong nor too weak for the European environment? [38]

We can parenthetically remark that the importance of the German problem stems from the fact that in systems with feedbacks each part of the system has veto power over the stability of the system as a whole. In other words, unless each and every part is "satisfied" with its own state, given the states of all other parts, the system will move or try to move away from its present state.

The Russian solution to the German problem is rather simple. It is also the only solution which keeps the net of links constant. It rests on the basic assumption that "the question of borders in Europe is solved finally and irrevocably." [39] Translated, this means that Polish-German, Czechoslovakian-German, and GDR-GFR borders are permanent.[40] Furthermore, the two German states have to be treated as sovereign states, neither of which has a legal basis for claiming monopolistic rights for representation of all German peoples. Thus Russia repeatedly calls for repudiation of the Hallstein Doctrine by West Germany.

The Russian design, then, is to keep Germany divided, probably indefinitely. West German efforts at achieving some degree of rapprochement with East Germany are constantly frustrated by Ulbricht's regime, but not to the extent that it is likely that future West German governments will completely give up the idea of an active Ostpolitik. It is impossible to assess how much of Ulbricht's policies are of his own design. We are inclined to believe that these policies are the result of what *The Economist* aptly calls "division of labour" in politics. The proof is as follows: the Soviet Union does not want to forgo the economic advantages of contacts with West Germany by completely alienating the German government. Next, it would like to see a less active Ostpolitik because it finds some East European countries willing to pursue a policy of rapprochement with Bonn. Lastly, because it thinks that "the threat to security comes not from Germany's being divided but from the attempts made to overcome it," [41] it would like to see the West German government agreeing de facto, and preferably de jure, to a division of Germany.

[38] Hassner, Part II, p. 2.   [39] "Bucharest Conference," p. 5.

[40] The Polish-German and the Czechoslovak-German border positions cannot, of course, be questioned. The Bucharest Declaration also mentions the possibility of reunification (*ibid.*, p. 7), which I discuss below, when I analyze the possibility of the reconstruction of Europe.

[41] Hassner, Part II.

If we combine military and political adjustments, we find that the Russian policy is to keep Germany divided and neutralized. In return Russia may be willing to pay the price of a disarmed East Germany. The last point was made clear by Ulbricht: "The governments of both German states sign a treaty through which they pledge themselves to accept together and simultaneously a status of neutrality for both German states, guaranteed by the Powers." [42]

From the Western point of view, neither part of the Russian design would be acceptable. Neutralization of the two Germanies does not reduce the military strength of WTO but does deal a deadly blow to NATO and to NATO's capacity to maintain an interest in West Berlin. It is conceivable that many Western European countries would in this situation seriously consider withdrawing from NATO and would prefer to sign bilateral treaties with the United States providing for their defense in the case of war. This could be the result of a further reduction in the assessment of the Russian threat, once one of the Russian demands were satisfied. Another factor might be that NATO is viewed as a channel through which European countries exercise control, however limited, over German armaments. Now there would be no German army and the need for control would disappear. Conceivably, then, the result in the long run of legitimization of the status quo could be Europe des Etats.

As we have observed, the possibility is very small that there would be a reduction in the level of conventional and nuclear forces in Europe which would not be a result of a more general political solution. However, an outgrowth of the American search for detente with the Soviet Union might be legitimization of the political status quo. This is becoming more and more a realistic proposition. The United States policy "moves from encouragement of Eastern European independence to an increasing stress on multilateralism—and on multilateralism which more and more includes the Soviet Union and less and less excludes East Germany." [43]

It is my opinion that the recognition of the German Democratic Republic (GDR) and guarantee of the seal of permanence to the division of Germany would be the most unwise course the United States could follow in Europe. First, it would further aggravate our relations with France, which would consider a decision such as another Yalta a "betrayal." Second, it would effectively destroy West Ger-

[42] *Archiv den Gegenwart,* I, 1967, p. 12896, cited in Hassner, Part II, p. 12n18.

[43] Hassner, Part I, p. 15.

many's belief in the value of close links with the United States, which would have failed even to initiate the move toward the reunification of the Germanies. West Germany would have a number of policy options, each of them detrimental to the interests of the United States or the Soviet Union or Western Europe—and most probably to all of them. West Germany could follow the road of "creating" the Independent Federal Europe (IFE), which would have its own nuclear deterrent and its own foreign policy (conceivably hostile to the United States). At the same time, this IFE could aggressively strive for the solution of the German problem, especially if it were indirectly dominated by West Germany as economically the most powerful member.[44]

It is doubtful whether this "Straussian" Europe would help realize the ultimate goal of reunification. And, it would certainly worsen relations between Eastern European and Western European countries. On the other hand, the Soviet Union would be even less inclined to let the GDR enter a new federation because it would bring a strong nuclear power, that is, Federated Europe, closer to its borders, and at the same time it would deprive Russia of the crucial "control variable," Berlin.

Other policy options include West Germany's creating its own nuclear deterrent, and the use of it as a means of extracting concessions from Russia. West Germany could also enter into direct negotiations with the Soviet Union, which might lead to a Russian-German dominance over Europe. The consequence of such dominance would be more tragic for Europe than domination by the Russian-French alliance described by Liska.[45]

There is, of course, the policy of "bridge building," of reunification through detente. This is the least destabilizing option, both in a political and military sense. It has, however, the undesirable feature of making Germany so deeply involved in its Eastern European affairs that it would be an easy target of Russian foreign policy. That is, the Soviet government would perhaps try to manipulate the German body politic with illusory offers and promises and simultaneously estrange West Germany from its Western allies.

[44] This type of IFE differs from the model described by Buchan (pp. 124–48), since in Buchan's model Independent Europe would not be conducive to a solution to the problem of reunification, and "Germany's integration in an Independent Federal Europe would imply her abandonment of West Berlin to East Germany or Soviet control" (p. 143).

[45] Liska.

This rather lengthy discussion has shown the specific characteristics of the Soviet concept of the status quo. Russia seeks a change in the existing situation through the legitimization and formalization of that situation, both political and military. The dynamic long-run effect of the consolidation of the status quo along the lines proposed by the Russians could lead to a complete revamping of political and military realities in Europe. Russia cannot solve the German problem in any but a highly unsatisfactory way for the West; the Russian plan disturbs the balance of power in Europe; finally, the plan would reduce, if not completely nullify, the American influence in Europe. It may well be as Hassner says that "a formalization of the status quo means reinforcing certain elements of the status quo while weakening the others." [46] What should not be overlooked in the West is that the Russian solution weakens those elements of the status quo which are favorable to the West while strengthening those favorable to the Soviet Union. This may seem obvious, but it is not always clearly understood. Theo Sommer aptly characterizes the Soviet proposals as "a continuation of the cold war by other means." [47] There are, no doubt, some valid points in the Russian proposals for European security. The major point stresses the dangers of West German access to the nuclear arsenal.[48] Even though well founded,[49] the Soviet position goes further than that of the West European countries. The Russians would like to see Germany excluded from the multinational nuclear schemes such as MLF, and most probably would vociferously object to the Independent Federal Europe in which European countries "decide to pool their resources and offer Germany equal participation in a European nuclear force." [50]

The West should also study closely the proposals for increased contacts, cultural and economic, between Eastern and Western Europe.[51] The usefulness of these channels for "peaceful penetration" of the East European regimes, leading perhaps to a political liberalization in Eastern Europe, is recognized by many writers.[52] There are

[46] Hassner, Part I, p. 6.

[47] Theo Sommer, "A Chance for Europe," in *Die Zeit*, March 28, 1969, reprinted in *Survival*, Vol. XI (June, 1969).

[48] "Karlovy Vary Conference," p. 212; also "Budapest Meeting Communique," pp. 4, 7.

[49] Ulam, p. 663.   [50] Buchan, p. 129.

[51] "Bucharest Conference," p. 161; "Karlovy Vary Conference," p. 212; "Budapest Meeting Communique," p. 5.

[52] Brzezinski, pp. 39–55.

a number of problems here. It seems improbable that Russia would relinquish its say in the extent of cooperation allowed. An increase in economic welfare resulting from accelerated economic cooperation could solidify the position of orthodox communist elites. According to the latest doctrine, the better off the people, the less revolutionary they are. This is not to say that increased cultural and economic exchange should be dismissed. We should try to establish contacts on a basis which is not detrimental to our long-run interests in Europe.

RESULTS, OR OUTPUT, OF THE SYSTEM

So far we have been primarily concerned with those Russian proposals which would leave untouched the existing links among European countries in the short run. This conforms to our second definition of the status quo, which requires constancy in the map of the European network. However important those proposals are for the Russians, they constitute only a basis for far-reaching changes the Soviet Union would like to see. Those changes directly involve rearrangement of the links among European countries and between European countries and the United States. In this context we should note that the mere restructuring of the system by rearrangement of the links does not necessarily produce a change in the behavior of the system. Indeed, it can be shown that there exists an infinite number of ways in which the system can be built and still exhibit the same pattern of behavior.[53] Thus, any transformation of the system's network which does not change the ultimate behavior of the system may be said to be preserving the status quo in the most general sense.

In all of the Russian proposals for European security we encounter the call for the "ending of the division of Europe into military groupings." [54] Those calls were particularly loud in the 1966 and 1967 declarations. In Bucharest the Russians expressed the strong conviction that

there can be no doubt that the aims of United States policy in Europe have nothing in common with the vital interests of the European peoples, the task of European security . . . the North Atlantic military bloc and military machine deepens the division of Europe and hinders the development of normal ties between Eastern Europe and Western Europe.[55]

In the Karlovy Vary Declaration the Soviet Union proceeded to identify NATO as the extension of American capitalism and as an

[53] Ashby, p. 53.   [54] "Bucharest Conference," p. 161.   [55] *Ibid.*, pp. 2, 3.

outlet for West German revanchism.[56] This was intended to aggravate the crisis in NATO and to promote the dissolution of NATO from within. If this were to fail, there was another plan, namely to negotiate the dissolution of NATO and WTO. This was to happen in two steps. First, the military organizations and then the alignments themselves would be liquidated. Dissolution of the alignments could, however, be delayed.[57] This plan carries no merit from the Western point of view: there is no use of a NATO stripped of its military role, whereas the Warsaw Pact could still serve as a means of controlling the Eastern European countries. Without a doubt, dissolution of NATO would create a power vacuum in Europe which could be filled, if only gradually, by the Soviet Union. This would be a direct result of the withdrawal of American troops from Europe. Thus,

there is everything to be said for keeping American troops in Europe . . . [since] American disengagement can only be the first step in a process of Sovietization (in its milder and more modern form of "Finlandization"), or the last step in a process of Europeanization.[58]

The latter possibility seems to lie in a rather distant future; but, on the other hand, it gives the only logical basis for the dissolution of the two alignments. Western Europe would have to pass through the stage of consolidation and development of its own deterrent. This could perhaps occur within the framework of the NATO alliance. The next step would be a physical disengagement of the United States from Western Europe and of the Soviet Union from Eastern Europe. Both super powers would remain, however, committed to defend their allies. The main goal of this new Europe would be the achievement of the "second stage of detente," that is, "the European settlement."

There is no doubt that European security must rest "on relations of equality and mutual respect among all states of the continent and 'peaceful coexistence.' "[59] It is my view that this mutual respect would be fostered if in the reorganized Europe Western Europe could counterbalance at least partially the military might of the Soviet Union.

Another problem, no less important, arises: Is the collective security system, as proposed by the Russians, workable, and if so, will it

[56] "Karlovy Vary Conference," pp. 208, 209; "Bucharest Conference," p. 3.
[57] "Bucharest Conference," pp. 5, 6.
[58] Hassner, Part II, p. 29.   [59] "Bucharest Conference," p. 6.

provide more security than the existing system, which relies directly on the military presence of the super powers? This question is thoroughly analyzed by Hassner;[60] I may add that from the cybernetic point of view, collective security systems may be extremely unreliable. This follows from the fact that the elements (i.e., countries) of the system are linked in the following manner.

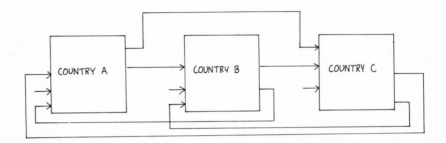

FIGURE 3

If each element is not completely reliable, then the whole system becomes extremely unreliable. In other words, any given country has some probability assigned to it that it will respond with "war" when this response is not warranted. If so, the system will find itself in a state of war more often than we would expect, because the probability of the system being at war is equal not to the average of the probabilities of the component countries but rather to the multiple of their probabilities. *A, B,* and *C* each have a probability of 0.5 of responding with "war." The whole system has a probability not of 0.5 but of 0.875 of being at "war."

There exist methods of increasing the reliability of such systems; but since we are not interested here in the optimal solution of the collective security system, suffice it to say that they rely on the manipulation of the links between the components.

Western interest in the restructuring of Europe stems from the desire to solve the German problem. There are some who would accept A. J. P. Taylor's diagnosis that "what is wrong with Germany is that there is too much of it"[61] and go along with the Russian proposals

[60] Hassner, Part II, pp. 21–24.

[61] A. J. P. Taylor, "German Unity," in *Europe, Grandeur and Decline* (London, 1967), p. 121.

to keep Germany divided. Much more prevalent is the notion that the German problem should be solved through some sort of confederation of the two Germanies which would in the future evolve into a wholly unified, presumably federal, nation. Unification could proceed without formal recognition of East Germany as a sovereign state by West Germany.

The Soviet plan for the reunification of Germany was outlined in the communiqué issued after the Bucharest Conference. The plan can be characterized only as vague and reflecting the lack of interest of the Soviet Union in the reunification of the two Germanies.

The long path toward reunification would have to begin with the "reduction of tensions and gradual rapprochement between two sovereign German states." [62] It is noteworthy that the sovereignty of the two German states is listed as a prerequisite for reunification. I already noted that recognition of East Germany is not feasible. Now one may ask what the reasons would be which would compel the Soviet Union to agree to reunification once the sovereignty of East Germany is secured. The most obvious one would be a desire to extend the socialist regime over the whole of Germany. Another, less probable, would be the development of isolationist tendencies within the Soviet Union resulting from internal difficulties, mostly of the economic type. Finally, this being a highly speculative reason, the Sino-Soviet dispute may reach such a level that Russia would have to seek accommodation with the United States. However, as the situation stands now, the United States would presumably seek concessions in Southeast Asia or the Middle East rather than in Central Europe.

The disarmament of both Germanies is the next prerequisite. It was analyzed above and found to be contrary to the interests of the United States and Western Europe, at least at the moment.

The plan mentions also the fact that the reunification of the Germanies is conditional upon disarmament in Europe.[63] This is difficult to understand. Obviously, the Soviet Union, a European country by any definition, would not like to bind itself to an all-European disarmament plan while the United States, which according to the Russians is not a European country, remains armed. Unilateral Western European disarmament is out of the question. Even if both Eastern Europe and Western Europe were to disarm, the situation would not change, since the balance of power would still move unfavorably

---

[62] "Bucharest Conference," p. 7.   [63] *Ibid.*

against Western Europe, with armed Russia, citing her non-European commitments, on the doorstep.

And even if Western Europe (and the United States) were to accede to the Russian disarmament plans, the reunification of the Germanies may never materialize. Reunification is conditional on the United German state being truly "democratic and peaceful," and the Soviets could use the withholding of their final approval indefinitely as a means of extorting further concessions from the U.S. or as a means of imposing a socialistic regime on the new German state. Solving the problems of arriving at definitions, procedures, and the like acceptable to both East and West would take years; and of course there are the conundrums of who is to do the bargaining and what weight is to be attached to the opinion of, say, France.

The Soviet attitude casts doubt on the realism of the Western proposals. Phillip Windsor's scheme seems to be the least objectionable to the Soviet Union, since it links the military and political aspects in a manner similar to that of the Russians.

The best approach to the whole problem seems therefore that of the arms-control agreements between the two alliances. A detailed policy of linking arms control with recognition and disarmament with reunification —even many years ahead, but within a specified time-table—would offer the best hopes of putting an end to the indissoluble problems of Germany and the cold war.[64]

Henry Kissinger's scheme would not find much approval in the Soviet Union. It admits the necessity of mutual troop withdrawals from East and West Germany, but the final outcome would be a demilitarized East Germany with NATO troops moved away from the Elbe line.[65] Similar ideas were expressed by Brzezinski, but his plan does not envisage moving NATO troops away from the GDR-FGR border.[66] He gives us a glimpse of the situation in which his plan may become acceptable to the Russians:

with the progressive evolution of the East German state, skillfully abetted by a conciliatory West, East Germany eventually may lose even its appeal as a buffer, and begin to resemble a Soviet Mozambique—a source of irritation to the East Europeans and of embarrassment to

[64] Phillip Windsor, "Berlin," in Evan Luard, ed., *The Cold War* (London, 1964), p. 138.

[65] Henry Kissinger, *The Troubled Partnership* (New York, 1965), p. 220.

[66] Brzezinski, pp. 27–28.

Moscow. Only then will the Kremlin consider the possibility of liquidating East Germany, and it is only the Kremlin, not the German communists, who can consider its liquidation.[67]

Rather than analyzing the possible solution to the German problem or pointing to the situation in which one or the other solution might be possible, I have tried to show the divergence of the Russian and U.S.–Western Europe goals. Russia's European policy is dynamic and forward looking. This may be due to the declining American interest in Europe, although President Nixon was trying to reverse this trend, or due to the dissipation, in the late 1960s, of dreams of Western European unification. Western Europe, faced with the possibility, however slight, of American disengagement from Europe, will seek accommodation with the Soviet Union. This accommodation is bound to be disadvantageous to Western Europeans, since they are unable at the moment to present a unified military and political front.

Moreover, the unstable relationship between Western Europe and the United States lends credibility to the Soviet inspired idea of "Europe for the Europeans," a "Monroe Doctrine for Europe." [68] "Spheres of influence" advocated by the Soviet Union in the late Forties, turned into a dynamic, evolutionary concept. The Russian sphere of influence may at some time be declared to stretch to the Atlantic.

This would leave the USSR with the problem of how to keep their new sphere of influence stable. There are two basic requirements for stability: first the Western European countries should be prevented from getting together in political and military matters. This could be achieved by systematically playing one country off against another. Second, the problem of German armaments has to be resolved. Since NATO, into which a German army can be integrated, is to be dissolved and since the U.S. is no longer to exercise direct influence over Germany, the natural solution is the total disarmament of Germany. Direct control of the Soviet Union cannot be substituted for American control. If this were possible, the Russians would not press the point of German disarmament. Finally, the disarmament of Germany at Russia's insistence may well earn Russia supporters in Western Europe.

This is the maximal plan the Soviet Union can hope for. The main

[67] *Ibid.*, p. 15.   [68] Hassner, Part II, p. 1.

objective of American foreign policy in Europe and Western Europe's policy toward Russia should be to prevent this plan from being realized by our default. I have shown that Russian policy is dynamic, and if it is to be controlled and influenced we must rely on methods appropriate for control and stabilization of dynamic processes. We should stop relying on stop-gap measures which treat every Russian move as a separate case—we should improve our "memory." We should develop a long-term policy which would concentrate on keeping the Soviet Union away from its optimal path in Europe. Basically this requires the evolution of the Atlantic alliance, perhaps along the lines recently proposed by Enthoven and Smith.[69]

[69] Enthoven and Smith.

Developmental Change in San Blas, Panama: A Comparative Community Study

PATRICIA L. REYNOLDS

Few places in Latin America have the social systems of communities continued to exhibit the flexibility and adaptiveness characteristic of the Cuna Indian villages in the Comarca de San Blas, Panama. While other and larger cultural groups have broken apart under the stress of contact with the world market, industrialization, and nation states, the San Blas Cuna have accepted their Panamanian citizenship and, with the support of the central national government, entered upon a controlled program of change and development without destruction of their cultural system. The strength and flexibility of San Blas social organization, the caliber of Cuna leadership, and an isolated physical domain have combined to foster a racial and tribal homogeneity, economic security, happiness, and hope that is unique among Latin American Indians. Therefore, this chain of coral-island communities along the eastern third of the Panamanian Caribbean coast affords a unique anthropological laboratory where may be studied the differential effects of penetration from the outside.

Strung out for 100 miles along the Continental shelf from Punta San Blas, 55 miles east of Colon, to the Colombian border are the 365 tiny islands constituting the Archipelago de San Blas, barely above sea level and within 5 miles of the mainland. The islands parallel a cliffed coast, along which extends a continuous range of axial mountains. The region of San Blas includes both the offshore islands and a strip of coastal lowlands and jungle. It is bounded to the north by the Caribbean Sea, to the south by the Bayano and Chucunaque Rivers, to the west by the Escribiano, and to the east by Port Sarsadi

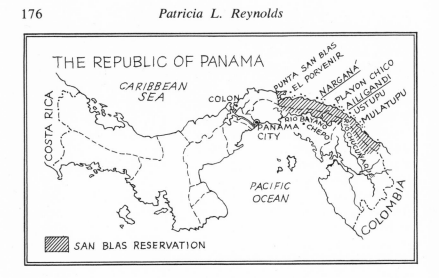

MAP 1

(see Map 1). The Cuna Indian Reservation occupies this approximately 700-square miles of humid tropical forest area and offshore coral islands. Today 19,242 [1] Cunas occupy this area as their own reservation, are granted by treaty with the Republic of Panama both local and tribal self-government, possess a chief (*cacique*) for the tribal area, and consider themselves essentially independent of the 9 provinces of Panama. By the Second Law of the National Assembly of the Republic of Panama of 1938, federal government authority was vested in an *Intendente,* or keeper of the Reservation, residing on Porvenir Island at the eastern end of the Comarca. The Intendente has the official legal title of governor and serves to inform the Cuna of changes in national law and instruct them in existing laws.

Of the 365 islets forming the Comarca de San Blas, only the 40 to 50 located near a mainland river are inhabited by the Cuna. While in 1900 all Cuna island-villages participated equally in the traditional Cuna way of life and there was very little difference among them except in size, today some villages are highly traditional and others are highly acculturated, as the Cuna villages of Ailigandi and Narganá

---

[1] According to the 1960 Census of the Republic of Panama, the population of San Blas is 19,242, or 6 percent of the total 1,067,766 population of the country.

manifest. Both Ailigandi and Narganá can be isolated together theoretically within the same ethnic group, both share common Cuna institutional and organization-and-structural characteristics, and both
are closed corporate communities. Yet Ailigandi represents a tradi-
tional-conservative community, while Narganá has undergone rapid
change.

Before exploring further the concept of developmental change
within San Blas as evidenced in the current cultural contrast between
Ailigandi and Narganá, the institutional and organizational structure
of each of the two communities must be delineated.

Both Ailigandi and Narganá are visible, identifiable communities,
in accord with Conrad Arensberg's definition: "the minimal group
capable of reenacting in the present and transmitting to the future the
cultural and institutional inventory" [2] of a human culture's distinctive
and historic tradition. Essentially a group of matrilocal extended
family households, each village functions as an organizational center
of Cuna Indian society. They are island villages whose community
boundary ends at the water's edge. Both family-held and commu-
nity-held farms are located on the adjacent mainland. The basis of
the subsistence economy is the plantain; the basis of the cash economy is coconut cropping. Opportunities for diversification of agriculture in both communities are limited by the absence of roads con-
necting the region with the cities of Panama.

Ailigandi is located 100 miles east of Colon. With an area of 2
city blocks, or twice the size of Narganá, Ailigandi is crowded to the
tidemark with 200 huts and 1,800 residents with an average, then,
of 9 persons to a dwelling unit. All Ailigandi dwelling units consist
of 2 traditional adjacent structures of cane walls and thatched roof,
the larger one (*nega*) for sleeping, entertaining, and storage, the
smaller (*sokaka*) for cooking. The physical layout of the community
is essentially one large cluster of huts separated by narrow alleys with
two main streets paralleling the windward and leeward edges of the island. Huts are well constructed, large, and roomy. There are several
house-construction *sociedades,* or cooperatives, of community members on the island. While Ailigandi has no central plaza, the Baptist
Mission Hospital, public elementary school, Cuna-owned-and-man-
aged Hotel Palmera, and several stores (*tiendas*)—all imposing concrete structures—are grouped in the southeast corner of the island

[2] Conrad Arensberg, "The Community as Object and Sample," *American
Anthropologist,* LXIII (1961), 253.

and form its commercial core (see Map 2). In contrast to Narganá, the community congress hall is cane and thatch, there is no Catholic Church, and community sociedades have been formed for the joint ownership and operation of two motor launches that carry passengers and supplies to and from Colon fortnightly at a slight profit for the village treasury. The Ailigandi airplane-landing strip and concrete waiting-shed are located on the mainland, ½ mile and a three-minute motorized-*cayuca* ride away. Following suit with Narganá, in 1966 Ailigandi buried their respected Chief Iglesias beside the airstrip in honor of his foresight and noble Cuna ideals. Community members, however, are buried in their hammocks in the mainland hilltop burial ground. Though the Ailigandi hospital generator does supply a feeble electric current for the hospital, hotel, and few nearby stores a few hours each night, there are no street lights, and none of the cane dwelling units has reliable electricity. Public facilities include the well-equipped and well-staffed Baptist Hospital with an American doctor in charge, a federal post office, and a public elementary school funded and staffed by the national government.

Narganá, in contrast, an island village of 600 inhabitants, is located 85 miles east of Colon, one third of the distance down the Comarca toward Colombia (see Map 1). The community was con-

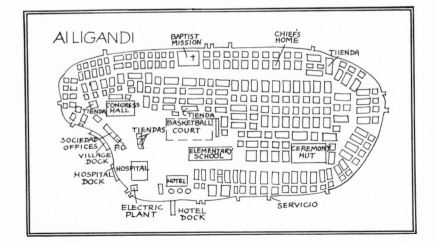

MAP 2

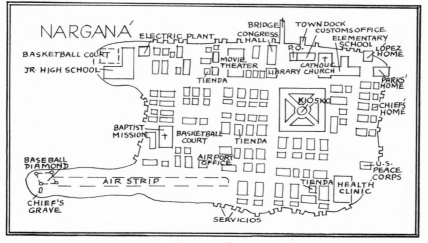

MAP 3

structed according to the typically Spanish rectangular plan with houses arranged on streets radiating out from a central plaza, or village square, on which is located the principal church (Catholic) and all the administrative buildings (the village town-meeting congress hall, library, post office, and "customs" office). In the center of the plaza is the most important commercial house, the community-owned-and-managed *kiosko* store-restaurant, where readymade rice, soup, and other food, as well as packaged and canned supplies, can be bought and the profits from which are contributed to the Narganá maternity ward and health clinic (see Map 3). Constructed on posts driven along the island edge are *servicio* outhouses, a structure not so commonly found on Ailigandi or the other traditional islands. With the exception of 4 cinder-block houses and 1 wooden house, all Narganá dwellings are the traditional 1-story cane and thatch structures with sand floors, no windows and 2 doors. Because the island no longer has a house-construction sociedad of local men and families in need of a new home must hire a sociedad from a neighboring island for a $150–$300 fee, Narganá houses are smaller, older, and shabbier than houses on less acculturated islands. Plastic *capotes,* patching holes in a roof, for instance, are much more frequently seen in Narganá than in Ailigandi. In 1949 Narganá was the first Cuna community to construct an airport and runway, and today it is the only one with its airstrip on the island itself. Progressive Narganá chiefs are buried in a special honorary cemetery at the tip of the airstrip; the village burial ground is located 3 miles upriver on the adjacent mainland, according to traditional Cuna practice, but gravesites are marked with whitewashed cement tombstones rather than the traditional Cuna dirt mounds and thatched huts, and the dead are buried in wooden caskets rather than in their personal hammock. Narganá is the most progressive Cuna community, also, in its electric-light facilities and its modern-style buildings on concrete posts—novelties none of which were present when anthropologist Henry Wassen made his first trip to Narganá in 1935.[3] In 1944 the Diesel generator was installed, and the small electric plant is run by a town-appointed Cuna. Today the village streets, open spaces, and the footbridge to the neighbor island of Corazón de Jesús, as well as most of the Narganá houses and buildings, have electric light between 6:00 and 11:00 P.M. Consequently, movie-going is a favorite weekend activity, and ironing with electric irons is an evening pastime for Narganá residents. Also, at the death of a community member, the light plant is left on all night for 3 nights in honor of the deceased and at the expense of the community treasury. Modern facilities on Narganá include a federally supported library, a federal post office, a government health clinic with Latin doctor, a movie theater, parochial (Catholic) elementary school, and the federally supported and only junior high school in the Comarca, *Primer Ciclo Esteben Oller*. Such facilities substantiate Henry Wassen's more recent statement that "It is quite obvious that Narganá is the leading community in respect to the introduction of modern elements among the San Blas Cuna." [4]

Though different in physical layout, the communities of Ailigandi and Narganá have similar village social and civic organization, in accord with Article 6 of the Sixteenth Law of the Republic of Panama of 1953. Both are politically organized through their own town meeting, which is conducted by the village first, second, and third chiefs and their town council, and in which all male community-members participate. In the town meetings common problems are discussed and decisions reached by consensus. Whereas in both communities village leadership is in the hands of a group of older men, in Aili-

[3] Henry Wassen, "Contributions to Cuna Ethnography," *Etnologiska Studier*, No. 16 (Gothenburg, Sweden, 1949), p. 4.

[4] *Ibid.* p. 16.

gandi these men achieve their positions of authority in the traditional way through mastery of Cuna religious and historical myths of the oral tradition, while in Narganá, since no community members qualify as religious specialists, the office of chief has been made elective, with a four-year term of office and universal adult suffrage. Also, while Ailigandi still holds periodic singing meetings during which the "singing chief" passes on the Cuna tradition and lore by chanting to community women and children, Narganá never holds singing meetings, and the Narganá town meeting is completely secularized.

It has been through these firm lines of authority and highly refined societal organization, on both the tribal and community levels, that Ailigandi and Narganá separately have entered upon a controlled program of change and development without destruction of their cultural system, though, as we shall see, the erosion of Cuna culture has been far more extensive and severe in Narganá. The functional demands placed on the community system in both these, as well as all San Blas, villages are very great: the community member asks from his system a modicum of personal, economic, political, religious, social, and emotional security and guidance. The community town meeting, or *congreso,* in response, exhorts the individual to follow the ideal patterns of behavior as laid down in Cuna myths and legends, makes decisions of policy in dealing with other islands and with the outside world, assigns cooperative village tasks, and, occasionally, settles disputes or controls transgressors where the household head is unable to act. The tribe is the institutional framework for organizing most interpersonal relations within each village; the daily town meeting is the adaptive mechanism through which such relations are directed and any developmental change is engineered.

The wedges for social change in both Ailigandi and Narganá have been numerous. Due to the relatively isolated geographic position of the islands, "cultural brokers" [5] have been of primary importance in linking the Cuna to the nationally and internationally oriented institutions and subcultures. During the past four centuries all Cuna communities have been in contact at different times with escaped Negro slaves, English pirates, French Huguenots, Scottish colonists, United States citizens, Panamanians, and Colombian traders. The Cunas consider their civilization decidedly preferable to that of the white or black man and have an almost fanatical zeal for keeping their blood

---

[5] Eric Wolf, "Types of Latin American Peasantry," *American Anthropologist,* LVIII (1956), 452–71.

lines pure. Until recently, women were prohibited to leave the islands unaccompanied by a Cuna man, very strict endogamy prevailed within each island, and all who visit the islands without permission of the chief are still required to leave before sundown by penalty of the law. Thus, in spite of their many and varied cultural contacts, the Cunas have retained a high degree of racial purity and cultural individuality and remain primarily dependent upon local natural resources for food and raw materials for construction and home crafts.

Although Cuna ethnocentrism has prevailed,

it has not been a deterrent to extensive cultural changes. Rather it serves as the starting point of the Cuna scale of rating other groups, for they place themselves first, Americans and English second, Spaniards and Panamanians third, and Negroes last.[6]

The prestige rating given to non-Cuna groups has strongly influenced the amount and nature of borrowings from those groups. Likewise, a number of covert cultural and social elements in community life of both Narganá and Ailigandi, such as race prejudices, moral code, and sex attitudes, as well as overt elements of functioning democracy and English rather than Spanish surnames, "have a greater correspondence to British and American culture than to Spanish-Panamanian." [7] Miss Annie Coope, the Baptist missionary who visited the islands in the early 1900s and was responsible for the Baptist high school education of 10 Cuna lads in the United States, is still today a person most Cuna remember with respect and talk of often. Federice Filos, present chief of Narganá, and Peter Miller, present pastor of the Ailigandi Baptist Mission, were two of the young men educated under Miss Coope's sponsorship: they returned to their island communities with outside experience, religious training, and educational knowledge and, as leaders, have functioned in their communities as brokers of the Baptist faith, American democracy, and an international world view.

Furthermore, as national institutions have penetrated Narganá and Ailigandi, they also have brought to both communities cultural brokers from the outside: Spanish-American Panamanian teachers, Panamanian and American health officers, United States Peace Corps personnel, American and Spanish Protestant and Catholic missionar-

[6] David Bond Stout, *San Blas Cuna Acculturation: an Introduction* (New York, 1947), p. 58.

[7] *Ibid.*, p. 109.

ies, and Panamanian politicians. To the degree that such outsiders equate becoming "civilized" with becoming "less Cuna," however, their very presence in the community is on a precarious balance. That is, while in general all San Blas communities are homogeneous internally, in that only people of Cuna race and culture identify with the community, the institutionalized resident stranger has become a feature of Cuna community life. Traditionally no non-Cunas have been granted permanent residence in Cuna communities, but the Narganá congreso has permitted 2 Panamanian *mestizo* families to take up permanent residence in the community: the Parks family occupy a concrete home and service the village with a well-stocked tienda and goods from Milton Parks's traveling-merchant launch; the Lópezes live in a wooden house, and Trinidad López works as secretary to the principal of the junior high school and as an active member of the Narganá town council. In Ailigandi, in contrast, no non-Cuna are permanent community members.

Moreover, the Catholic Church has made firm inroads into Narganá, while the community of Ailigandi forbids any Catholic even to sleep overnight on their island, by penalty of the law. In Narganá the Spanish *padre*, Padre Jesús, and 6 Spanish *madres* have been "new cultural brokers" since the beginning of the century, "working generally for change" [8] and teaching the Spanish language and Panamanian national cultural forms in the well-attended elementary school. The 5 mestizo Panamanian *profesores* in the junior high school on Narganá have functioned in a similar role. In contrast, education in Ailigandi is conducted by Cuna teachers only, though they are essentially "native son cultural brokers . . . fully aware of the traditional values and of the local social system" yet having "lived in and learned something of the larger [Panamanian] society and . . . accepted the values of the outside world." [9] Padre Davis, the first and only Cuna priest, and currently a junior high school English professor, functions on Narganá in this role of a "native son cultural broker."

The number of Cunas who have returned to Ailigandi and Narganá in this manner after already consciously becoming a part of the larger Panamanian or American society substantiates the proposition that even Cunas most favorably inclined toward social change still tie

[8] Charles Wagley, *The Latin American Tradition* (New York, 1968), p. 152.
[9] *Ibid.*

their identity to their tribe. As Cunas, their existence is dependent upon the preservation, in some sort of identified wholeness, of the small communities which they have built. Like the community chief, the native son cultural broker has a role that curiously combines that of the "traditional broker," as an influence for continuity of the Cuna way of life, with that of the "new broker," relating influences from the larger outside Spanish-American and North American societies to local community and tribal life. Developmental change here is the means to a traditional goal of preserving tribal homogeneity, integrity, and national respect.

While the wall of isolation the Cunas built around themselves has cracked just enough to let a few in, recently increased mobility and communication with the world outside have narrowed significantly the breach in isolation of the tribe and have been important wedges for change in both Ailigandi and Nargana. While fifty years ago the Colombian coconut boat was their chief contact with the world beyond San Blas, today there are two-way radios to the Canal Zone on both islands, mail and newspapers arrive regularly on the early morning planes, and the daily flights into Panama City are well enough within Cuna budgets that they are very popular for shopping trips or even vacations and visiting one's relatives in the nation's capital. Furthermore, the airstrips have served as open invitations to transient American dentists, Canal Zone military pilots, flying meat-and-dairy-product merchants, lobster purchasers, and frequent tourists who, as Nargana and Ailigandi community members become more continually exposed to them, are driving the wedge for social change still further into Cuna life. Thus one justifiably can predict, with Northwestern University anthropologist, Regina Holloman, that "The most likely source of future development in San Blas is tourism," [10] while Cuna urbanites who fly back to Ailigandi and Nargana increasingly will offer to the community congresos modern urban values and practices to be juxtaposed on traditional Cuna community life.

However, the history of San Blas modernization in this century has not been one solely of gradual, progressive change. Because of the dominant role of the town meeting, individual cultural brokers have had significant impact on the communities, as David Stout recognizes: "The personality of one individual may be a decisive factor

[10] Regina Holloman, "Acculturation and the Cuna," *Field Museum of Natural History Bulletin*, XL (July, 1969), 5.

in the amount of changes or the course that they take." [11] As a striking example of this fact, Narganá's present status as the most acculturated Cuna community is due wholly to the initial acts of one community member, Chief Charlie Robinson, who, in inviting a missionary to his island in 1907, set off a series of changes more numerous and far-reaching than on any other island. He was able to do this because of both the high value Cuna culture places on esoteric knowledge of any sort and his chiefly authority: he had been elected chief because of his store of knowledge of, and experience in, the outside world gained while a sailor on American and English ships for many years. Stout alleges that "He acted as he did because he was in reality a marginal person, more habituated to Western culture than to his own, and wanted to 'civilize' the island." [12] Therefore, in 1915–25 when the Panamanian government enforced an Indian policy that aimed at economic incorporation of the Indian regions within the national system and rapid acculturation of the various tribal populations, Narganá became the central station for Panamanian National Guardsmen in San Blas, cooperated with the government, and doffed the Cuna costume and nose ring at the Guard's request and Robinson's exhortation. Ailigandi and the other San Blas villages became increasingly hostile as land alienation proceeded and abuses by the guardsmen increased, and in 1925 a large group of islands successfully revolted, massacring or routing all of the National Guard in the region and restoring San Blas's political autonomy and territorial integrity.

These years from 1925 to 1930 were decisive in establishing the direction which San Blas modernization would take over the next generations. Since 1925 Narganá has undergone rapid change and acculturation while Ailigandi has remained a traditional and conservative Cuna community.

The principal results of acculturation in Narganá evident in the present situation, briefly, have been: increased conflict between competitive techniques and cooperative patterns; decreased interest in subsistence agriculture and substitution of foods bought at stores for foods once grown by every family; a growing disintegration of the extended family organization into its component conjugal units; the growth of national political party factions and an increasing dependence on the external national government, especially for pay checks

[11] David Bond Stout, "San Blas Cuna Acculturation," *Social Forces,* XXI (October, 1942–May, 1943), 89.
[12] *Ibid.*

and protection of property; a spreading substitution of school education for training in the indigenous occupations, specialties and skills;
a growing loss of interest in Cuna ceremonial details (e.g., the *Inna*
ceremony) and heightening interest in gala national holiday fiestas; a
growing number of men who are at ease in the cities and in their
dealings with whites, and the beginnings of this phenomenon among
women; a rapidly increasing number of individuals, mostly males,
who are frustrated and maladjusted because of their marginality or
incomplete participation in white and Cuna cultures. In his suggested
folk-urban transition, Robert Redfield warns of this "disorganization
of the culture, secularization and individualization" [13] that accompany the impact of modernity upon folk culture.

More specifically, the Inna, the most important of traditional Cuna
ceremonials held in connection with female puberty, and traditional
dances enacting Cuna myth and lore with flutes and rattles much in
the style of our American square dance, are no longer engaged in
Narganá. Rather, patron saints' days and Panamanian national holi-
days are celebrated in all-night fiestas with Panamanian and Colombian music, stereo phonographs, a local community *reina,* new shiny
dresses, starched white shirts, hair styling, perfume, romance, and the
donning of shoes for dancing the *cumbia* and *pata-pata* in the cement
congress hall. Stout notices that

Phonographs, which are most common at Carti and Narganá, are played
for amusement but also serve as a display item. They have had a noticeable effect on the indigenous instrumental music, for not nearly so many
young men know how to play the pan-pipes and flagelots as formerly;
these instruments are rarely heard.[14]

Moreover, Narganá community members have public entertainment
not found in Ailigandi, including weekend movies, school plays,
queen coronations, and school graduation exercises. Such loss of traditional dances and emergence of public entertainment is indicative
of the encroachment of civilization, Redfield maintains:

In the precivilized society the dramatic and lyric arts are inseparable
from the religious or from the mythic content of the local culture, and
secular professional entertainment is unknown.[15]

[13] Wagley, *The Latin American Tradition,* p. 113.

[14] Stout, *San Blas Cuna Acculturation: an Introduction,* p. 72.

[15] Robert Redfield, *The Primitive World and Its Transformation* (New
York, 1953), p. 35. Used with the permission of Cornell University Press.

Also, while Narganá community members are not as conscious of social ranking as Latin Americans are, Narganá, in contrast to Ailigandi, has developed social strata, "whose principal criterion is wealth but which are also differentiated by their degree of adherence to ideal behavioral patterns."[16] School teachers, priests, nuns and pastors form the top strata; members of the community civic hierarchy (chiefs, town-council members) and individuals receiving national government paychecks form the second strata; institutionalized nonresident strangers (U. S. Peace Corps Volunteer, non-Cuna doctor) form the third strata; and the general community members constitute the large lower strata in Narganá. In Ailigandi the conscious distinction made between such strata is very slight: members of the civic and religious hierarchy and teachers are respected above other community members, yet they engage in all the normal traditional daily tasks and chores of Cuna life like anyone else without feeling such activity to be degrading at all. Specific evidence of traces of social class in Narganá is the Morris household, where a Cuna babysitter-maid is hired while Sr. Morris teaches during the day in the junior high school and Sra. Morris works in the community health clinic, both receiving a government paycheck from Panama at the end of the month.

In Ailigandi behavioral patterns reflecting all the major values and attitudes in traditional Cuna culture are evidenced, such as prudish modesty concerning all sex matters, modesty concerning one's own actions and achievements, status achievement through industriousness, learning and experience, hospitality, generosity, and consideration for others. In Narganá, on the other hand, all these patterns have been modified, and new institutions have emerged, such as romance learned from the movies, emphasis on strong odors and sweet fragrances, cleanliness of person, individual freedom of movement, a general "property sense," and status achieved through national political consciousness. Certain of these patterns, of course, are contradictory and reflect divergencies and strains within Narganá community life. For instance, while cooperation is a constantly recurring feature in the labor of San Blas communities—since every man in a village is liable for helping in housebuilding, for contributing food and fuel to ceremonies, for assisting his relatives in agriculture, and for giving his share of work or money to village enterprises—conversely, there

---

[16] Stout, *San Blas Cuna Acculturation: an Introduction*, p. 108.

are relatively few techniques for channeling wealth toward individuals at the expense of others, entrepreneurs are limited to a few storekeepers, and property inheritance extends to all children. As a result, Narganá men energetically seek out Panamanian government extension jobs, preferring to sit idly as *botellas* in their government post and wait for the monthly paycheck rather than "get their hands dirty" or lower themselves to planting rice, pineapple, and yuca on their family's mainland property, farming the coconut *finca,* or fishing; they choose to "cooperate" by paying the community monetary fine for not participating in town workdays. The result has been a startling deficiency of locally grown fresh food on Narganá, a noticeable inferiority in the quality of house construction due to lack of labor, and a decline in the intensity and frequency with which dyadic contracts are reinforced by exchange of food. (In Ailigandi, for instance, every visitor always is served a beverage upon entering a home, while in Narganá this custom is not always followed.) These "modern" Narganá Cuna, adopting the Spanish-American's characteristic reluctance to make a living from farming and reliance on outside forces and fate rather than initiative, manifest a distinctive shift in the man-land attitude from one of vigorous and direct involvement to a "let George do it" laziness: they let the other community members farm and fish while they buy canned Vienna sausage and rice imported from Colombia at the half-empty town tienda. Margaret Mead notes the regularity with which "most people who change from a life of highly traditional handicraft to one of dependence on the purchase of European-manufactured objects become slum dwellers." [17] Thus, was the Cuna social organization adaptive mechanism not so flexible and adequate, as delineated below, such fragmented patterns of change here described could be seen as portentous.

In addition to the above-delineated changes in community activities ushered in to Narganá through acculturation, since the National Guard's equating "civilization" with becoming "less Cuna" in the 1920s, Narganá also has experienced a general trend of deculturation, in the sense that the community has lost a number of religious and aesthetic complexes of an essentially Cuna character with a resulting convergence toward the Spanish-American Panamanian pattern. Most vividly, this deculturation is manifested in dress: Narganá

[17] Margaret Mead, *New Lives For Old* (New York, 1957), p. 448.

women's dresses of cheap cotton peddled by Colombian traders, homemade on sewing machines, fading quickly in the tropical sun, and lasting only about four months contrast sharply with Ailigandi women's traditional, colorful, individually designed and hand stitched *mola* blouses, *saboret* blue and green wraparound skirts of cloth imported to Colon from England, and bright orange and yellow *wini* bead wrist and ankle bands. The deculturation is manifested also in tribal crafts: ancient ornamentation (gold jewelry, beadwork) and featherwork have disappeared in Narganá, and the highly sophisticated and uniquely Cuna art of sewing the reverse-appliqué *mola* blouses on which Cuna myth is depicted has been lost almost completely there. The National Guard's literally "chopping out" these Cuna cultural elements from Narganá life in the 1920s dealt a monolithic blow to the religious and aesthetic complexes of Cuna culture on Narganá.

The general outcome of this rapid deletion "has been adaptation, in contrast to assimilation or reaction," Stout perceptively states.[18] The total Narganá culture is a mosaic of aboriginal, foreign, and indigenously developed traits, complexes, and patterns, among which there is a considerable degree of adjustment. Stout describes this phenomenon as a

diffusion on a rather large scale between cultures immediately involved; its logical conclusion is assimilation, though in actuality the latter state is not always reached but instead the societies involved arrive at a point of adjustment and thereafter retain their cultural uniqueness.[19]

Narganá has reached this "point of adjustment." There is today a curious, sometimes comic and surrealistic, sometimes sad, juxtaposition of the modern urban values and practices on Cuna traditional life: the teen-ager with "mod" sunglasses bathes in vines-and-water Indian medicine; the khaki shirt of the funeral *nele,* chanting before corpse and cacao brazier, has U. S. CANAL ZONE stamped in black stencil letters across the back. What change that has occurred, then, has been of fragmented patterns.

Listed briefly, the differences in cultural elements of the two communities today are: Ailigandi's monolingualism vs. Narganá's bilingualism and frequent trilingualism; Ailigandi's retention of distinctive costume vs. Narganá's Western dress; Ailigandi's variety of

[18] Stout, *San Blas Cuna Acculturation: an Introduction,* p. 107.
[19] *Ibid.,* p. 87.

fresh food crops vs. Narganá's decreasing interest in agriculture; Ailigandi's cultural stability and conservatism vs. Narganá's fragmented progressivism; Ailigandi's intentional cultural isolation vs. Narganá's lesser insulation and greater loss of individuals to Spanish-American Panamanian low- and middle-urban classes.

Such contrasts substantiate the proposition that there is a fundamental disparity in culture content of the two communities. However, Narganá, despite its deletion of many fundamental Cuna cultural elements, has been able successfully to retain the essence and major portion of the common Cuna culture that it always has shared with Ailigandi and the other San Blas communities, involving a large body of cultural traits (e.g., folk beliefs, superstitions), common structuring of these traits into behavioral and value patterns (e.g., elaborate patterns of complementary reciprocity in dyadic contracts), as well as a common specific social and economic relationship with the outside world (e.g., marginal to the world market for coconuts and therefore subject to international price fluctuations).

More specifically, Narganá residents, in contrast to those of Ailigandi, do share with mestizo Panamanians certain important attitudes, values and ideals, or "ideal patterns" [20] of behavior: hypocrisy and saying "yes" when they mean "no"; the double-standard relation between males and females; a separate male and female ethos; the *compadrazco* system; national fashions, values and aspirations, such as "mod" clothes, literacy as an aid in social and economic mobility, and desire to obtain a job with monetary income. However, Narganá community members value manners less than Latins do, are not so sensitive to "pride" or "loss of face," consider cooperation and industriousness as major behavioral values, and hold modesty as an essential aspect of the ideal personality. Furthermore, these distinctively Cuna values are promulgated and reinforced through the town meeting: cooperation among members of the community, for example, is maintained in the usual Cuna manner of invoking principles of reciprocity, ridicule, and guilt.

That is, because of having retained the uniquely Cuna adaptive mechanism of the town meeting, Narganá, despite significant acculturation and partial deculturation, still remains within the San Blas Cuna ethnic group. While its traditional religion has been highly syncretistic with the Baptist and Catholic, it has retained, along with

[20] Eric Wolf, *Peasants* (Englewood Cliffs, N.J., 1966), p. 76.

Ailigandi and the other San Blas communities, a civil hierarchy that is distinct from the Spanish-American Panamanian form and a community membership that is racially pure and culturally distinctive.

The alarming erosion of Cuna culture in Narganá, in comparison with Ailigandi and the other traditional island-communities, is portentous evidence of what will happen to Cuna communities if and when the relationship between the Cuna and their chiefs, which exists through the town-meeting system and has served them so well as an adaptive mechanism for social change, is broken, as it partially was in Narganá during the 1915–25 *Guardia Nacional* oppressive occupation.

In the breathing space created by the success of the 1925 revolt, the town meeting in Narganá again became the important institution for the community's social engineering and direction of change, in response to the exhortations of Nele Kantule, that "remarkable [Cuna] man who more than any other individual was responsible for the ideas and innovations which facilitated San Blas' modernization over the past generation." [21] Though Spanish-American culture had made ineradicable inroads into Narganá life-style, Cuna social organization and community structure proved resilient to Latin influence. Redfield asserts: "The primitive and precivilized communities are held together essentially by common understandings as to the ultimate nature and purpose of life." [22] It is through the town meeting that these "common understandings" are, and have been, transmitted to community members by the village chief. Through exhortations to the individual to follow ideal patterns of behavior as laid down in the myths and legends, making decisions of external relations policy, assignment of cooperative village tasks, and, occasionally, settlement of household disputes, the Cuna town meetings, in both Narganá and Ailigandi, have provided "effective and flexible cultural devices for handling problems arising from a continually changing social environment." [23]

It is because of this mechanism inherent in their community structure that the Cuna, uniquely among Latin American aboriginal groups, have been able to retain the racial purity and cultural identity of their tribe. Furthermore, "We are not used to looking for evidence of social engineering and directed change in preliterate societies." [24] The unusually high caliber of Cuna leadership coupled

[21] Holloman, p. 8.   [22] Redfield, p. 12.   [23] Holloman, p. 9.   [24] *Ibid.*

with the dominant role of the town meeting in community life constitute a recognizably unique and highly effective adaptive mechanism.
Cuna leaders are often illiterate, monolingual, and not acculturated,
though farsighted and the product of the excellent traditional oral
Cuna education system. Through the town meetings they convey to
community members their recognition of the fact that Cuna problems
in the early part of this century had their roots in the increasing de-
pendency of their people on outsiders for goods and services. The
leaders' solution does not take the form of a movement to eliminate
foreign cultural influences and return to some version of Cuna life in
the past, but instead they encourage the local town meetings to continue undertaking many secular activities within the community—
such as construction and maintenance of the community airstrip, re-
pair of the village docks, installation and regulation of a community
electric plant, construction of houses for cultural brokers such as a
Peace Corps Volunteer or Spanish-American doctor, or painting the
community tienda façade—and they exhort people of the village to
undertake the organization of many commercial activities, such as sociedades, or commercial cooperatives, so as to reduce dependence on
outsiders. They preach to their community members that Cuna political and economic independence in the future will depend upon the
ability of the Cuna population to master basic technical and literary
skills.

That is, to community leaders in both Narganá and Ailigandi
modernization is not a goal, as it had been for the National Guard
during their occupation in the 1920s, but a means to a traditional
goal, namely the continued preservation of the Cuna way of life. This
attitude is unique among primitive peoples, for, according to Redfield, in most primitive societies characteristically "the future is seen
as a reproduction of the immediate past." [25] Such realistic introspec-
tion and responsible foresight by Cuna leaders constitute a recognizably unique and remarkably effective mechanism for their grappling
productively with problems that accompany developmental change.

So long as San Blas remains recognized as a reservation for the
Cuna, any future change in Ailigandi and Narganá society will continue to be gradual and individual, and the viability of the tribe will
be maintained vigorously. The most ominous current threat to their
very existence is the proposed plan for a new sea-level trans-Isthmic

[25] Redfield, p. 120.

canal, which could deal a monolithic blow to the civic structures and adaptive mechanisms of every Cuna community, including Ailigandi and Narganá.

After fifty years, the present Panama Canal is too small. Of 30 possible routes for a new canal, 6 were selected for two-year aereal and ground reconnaissances: 1) the Tehuantepec Route, 2) the Nicaragua Route, 3) the present Canal Route, 4) the Bay of San Blas Route, 5) the Caledonia Bay Route, and 6) the Atrato River Route (see Map 4). While the Canal Zone Company will not reach a con-

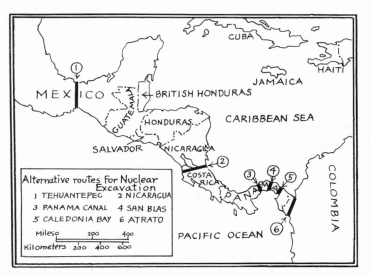

Map from David Howarth, *Panama: 400 Years of Dreams and Cruelty* (London, 1966), p. 276.

MAP 4

crete decision for several, perhaps five, years, David Howarth determines that "it seems most likely that the chosen route will be Caledonia Bay." [26] If this is the choice, the Cuna of all the San Blas communities will have to be relocated temporarily for an undetermined period of time during the blasting and settlement of radiation,

[26] David Howarth, *Panama: 400 Years of Dreams and Cruelty* (London, 1966), p. 283. Used with permission of McGraw-Hill Book Company.

the entire San Blas region will be altered physically, and unquestionably Cuna community structures will be influenced. More specifically, the island community of Mulatupu, which lies directly opposite the mouth of the planned canal in Caledonia Bay, will line an international anchorage full of ships. A canal through either the Caledonia Bay or Atrato River routes will require the establishment of a small town at the Caribbean end and completion of the axial Pan-American Highway from Chepo, Panama, to Colombia.

The view taken here is that such a highway would open up the entire region of eastern Panama to tourism and migration of Panamanian farmers, already discouraged with low yields from their exhausted tropical soils in central and western Panama. While presently only 1 percent of the land east of the canal is used agriculturally, this uninhabited jungle is rich in resources: the Darien Province is a "vast reservoir of only partially explored land suitable for agricultural expansion." [27] Furthermore, Darien jungle gold and mahogany resources, while quite considerable, remain as yet unexploited because of inaccessibility. This is the jungle of which the Cunas have only pierced the fringe and whose vicious cat animals and voracious growth already have halted completion of the Pan-American Highway several times before. But presently surveying crews are stationed throughout the Darien, and a wide path has been bulldozed away. With completion of the highway, inevitably, towns will spring up alongside, and deforestation, unless governmentally checked, will push back the jungle to, someday, San Blas. Basic infrastructures facilities of roads, ports, communications, and public power will be developed. Roads will extend to the coast, and Cunas will find unexpected accessibility to markets for buying and selling, while tourism to San Blas will increase. It is not unfair to predict that, with access to different raw materials, specialization will be induced and the Cunas will enter into the mainstream of a money economy where an individual may produce the commodity in which he has the comparative advantage.

Precisely what effect such drastic geographic and organizational alterations will have upon the community structures of Ailigandi and Narganá it is impossible, of course, to foresee. Assuming the Cuna were to return to their respective islands after a couple of years of temporary relocation elsewhere in Panama during the blasting, it is

---

[27] *U.S. Army Handbook for Panama* (Washington, D.C., 1965), p. 387.

justifiable to speculate that, with the opening up of the Darien jungle, Ailigandi and Narganá will mutate from closed corporate-type communities to open communities. Regina Holloman, noted Cuna anthropologist, substantiates this proposition with the assertion that "in the long run, a new Colon will grow opposite Mulatupu, and the Cuna at that end of the Comarca will be absorbed." [28] However, the reestablishment of Cuna island communities on the present model would depend ultimately upon whether the Cuna, during relocation outside of San Blas, were able to retain in some form their town meeting and tribal chieftains' congreso institutions, which have served them so effectively as mechanisms for adapting to various other types of change already. If this backbone of the community and tribal organizational structures breaks down, the racial purity and cultural vigor the Cunas have been able to maintain so far will be lost, as the Indians become absorbed into the encroaching Spanish-American Panamanian society.

Whether or not a sea-level canal is constructed near San Blas, one can predict with near certainty that "in the short run, San Blas will probably develop true towns (as contrasted to villages)." [29] As the growing Cuna population increases its pressure on the tiny islands, as it already is on Ailigandi, several of the village communities will become towns with distinct class stratification, functioning as service centers for the overflow of community members that move onto nearby islands in the surrounding areas. To some degree already Narganá is beginning to function as a town, a slight class stratification begins to be seen, as described above, and as residents of the adjacent island, Corazón de Jesús, and the nearby islands of Tigre and Rio Azúcar make frequent trips to Narganá to see a movie, attend a dance, sell lobster, or board a plane. In the near future Narganá will become a true town, as will Ailigandi and some of the other major villages, such as Carti-Sugtupu, Rio Cidra, San Ignacio de Tupile, and Ustupu.

In contemplating the future of Ailigandi and Narganá in light of the present disparity in their degree of acculturation, one can only agree with Erland Nordenskiold, the foremost Cuna anthropologist, that

The independent Cunas are at present time endeavoring to consolidate their position in every way. They are exceedingly anxious to be consid-

[28] Correspondence with this author dated December 16, 1969.   [29] *Ibid.*

ered a civilized people, and they take keen interest in other countries. . . . It is to be hoped that the tenacious struggle that the Cunas for more than four centuries have been putting up for their liberty will not have been in vain.[30]

Never having experienced Spanish Conquest domination, the Cuna are a vigorous, prosperous, happy and spirited tribe, not a downtrodden mass like most other Latin American aboriginal groups. Despite Wagley's affirmation that "Tribal subculture types will probably disappear well within the next hundred years," [31] one hopes that the rich Cuna culture, unique in twentieth-century Latin America, will not be exterminated through the diluting effects of acculturation. So long as San Blas remains a reservation for Cuna only, the essence of this cultural richness will be maintained vigorously by the Cunas themselves: as long as the Indians can retain control of the islands, they will resist major change, as William Stein's study proved of the Indian peasants in Hualcán, Peru.[32] But if Ailigandi or Narganá or any other San Blas community mutates from a closed-corporate to an open-community type—the town meeting ceasing to exercise jurisdiction over free disposal of land, ceasing to act as rallying point and symbol of collective unity, ceasing to define community boundaries through the political-religious system as a whole, easing its unwillingness to admit outsiders as competitors for land or as carriers of cultural alternatives—then, inevitably, Cuna culture will be lost, in accord with Wolfe's warning:

Persistence of "Indian" culture content in corporate communities had depended primarily on the structure of the community: where the structure collapses, traditional cultural forms quickly give way to new alternatives of outside derivation.[33]

Narganá is a vivid example of the relevance of this proposition to Cuna communities. With the National Guard's occupation in the 1920s, Narganá suffered the breakdown of the traditional Cuna educational system, even though it was able to retain the town meeting. The Cuna educational system has always been one of the most important institutions of Cuna society, whereby aspiring village leaders

---

[30] Erland Nordenskiold, *An Historical and Ethnological Survey of the Cuna Indians* (Gothenburg, Sweden, 1938), p. 7.

[31] Wagley, *The Latin American Tradition*, p. 116.

[32] William Stein, 1957:19.

[33] Wolf, "Types of Latin American Peasantry," p. 456.

study under Cuna savants to learn the traditional lore and myth that defines the Cuna ideal behavior which they, later through the town meeting, will exhort their community members to emulate. That is, half of the uniquely Cuna institutional adaptive mechanism broke down in Narganá: knowledge of Cuna lore is no longer a prerequisite for Narganá chiefs nor do Narganá lads aspiring to be community leaders ever study Cuna tradition under elder savants now. The result has been drastic to Cuna culture in Narganá, as delineated in length above. The only reason Narganá has been successful in retaining what essence of Cuna culture that still does exist within its community is because the other vitally important half of the adaptive mechanism, the town meeting, was never destroyed. Under the National Guard's occupation the traditional Cuna education system in Narganá withered, while the more resilient town meeting remained as a functioning element of Narganá community structure. In Ailigandi, of course, both parts of the institutional adaptive mechanism have remained strong, and the richness of Cuna culture consequently has not been diluted there.

This comparison has clear implications: only so long as Cuna communities are able to retain both their traditional education system, even if in modified form, and their town meeting will they be able effectively to maintain the viability of their tribe and flexibly to handle the problems arising from a continually changing social environment.[34]

[34] Readers interested in a further investigation of the subject of this article may wish to consult:

Adams, Richard. "The Cultural Components of Central America," *American Anthropologist,* LVIII (1956), 881–907.

Arensberg, Conrad H. "The Community Study Method," *American Journal of Sociology,* LIX (1954), 109–24.

Harrington, Richard. "San Blas Indians of Panama," *Canadian Geographic Journal,* LV, No. 1 (July, 1956), 14–23.

Keeler, Clyde E. *Secrets of the Cuna Earthmother.* New York, 1960.

Kelly, Joanne H. *Cuna.* New York, 1966.

Marino Flores, Anselmo. "Indian Population and Its Identification," in *Handbook of Middle-American Indians.* Austin, 1967. VI, 12–25.

Torres de Ianello, Reina. *La Mujer Cuna de Panama.* Mexico, 1957.

Wagley, Charles, and Marvin Harris. "A Typology of Latin American Subcultures," *American Anthropologist,* LVII (1955), 428–51.

Maintenance of the NPT in the 1970s: The Asian Dimension

DARIOUSH BAYANDOR

Former President Johnson once described the Treaty on the Non-Proliferation of Nuclear Weapons (NPT) as "the most important international agreement in the field of disarmament since the nuclear age began." [1] One can argue that the Johnson Administration had at the time (June, 1968) every reason to dramatize its achievements. This statement, nevertheless, can hardly be rated as an overestimation. For one thing, the Treaty brought a stabilizing effect to bear on the international situation at a time when it was faced with the threatening prospect of the emergence of a new chain of nuclear powers. By freezing the world-power configuration, the Treaty also provided the super powers with leverage to act on arms-control measures from a solid and safe starting point. This is not, however, to say that the problem of proliferation of nuclear weapons has, in any conclusive or irreversible manner, been disposed of by the coming into force of the NPT. A formidable task of implementing as well as consolidating the agreement still lies ahead.

To begin with, the achievement of a convincing degree of success in arms-limitation talks is essential for the viability of the NPT, whose operation will become the subject of close scrutiny by the review conference which will be convened less than five years from now. The task of the review conference will be to assure that the purposes (of the preambles and the provisions) of the Treaty are being realized. Article VI of the Treaty binds parties to "pursue negotiations in good faith on effective measures relating to cessation of the nuclear arms race at an early date and to nuclear disarmament."

---

[1] Speech before the Resumed Session of the Twenty-second Session of the United Nations General Assembly on June 12, 1968, document A/PV.1672.

The emphasis laid by a number of potential nuclear powers on the implementation of Article VI strongly suggests that this issue would be a focal point in the debate over the operation of the Treaty. Japan, for instance, has declared [2] that when it decides to ratify the Treaty as well as when it participates in the review of its operations, it will concern itself most vigorously *inter alia* with the developments in the field of arms control and nuclear disarmament. The Federal Republic of Germany, in the same vein, has emphasized its interest in the "effective implementation" of the provisions of Article VI, by calling the achievement of this goal a "natural supplement" to the Treaty. [3]

The present course of events, however, does not seem to be moving in that direction. Not only does the momentum of strategic arms-limitation talks seem to have been lost, but its outcome has increasingly become the subject of pessimistic prognostication. The decision of the Nixon Administration for an early deployment of Multiple Independently Targeted Re-entry Vehicles (MIRVS) and the inclination of the Soviet Union and the United States to go ahead with Anti-Ballistic Missiles (ABM) programs might already have stripped the strategic arms-limitation talks of their substance.

The extension of war into Cambodia is only the last in the series of blows dealt to the Strategic Arms Limitation Talks (SALT). Though the effects of this latter development cannot yet be determined, Kosygin's statement of May 5, 1970, suggests that it may affect the present round of talks in Vienna. If, nevertheless, some success is achieved by SALT, it still remains to be seen to what extent such agreement would strike the threshold powers as promising an eventual elimination of nuclear stockpiles.

A limited agreement that does not include major strategic-weapons systems might be viewed by non-nuclear states as a bilateral enterprise conforming only to the military and strategic needs and interests of the super powers and as such would fall short of their treaty expectations.

---

[2] "Statement of the Government of Japan on the occasion of the signing of the Treaty on the Non-Proliferation of Nuclear Weapons," February 3, 1970, released by the Permanent Mission of Japan to the United Nations.

[3] "Statement by the Government of the Federal Republic of Germany on signing the Treaty on the Non-Proliferation of Nuclear Weapons," Courtesy Translation released by the Office of the Permanent Observer of the Federal Republic of Germany to the United Nations.

The question of safeguard agreements envisaged in Article III of the NPT presents another major problem to the implementation and the maintenance of the Treaty. West Germany, for one, has made ratification of the Treaty dependent upon the satisfactory negotiation of a safeguard agreement between the Commission of Euratom and the International Atomic Energy Agency (IAEA).[4] Japan is equally concerned about industrial espionage and keeps a vigilant eye on the Euratom-IAEA negotiations to ensure that she will not be discriminated against with regard to safeguard procedures. Japan has already hinted that her decision to ratify the Treaty might be affected by the outcome of the negotiations.[5]

A more complex issue in the realm of implementation is the problem of peaceful application of nuclear explosions envisaged in Article V of the Treaty. Under this article, nuclear-weapon states undertake to cooperate to insure that potential benefits from any peaceful application of nuclear explosions will be made available through appropriate international machinery and under international supervision to non-nuclear parties to the Treaty. Once the technology of peaceful nuclear explosions becomes fully developed, non-nuclear weapon states will be eligible, pursuant to a special international agreement, to receive nuclear-explosive services through an international body. It appears to be agreed on all sides to entrust this task to IAEA.[6] Yet a glimpse of disagreement over modalities of international observation of peaceful explosions has already appeared on the horizon. United Nations resolution 2456 C (XXIII) of December 20, 1968 raised a controversy by implying, among other things, that peaceful explosions shall be put under "international control" rather than "international observation" prescribed in Article V of the Treaty.[7] Both the United States and the USSR refused to support the resolution. The issue has far-reaching implications. Supporters of the resolution implied that the procedure for the conduct of peaceful explosions should include safeguards against possible abuse of test results for military purposes. The issue will take on particular significance if a comprehensive test ban should eventually be negotiated. The follow-up resolution last year, however, toned down the contro-

[4] *Ibid.*   [5] "Statement of the Government of Japan."

[6] UN General Assembly resolution 2456 C (XXIII) of December 20, 1968, *UN General Assembly Official Records,* Twenty-third Session, Suppl. 18 (A/7218), p. 14.

[7] See UN document A/C.1/PV.1643, pp. 18–20 and 43–52.

versy by assigning the study of the "character of international observation" to the IAEA.[8]

The above observations indicate that, as suggested before, a formidable task of implementation confronts the NPT. Yet the real threat
to its workability lies in the likelihood of a chain reaction if a sixth
power should decide to develop nuclear weapons.

Maintenance of NPT therefore presents a twofold problem. On the
one hand, there is the problem of implementation, with an implied
threat of disintegration of the Treaty, should the fulfillment of its
provisions prove less than satisfactory to potential nuclear powers;
on the other hand, there is a looming threat that a sixth power may
break the ice by adopting a nuclear posture, thus setting in motion a
chain reaction which would lead to ultimate failure of the NPT.

To evaluate the Asian dimension of that threat, let us focus on the
attitude of three countries, one of which—Japan—has already
signed the Treaty (framing her understanding of its provisions in an
elaborate Declaration). The other two—India and Israel—have not
shown any inclination to forgo the nuclear option. If technical capability, political desirability, economic feasibility as well as security
contingencies might affect the decision of these states with regard to
the development of nuclear weapons, then an examination of these
factors should permit us to determine whether all these states may already have decided to follow a policy, latent in which is the development of such potential that could be converted, in short notice, to a
credible nuclear posture.

Israel

ORIENTATION OF NUCLEAR PROGRAMS

When Ben Gurion reassumed the post of Defense Minister in
1955, one of the goals he set for modernization of the army was to
expand the ministry's scientific and armament industries and develop
a nuclear capability for Israel in order to deter growing Arab military forces.[9] Peres Shimon, a close associate and disciple of Ben
Gurion, who was at the time Director General of the Defense Minis-

[8] UN General Assembly resolution 2605 B (XXIV) of December 16, 1969.

[9] Amos Perlmutter, *Military and Politics in Israel: Nation Building and
Role Expansion* (London, 1969), p. 92.

try and in charge of supply of arms and ammunition,[10] successfully negotiated an agreement with France for the building of a version of France's EL-3 experimental reactor at Dimona in the Negev. This was done in almost complete secrecy.[11] What is even more important is that the agreement envisaged no safeguards to assure peaceful use of the material produced.[12] The military orientation of Israel's nuclear activities is further suggested by the fact that nuclear research and development were initiated by the scientific branch of the army called *Hemed*. Under Shimon's direction this branch, and with it nuclear research and development, was later incorporated into the Ministry of Defense.

This is not, however, to say that peaceful application of nuclear energy was abandoned or was secondary in importance. A fact to be borne in mind is that in Israel science has always been closely linked to security.[13] In fact, the immense need for electric power (Israel does not have any traditional source of energy within its own territory) and an even greater demand for water supplies clearly justify greater effort in the field of reactor construction to meet the civil requirements of Israel's agriculture and industry. Yet, the government's official silence, matched by a patent reluctance to take steps to remove uncertainties about its nuclear programs suggest that if Israel has not in fact embarked upon production of nuclear weapons, she certainly had not been keen to dispel the doubts.

Ironically it was the Americans who first became suspicious of what was going on at Dimona. Beaton writes: "Repeated requests were made by American Embassy officials about what the facility was . . . and evasive contradictory replies were given." [14] At last Israel, most grudgingly,[15] yielded to American demands to make

[10] This was a parallel office to that of the Chief of Staff of the Army, under direct supervision of the minister, whose responsibility was "supplying and arming the military" (*ibid.*, p. 55). Peres guided the Ministry of Defense into the areas of applied military science and technology. Thus the ministry took over from the army the armament industry and aviation industry, etc. (*ibid.*, pp. 70, 74–75).

[11] Leonard Beaton, "Why Israel Does Not Need the Bomb," *The New Middle East*, April, 1969.

[12] George H. Quester, "Israel and the NPT," *Bulletin of Atomic Scientists*, June, 1969. See also Beaton, "Why Israel Does Not Need the Bomb."

[13] Perlmutter, pp. 74–75.

[14] Beaton, "Why Israel Does Not Need the Bomb."

[15] Quester writes in this respect "There has moreover been a general aver-

inspections at Dimona, but the suspicion of American officials, according to the report by the New York *Times* persisted even after inspections were carried out.[16]

CAPABILITY

The Israeli reactor at Dimona is a 25-thermal-megawatt experimental reactor capable of producing about 6 kilograms of plutonium a year. This is roughly enough to produce one bomb a year.[17] The reactor employs natural uranium. This fact lends further weight to the argument that the Dimona reactor was built with military rather than civilian considerations in mind. A light-water reactor that consumes enriched uranium would have made Israel dependent on source material from foreign countries. Uranium enrichment technology is extremely difficult and costly and, at any rate, beyond the present capacity of Israel. Natural uranium, however, can be extracted economically and in sufficient quantity for the Dimona reactor, from Dead Sea phosphates.[18] Israel thus seems to have acquired self-sufficiency in the supply of source material.[19] Another military advantage of a natural uranium-fueled reactor over a light-water reactor is its increased ratio of plutonium output.[20] The natural uranium reactor, moreover, diminishes the cost operation of a reactor whose production of plutonium is intended for weapons programs.[21]

Plutonium 239 is produced as a by-product of natural uranium

---

sion even to American inspections of the reactor at Dimona. American visits, when tolerated, are kept quiet, never to be dignified with the legal status of inspection."

[16] New York *Times,* March 14, 1965.

[17] Leonard Beaton, *Must the Bomb Spread* (Middlesex, England, 1966), p. 79.

[18] Beaton, "Why Israel Does Not Need the Bomb."

[19] According to the account given in 1966 by Beaton (*Must the Bomb Spread*), Israel had planned to increase its "production of uranium from the phosphates from ten tons to fifty tons a year." Even if this expansion is made halfway through, Dimona should have become entirely self-sufficient.

[20] Victor Gilinsky, "Military Potential," paper presented to the *Conference on Civil Nuclear Power and International Security,* p. 10. See also Beaton on "Military Implications of Contemporary Trends in Civilian Nuclear Power Programs," paper prepared for the same Conference.

[21] Technical explanation seems to be that a natural-fueled reactor need not be shut down for changing the fuel rods which ought to be frequently done in military programs to keep the admixture of isotope 240 with isotope 239 at a low level.

(U-238) in ordinary reactors. In order to create a fast chain reaction necessary for an explosion it needs to be reprocessed by chemical methods. There is no evidence that Israel has in fact an operational chemical separation plant; yet this somewhat negative conclusion needs to be supplemented by a few observations. To begin with, a chemical separation plant does not have to be a major facility. It is not a costly project requiring technological sophistication. Beaton observes:

there have been rumors about suggestive orders for equipment being placed in the Western world; and certainly it would be surprising if Israel tried to put together such a [chemical separation] plant without ordering much of the necessary equipment from others. . . . My own hunch, and it is only a hunch, is that . . . Israeli authorities have probably provided themselves with some separation capacity at a laboratory level.[22]

In his earlier work, *Must the Bomb Spread,* Beaton makes the point that "it might be possible to build a chemical separation plant secretly, especially if it was designed to handle only the quantities of plutonium which will be produced by Dimona."

One factor intrinsically relevant to an evaluation of the potential of states for production of the bomb is the method of production of plutonium. Gilinsky argues that "civilian plutonium is generally not suitable for simple, predictable, efficient weapons." [23] The basis of this assertion is that infrequent change of fuel rods of a reactor results in an increase in the isotope 240 content of plutonium which detracts from its military effectiveness. The bearing of this is that countries with scarce resources of uranium and, more important, with modest reprocessing and fuel fabrication capability, or lacking sophisticated measuring devices, might not be able to take advantage of plutonium produced from their reactors for military purposes since they cannot cope adequately with complications resulting from a disproportionate admixture of plutonium isotopes. This difficulty, however, *if at all real,*[24] is more relevant to countries operating light-water reactors that employ enriched uranium rather than natural uranium as does the Dimona reactor.

---

[22] Beaton, "Why Israel Does Not Need the Bomb."   [23] Gilinsky, p. 11.
[24] Beaton refutes this theory. Basing his argument on a study done by Arnold Kramish, formerly of the Rand Corporation, he concludes that "all plutonium must henceforth be assumed to be a potential explosive." *Must the Bomb Spread,* pp. 97–98.

Finally, Israel, unlike India, need not be concerned about the problem of "delivery systems." All target points in the neighboring Arab countries are within striking distance of Israeli Phantoms which are capable of delivering nuclear warheads.[25] The cost element, therefore, can be eliminated as an insurmountable factor in calculations related to the development of a nuclear-weapon system.

COMPULSIONS AND INHIBITIONS

The argument mostly articulated against the likelihood of an Israeli nuclear build-up has been the patent superiority of Israel in conventional warfare. If she decides to introduce nuclear weapons in the Middle East scenario, it would "in effect be changing the game when she had been winning under the old rules." [26] Beaton takes a similar line by arguing that "a build-up of nuclear weapons on both sides would remove Israeli superiority in major conventional war, which is the present basis for her security." [27] This argument, persuasive as it is, entails two rather equivocal assumptions. First, that the weapons, if developed, need to be tested. That is neither indispensable nor quite consistent with the occult nature of Israel's nuclear programs. The second presupposition, which is the corollary of the first, is that Israel's bombs would presumably elicit a similar response from Egypt. However, given the Soviet predilections for preservation of NPT the preferable choice, for both the Arabs and the Soviet Union, would be more likely a guarantee set up in line with NPT security arrangements, yet credible enough to deter and neutralize Israel's nuclear force. Arabs, anxious to involve the Soviet Union increasingly in the Middle East conflict, might demand a Soviet-controlled nuclear base in Egypt or Syria. The Soviet Union might welcome this occasion to consolidate its strategic hold in the area without risking a "catalytic" war with the United States (since its move would be justifiable in terms of NPT security arrangements).

If Israeli superiority in conventional war is not a compelling reason to deter it from making the bomb, inferences to the contrary may well be no more than speculative and illusionary. In fact if Israel does possess the bomb, the United States must certainly have been kept in the dark. President Nixon's acquiescence in the sale of 50 Phantom jets to Israel, which had been agreed upon during the John-

[25] Beaton, "Why Israel Does Not Need the Bomb."
[26] Quester, "Israel and the NPT."
[27] Beaton, "Why Israel Does Not Need the Bomb."

son Administration, is viewed by some observers such as Beaton as further evidence that American requirements on nuclear issues were met by Israel. In the same vein the relative silence maintained by the Arabs on this issue has been attributed to assurances they might have received from American sources.[28] Certainly the fear of American retaliation could well form a stumbling block in the making of the bomb by Israel if its concealment from American eyes proves impossible. Such a move, Quester observes,

> would shock and immobilize the American Jewish community and generally antagonize much other pro-Israeli opinion in America as well as in Britain and Europe. No one can definitively predict the U. S. Government reaction. If an American administration were at all anxious to disengage from commitments to Israel, opposition to nuclear weapon production might uniquely enable it to do so. If it conversely chose to remain responsible for peace in the Middle East, the United States might, nonetheless, decide that such nuclear activity requires severe retaliation, as with a freezing of American private monetary transfers to Israel.[29]

So long as Israel maintains the nuclear option, she certainly holds a bargaining asset that could help her to obtain qualities and quantities of weapons that would insure her conventional superiority vis-à-vis the Arabs. Though preservation of such an option is no doubt plausible and one that, with great probability, will continue in the foreseeable future, yet the possibility of a covert stockpiling of a few warheads that could escape the attention of American inspectors cannot entirely be overruled.

Long before anyone had any glimpse of active Soviet participation in the defense of Egypt, Quester had conceived a deterrent relationship between Israel's bomb and the specter of Soviet military involvement in the fighting in the Middle East. "It is plausible," he had contended, "that Israeli nuclear weapons would force the Russians to commit combat personnel to Syria and the UAR, along with a greater naval and air presence. It is also possible that fears of Israel going nuclear would deter the Russians from this much of a commitment." [30]

Such a fear, however, has not inhibited the Soviets from committing their pilots to flying missions in central Egypt. This move has

[28] Beaton, "Military Implications of Contemporary Trends in Civilian Nuclear Power Programs," p. 10.

[29] Quester, "Israel and the NPT."   [30] *Ibid.*

certainly enhanced Israel's bargaining position with regard to the purchase of 100 Skyhawks and 25 Phantoms. President Nixon has already announced that he will reconsider his decision on the sale of the plane in the light of new circumstances. Israel is reported to have asked President Nixon to warn the Soviets—either in public or privately—that the U.S. would act if the Russians intervened in the battles along the Suez Canal.[31] A dispatch from Jerusalem reported that "the Israelis are not sure that the U. S. will respond to their request at least in those terms *because they are not certain what the U. S. would do if the Russians become further involved.*"[32] U. S. reaction would probably await clarification of Soviet intentions. If, as is hoped, the Russians confine themselves to the defense of Central Egypt, the United States might not, in the face of Nasser's threat of curtailing U. S. oil interests in the Middle East,[33] take any provocative counteraction. This in turn might intensify Israel's sense of self-help from which a precipitate, though inexorably covert, build-up of a small nuclear arsenal cannot be excluded.

India

CAPABILITY

As early as 1965 an Indian representative to the First Committee of the UN General Assembly, quoting official statements, declared that "India had refrained from manufacturing nuclear weapons although it had had the capacity for quite some time."[34] He went on to say that India was the only country among non-nuclear weapon states that possessed such capacity. The fact was that India had just finished a chemical separation plant at the Bhabha Atomic Research Centre (BARC) in Trombay near Bombay with a capacity of processing 30 tons of irradiated uranium. When the government's mo-

[31] New York *Times,* May 10, 1970.

[32] *Ibid.,* May 8, 1970. Italics added.

[33] In a speech delivered on May 2, 1970. President Nasser warned that any move by the U. S. to assure "military superiority for Israel would damage U. S. interests in the Arab world." See *ibid.,* May 3, 1970. To substantiate his threat Nasser dispatched emissaries to Arab capitals to ensure a harmonized Arab reaction to a possible U. S. response to the Soviet move. See *ibid.,* May 7, 1970.

[34] Statement by Mr. Trivedi, *UN Official Records of the First Committee,* Twentieth Session, 1363d meeting, October 26, 1965.

tives for the establishment of such a facility were questioned by Pakistan,[35] the Indian representative gave this explanation:

With regard to the reasons why India had a chemical separation plant, it should be noted that atomic energy was today the most important thing for developing nations in connexion with their energy resources, particularly for large countries where normal fuel, such as coal, was not available. It was for that reason that India had a programme of electricity production by means of atomic reactors. Those reactors required plutonium, and in order to treat the deposits it had, India needed a chemical separation plant. The electricity produced in that way was cheaper than conventional electricity.

The explanation is somewhat blurred. It is hardly convincing that India, with abundance of source material, and nuclear facilities primarily based on natural uranium-fueled reactors, finds it necessary to process plutonium for power reactors.

It is, moreover, doubtful whether production of electrical power by nuclear energy for a country like India, whose total output of electricity at the time was in the neighborhood of 7,000 megawatts, would be economical. Beaton regards the establishment of nuclear power stations for countries such as Australia or India an "immense extravagance." [36] A possible explanation for production of plutonium, that might have been implicit in the latter part of the Indian representative's statement, might be its use in thorium-fueled reactors, the technology of which requires treatment of thorium with plutonium for conversion into uranium 233 that fissions. India, with the largest deposits of thorium (about 500,000 tons) has taken a keen interest in thorium technology.[37]

If one were to believe, however, the official explanation given in respect of the chemical separation plant, the least to say about it is that the decision had been squarely a premature one.[38]

[35] Statement by Mr. Shahi, *ibid.,* October 29, 1965.
[36] Beaton, *Must the Bomb Spread,* p. 96.
[37] A 10-megawatt experimental thorium-plutonium reactor at the Kalpakkam Nuclear Power Station has been planned, see S. K. Ghasmala, "Atom in India," *Science News,* Vol. XXIV (August 10, 1968). A chemical separation plant for the resulting uranium 233 had also been considered, see Beaton, *Must the Bomb Spread,* p. 75.
[38] Conclusion drawn on the basis of a technical question put to Professor Leon Lidofsky, Professor of Nuclear Science and Engineering, Columbia University.

The first agreement between India and Canada under the Colombo plan was reached before the IAEA came into existence.[39] No safe-guards were contemplated, though India promised to use the facility exclusively for peaceful purposes. The second agreement with Can-ada to build a 400-megawatt power station in Rajasthan (concluded in 1963 after the creation of IAEA) was different in this respect. The Indians were anxious to avoid inspections, whether conducted by Canada or under the IAEA safeguards system.[40] Inspections were re-sisted on the ground of infringement upon their national sovereignty. Though a face-saving solution was finally devised,[41] in essence, the agreement for the Rajasthan station contemplated a strict system of inspection.[42] It was, moreover, agreed that the conduct of inspections be eventually transferred to the IAEA. The reactor employs natural uranium.

Another reactor, this time with U.S. technical and financial assis-tance, has been built in Tarapur. This is a 388-megawatt power reac-tor employing enriched uranium which makes it of little value as far as military application is concerned.[43] India does not have facilities for uranium enrichment and therefore depends for fuel supply for the Tarapur reactor on the United States. She has, however, planned to build a large chemical separation plant at the cost of $7.5 million at Tarapur. This is partly to bring the plutonium reprocessing capacity up to the level where it can handle the increased output of plutonium produced in the reactors. A more ambitious program, with a mini-mum amount of foreign assistance, has been embarked on with con-struction of 2 Candu-type 200-megawatt reactors at Kalpakkam Atomic Power Station near Madras. These reactors are wholly Indian-built with almost 80 percent indigenous content.[44]

It is obvious, therefore, that India shall soon be in a position to stockpile, free from international obligations, sufficient amounts of

[39] Statement by Mr. Burns, Representative of Canada at the First Commit-tee of the Twentieth Session of the UN General Assembly, October 29, 1965.

[40] Beaton, *Must the Bomb Spread*, p. 72.

[41] It was agreed that Canada and India would mutually inspect this reactor and a similar-type reactor built in Douglas Point, Ontario. See *ibid*.

[42] Statement by Mr. Burns, Twentieth Session, UN General Assembly, Octo-ber 29, 1965.

[43] Beaton, *Must the Bomb Spread*, p. 72. The reactor was inaugurated on January 19, 1970.

[44] "Peaceful Uses of Atom," *Indian & Foreign Review*, Vol. VII, No. 15 (May 15, 1970).

plutonium to produce roughly 20 bombs of the Hiroshima-type a year. (This figure should be raised to 100 bombs if plutonium from Indian-Canadian and Indian-American reactors were to be used.)

At this stage, however, if a decision to explode a bomb were taken, it would not be without embarrassment for India since the critical mass of plutonium used must have necessarily come from facilities pledged to be used for peaceful purposes.[45]

THE NATURE OF THE THREAT

Twice during the decade of the Sixties India became engaged in military hostilities with its border states. In 1962 a clash with the People's Republic of China resulted in the military humiliation of India. The shock effect was immense. In a matter of days the ideological ground upon which the concept of nonalignment had been built and prospered, pathetically crumbled, awakening India to the sad reality of having to look, for its security, to outside powers. The Indian governments have since made nostalgic efforts to recapture the spirit of the Nehru era. That has been in vain.

Since the military defeat in 1962, and more particularly after the Chinese nuclear blast in October, 1964, the climate of opinion in India, particularly among the younger generation, has shifted toward a greater degree of self-assertiveness (a point further discussed below). Suffice it to say, at this stage, China's adventure brought about a feeling of insecurity, together with an emerging obsession for power. Retired Major-General Dutt said: "China has laid claim to well over 50,000 square miles of Indian territory along the Himalayas bordering on Tibet," and continued:

They are few in India who doubt that it is China's intention in the future to exercise direct influence over Nepal, Sikkim, Bhutan and the NEFA. . . . If China has strategic options which India does not have—or denies herself—then not only is China likely to win the psychological game, but she could precipitate a crisis over the border states or elsewhere in which India could be blackmailed into paralysis.[46]

This sample of opinion, from a man who had been the Director of the Institute for Defense Studies, to some degree typifies the way the

[45] Beaton, "Military Implications of Contemporary Trends in Civilian Nuclear Power Programs," p. 8.

[46] D. Som Dutt, "India and the Bomb," *Adelphi Papers,* The Institute for Strategic Studies, London, No. 30 (November, 1966), p. 7.

threat from nuclear China is conceived by the pro-bomb faction within the intellectually higher stratum of Indian society.

An equally real, yet less appalling threat, comes from Pakistan. The 1965 military clash showed that though Pakistan cannot pose a parallel threat to India's security, it is nevertheless a determined and a more obstinate adversary than is China. There is, moreover, a growing concern both within India's Parliament and government circles that Pakistan might secure atomic bombs from China.[47]

THE SEARCH FOR AN ALTERNATIVE
TO A NUCLEAR POSTURE

Both the Shastri and Indira Gandhi governments had initially sought a form of nuclear protection against possible Chinese nuclear blackmail. Both governments, however, strived to achieve this goal in a manner compatible with India's nonaligned posture.[48] In December, 1965, Premier Shastri demanded that a guarantee be extended not only to India but to all non-nuclear countries. This line of policy was pursued by Mrs. Gandhi's government. Defense Minister Swaran Singh had stated that a guarantee through the United Nations would be preferable to bilateral guarantees, "since the latter would be tantamount to military alliances." [49] The United States was prepared to go halfway to meet India's security requirements. President Johnson, on repeated occasions, in the course of 1966, made statements to the effect that non-nuclear states forgoing nuclear weapons will have the "support of the United States against nuclear blackmail." [50]

---

[47] An half hour special debate over this issue in the Lok Sabha (the Indian Parliament) took place on April 24, 1970, during which Mr. Salve, an M.P., called for guarantees from the U.S.A. and the USSR that they would retaliate on Pakistan in such an event. The Deputy Foreign Minister replied that the government shared concern over resumption of the supply of arms by the United States, the USSR and China to Pakistan, but no country in the world will give such a guarantee. India's defense capability should be brought to such a pitch that no country in the world can cast "evil eyes" on her territory. See *The Statesman,* Calcutta, April 25, 1970.

[48] *Stopping the Spread of Nuclear Weapons,* a report of a National Policy Panel established by the United Nations Association of the United States of America (New York, November, 1967), p. 20.

[49] *India's Search for a Nuclear Deterrent,"* a study prepared by the South Asian Institute, Columbia University, p. 9 (unpublished).

[50] Johnson's statement is quoted in UN document A/CONF.35/Doc.12, p. 7. See also McNamara's testimony on nonproliferation of nuclear weapons be-

These statements as well as the security formula eventually emerging from the Eighteen-Nation Committee on Disarmament (ENDC) in conjunction with NPT, were for all intents and purposes made to suit India's security requirements.[51] By April, 1967, however, India had shifted its position in favor of obtaining bilateral guarantees from the United Kingdom, the United States, and the USSR.[52] When finally the security guarantee offered to the non-nuclear states became geared to the NPT, India reluctantly abandoned its search for assistance from the three major powers.

INHIBITIONS IN MAKING THE BOMB

Despite failure to obtain an assurance of security vis-à-vis China, the government has steadfastly retained its original position not to embark on a nuclear military program. As late as April 28, 1970, Defense Minister Singh, in the face of mounting pressure on the government to change its nuclear policy in the aftermath of the Chinese satellite orbiting, iterated to Lok Sabha (the Indian Parliament) in unequivocal terms the government's policy not to use nuclear energy for nonpeaceful purposes:

There was no change in the "clearly and concretely" stated policy in that regard. Nor was there any change in the Government's policy not to sign the non-proliferation Treaty (NPT) which, he repeated, was unequal and discriminatory and sought to create an exclusive club of nuclear powers while preventing the non-nuclear countries from using nuclear energy for peaceful purposes.[53]

Before dealing with recent developments, however, it is essential to examine inhibitions that so far have deterred India from adopting a nuclear posture. It is not far-fetched to assume that the overriding factor has been economical.

Soon after China's nuclear blast Premier Shastri made a revelation of his thoughts in discussing the question of the "Bomb" with the

---

fore the Joint Congressional Committee on Atomic Energy, on March 7, 1966 (S. Res. 179), p. 85. McNamara refused to elaborate, under questioning from Representative Hosmer, on the President's statement and as such it is not known why in all statements made by the President, the pledge of support is against "nuclear blackmail" rather than "nuclear attack," see pp. 94–95.

[51] For an elaboration of this point see Richard Hudson, "The N.P.T.: Nuclear Watershed," *War/Peace Report* (April, 1968).

[52] "India's Search for a Nuclear Deterrent," p. 10.

[53] *The Statesman*, Calcutta, April 29, 1970.

members of Lok Sabha. Virtually all of his remarks centered on the uncertainty of cost estimates and its effect on India's economy.[54]

The question of cost estimates has been closely linked to the requirements of an operational and credible strategic nuclear force. Defense analysts in India have been unanimous in their assessment of the requirement of a second strike capability if India were to adopt a credible nuclear posture. Proceeding from this assumption, the cost estimates have ranged from $2 billion to $15 billion. General Dutt, basing himself on estimates provided by Leonard Beaton in his study on "Capabilities of Non-Nuclear Powers," believed that a modest retaliatory force with a sophisticated delivery system would cost something around $2,300 million over a period of ten years.[55] Another study makes a quantum jump in cost estimates by raising the ten-year bill to something in the order of magnitude of $10 billion to $15 billion.[56] A report of the UN Secretary-General published in 1967 puts the cost of a small but high quality nuclear force at $560 million a year.[57]

The impact of a military nuclear program on the Indian economy is not, however, confined to costs incurred. Such an undertaking might alienate and antagonize both the United States and the USSR, provoking them to retaliate by cutting off the much-needed aid programs. A reallocation of manpower resources from peaceful sectors to a military sector might, moreover, have considerable repercussions on the Indian economy.[58]

But apart from economic considerations there are a number of other factors that have influenced the government's decision. One is the nature of China's threat which is conceived of as a subversive and as a "conventional menace." [59] There are also indications to sug-

[54] Shastri's statement is partly quoted on p. 8 of "India's Search for a Nuclear Deterrent."

[55] Dutt, p. 7.

[56] *A Strategy for India for a Credible Posture against a Nuclear Adversary,* a study by the Institute for Defense Studies and Analyses, New Delhi, November, 1968, p. 57.

[57] *Effects of the possible use of nuclear weapons and on the security and economic implications for States of the acquisition and further development of these weapons,* report of the Secretary-General transmitting the study of his consultative group, UN document A/6858, p. 27.

[58] Earnest Weatherall, "Voices Rise for A-Power in India," *The Christian Science Monitor,* July 10, 1968.

[59] Defense Minister Chavan reported to Lok Sabha: "In the preliminary assessment that the Chiefs of Staff made about the nuclear capabilities of China,

gest that Indian leaders have been counting on a tacit nuclear guarantee by the super powers, should India become confronted by a nuclear threat from China.[60] This reliance on super-power support has, however, been subject to erosion because China's advancement in ICBM capability brings American cities within striking distance. The shift of the American ABM program from Sentinel to Safeguard might have a disquieting effect on India's strategic thinking.

There are still other factors that might have influenced the government's decision. Development of nuclear capability not only is a break with India's past traditions but might incur a loss in its reputation as a trustworthy and responsible state. It might be recalled in this respect that India's present stockpile of plutonium is not free from international obligations.

Last, but not least, is the reaction of Pakistan. Few in India doubt that an Indian bomb would precipitate a crash weapon program in Pakistan.

ARGUMENTS IN FAVOR OF THE BOMB

Since the explosion of China's first nuclear weapon in 1964, a strong climate of opinion in favor of development of nuclear bombs has grown in India. The pro-bomb factions have drawn most of their enthusiasts from among the younger generation.[61] Dissension has split all ranks of government and society. Sparing not even the Cabinet itself, the schism over the bomb issue has divided the military, the governing party, the Communist Party, and virtually all institutions within Indian society.[62]

At the heart of the yearning for the bomb lies not so much a fear of a nuclear China as a passion for the power and prestige associated with possession of the bomb. This, however, is not openly expressed;

---

they particularly took account of the nature of the immediate threat. According to them, the immediate and real threat is a conventional threat." Quoted, "India's Search for a Nuclear Deterrent," p. 24.

[60] Mrs. Gandhi was reported, at the time of Nixon's visit to India, to have believed that India was protected from nuclear attack since the major powers would automatically become involved in any nuclear confrontation. *Ibid.*, p. 10.

[61] Stephen P. Cohen, "The Indian Defence Policy Process," p. 52 (unpublished).

[62] For an excellent and thorough survey of opinion on the bomb in India, see "India's Search for a Nuclear Deterrent." For the rift within the ranks of Indian communists, see also Cohen, p. 53.

and on the surface, pro-bomb opinion seeks to justify itself by dramatizing China's threat. China is viewed as a domineering power trying to assert itself as the arbiter of Asia. India stands in the way of its ambitions and is therefore the likely target of nuclear blackmail. India, they argue, can afford raising its military expenditures to meet the cost of acquiring a second-strike capability. One study contends, for example, that India can double the percentage of GNP presently allocated to military expenditures by raising it to 6 percent. This would enable India to meet a $10 billion to $15 billion ten-year program for the build-up of a sophisticated nuclear arsenal.[63] A view particularly advocated by the younger generation is that the Gandhi and Nehru legacies are no longer applicable to India's present dilemma.[64] India cannot possibly remain dependent for its defense on major nuclear powers whose guarantees at best are dubious and at worst non-existent.

The argument that carries the greatest weight and is no doubt foremost in the minds of the military is the widening technological gap between India's and China's military capacity.[65] One growing concern in this respect is the development of delivery systems. India has very little experience with missiles. High-altitude research rockets have been tested by the India Atomic Energy Commission, but it is a long way from there to IRBMs.[66] India has Canberra bombers capable of carrying bombs weighing 4,000 pounds. But to reach their targets in China they require refueling over hostile territory.[67] They do not provide an adequate system of delivery. Most recently the concern in this respect was expressed by Defense Minister Swaran Singh when in reply to questions put by an M.P., said that "China was clearly ahead of India both in the matters of space technology and nuclear know-how." "The only course open to India," he added, "was to make greater efforts to cover the deficiencies." [68]

It is in response to this dilemma that a number of Indian strategists, conscious of India's obvious economic limitations, have pro-

[63] Study by the Institute for Defense Studies and Analyses, pp. 6–7.

[64] "India's Search for a Nuclear Deterrent," p. 4. See also Cohen, p. 53.

[65] *The Statesman* reported on March 15, 1969, that the New Delhi military establishment is unhappy about the widening technological gap between India's military capacity and China's.

[66] Study by the Institute for Defense Studies and Analyses, p. 8.

[67] Beaton, *Must the Bomb Spread.*

[68] *The Statesman,* "India's Space Plan to be Accelerated," April 29, 1970.

posed a new approach to the development of India's strategic capabilities. The writers of *A Strategy for India for a Credible Posture
against a Nuclear Adversary,* for example, propose that instead of
starting with a test explosion and declaring the country a military
nuclear power, priority should be given to R & D, on delivery systems, stockpiling a fissile material, and solution of the engineering
problems of the bomb and warheads without immediate testing.[69] A
similar strategy is proposed by Brigadier E. A. Vas:

It suits our proposed strategy to reverse our priorities and manufacture a
missile before the bomb. *The development of an IRBM with a range of
2,500 miles is required for the legitimate purpose of developing an Indian
space communication satellite and can be undertaken immediately without offending world opinion or contravening any self-imposed ban.*[70]

There are strong indications that the government is in fact pursuing a policy along these or similar lines to cope with the problem of
the widening technological gap. The stormy reactions to the recent
orbiting of China's 173-pound satellite confirm not only that India
takes a frenzied view of this triumph but also (the contention made
here) that the path chosen by the present government is one of inte-
grating peaceful and military programs to keep the country prepared
for future contingencies. This line of policy was strikingly revealed
by the government's reaction to the Chinese space event.

REACTION TO CHINA'S SPACE FEAT

The political correspondent of *The Statesman* wrote: "It is clear
that, psychologically, the Chinese space vehicle has come as a shock
—almost as big as the first explosion of the Chinese nuclear bomb."
The verdict of a majority of members from Mrs. Gandhi's party in
Parliament was that India should go ahead with producing the atom
bomb. Anxious M.P.'s demanded that the government explain its position in the light of the new developments.[71]

A seminar held in New Delhi to consider the implications of
China's space triumph to India's security overwhelmingly concluded

[69] Study by the Institute for Defense Studies and Analyses, p. 11.

[70] "A Nuclear Policy for India," quoted in the study by the East Asian Institute, p. 29. Italics added.

[71] *The Statesman,* "India Must Go Ahead with Atom Bomb," April 28,
1970.

that the development of the bomb is economically feasible, politically desirable, and strategically imperative.[72]

On April 28, Swaran Singh speaking before Lok Sabha announced that India will reexamine her ten-year space program to see whether it can be speeded up. The defense Minister had gone before Parliament to explain the government's reaction to the Chinese satellite.[73]

The present mood in Lok Sabha is reported to be strongly pro-bomb. There have been suggestions that despite the government's denials, an A-bomb explosion might be timed to have maximum propaganda effects for the government at the forthcoming elections. These suggestions are, however, more of a speculative nature.

India is pressing for self-sufficiency in conventional weapons [74] and there seems to be no disposition to curtail expenditure on such weapons to divert resources to nuclear weapons. All appearances, however, suggest that India will pursue, without great restraint on her economic development, a policy to acquire a technological base that could back a credible nuclear posture should developments in the future warrant such decision.

Japan

NUCLEAR CAPABILITY

It is superfluous to spend much time explaining Japan's potential for the production of nuclear weapons. Japan is one of the leading industrial powers of the world, possessing both technical know-how and financial resources to build up a significant nuclear strategic force in a magnitude comparable to that of France and England soon after a political decision in this respect was made.

In ten years' time, Japan's GNP might reach somewhere in the neighborhood of $600 billion.[75] At the moment it spends roughly 1

---

[72] Information supplied by the Press Attaché of the Indian Mission to the United Nations.

[73] *The Times of India*, "India's Space Programme May Be Speeded Up," April 29, 1970.

[74] *The Times of India*, "India Venturing into Sophisticated Fields of Arms, Self-reliance Reached in Traditional Items," April 28, 1970.

[75] See Statement made by Premier Sato in the Diet on Feb. 14, 1970, *Japan's Report*, Vol. XVI, No. 6 (March 16, 1970).

percent of its $200 billion GNP for defense purposes.[76] For all practical purposes this figure could be raised to 6 percent in ten years' time, putting up a military budget in proportions comparable to the present U. S. military expenditure of $70 billion.

As to its present nuclear capability, at the 1969 rate of power-reactor construction, Japan was estimated to be able to reach a bomb-a-week rate by diversion of plutonium from peaceful facilities, "even with the best of safeguard technology available." [77] Even if diversion of plutonium be completely ruled out, Japan still can produce domestically sufficient amounts of plutonium for bomb production. In June, 1968, Japan's Atomic Energy Research Institute disclosed production of a homemade 18-gram experimental sample in its Tokai Village laboratory.[78] Japan has, moreover, negotiated with France the construction of a -0.7-metric ton uranium-chemical reprocessing plant scheduled to be completed by 1972. A 1-ton-a-day nuclear fuel-reprocessing plant is planned for completion in 1977 at the cost of $55.6 million.[79]

More importantly, Japan has embarked on an ambitious program of uranium enrichment. According to a 1969 Report from the U. S. Atomic Energy Commission, "a Japanese research group claims to have made significant gains both in the production of *gaseous diffusion* barrier material and in the successful isotopic separation of small amounts of uranium using *gas centrifuge* equipment." [80]

Japan's drive for uranium enrichment has of course a technical explanation. Except for the Tokai 160-megawatt power reactor that is fueled with natural uranium, Japan's nuclear-power programs are based on enriched uranium reactors.[81] Japan presumably does not want, in the long run, to remain dependent for its fuel supply on the U. S. or any outside power. Admittedly, Japan's uranium resources are scarce. But the supply of natural uranium in the world market is abundant. There are reports of a joint Japanese-Italian agreement for extraction of Somali uranium resources. Having signed the NPT,

[76] J. K. Emerson, "Japan—Eye on 1970" in *Foreign Affairs,* January, 1969, p. 350.

[77] Ryukichi Imai, "The Non-Proliferation Treaty and Japan," *Bulletin of the Atomic Scientists* (May, 1969).

[78] "Japan Joins Club—Proliferation of Plutonium," *Science News,* Vol. XCIII (June 1, 1968).

[79] U. S. Atomic Energy Commission, *The Nuclear Industry* (1969), p. 231.

[80] *Ibid.,* p. 61. Italics added.   [81] Gilinsky, p. 21.

moreover, Japan will not have to preoccupy itself with the supply of either natural or enriched uranium.

One last point with regard to Japan's nuclear capability deserves mentioning. Unlike India and Israel, whose capability in this respect is uncertain, Japan is known to possess devices for measurement of the critical amount of plutonium (the 239 isotope ratio contents of plutonium) and has electronic capability to make a trigger for an atomic bomb.[82]

DELIVERY SYSTEM CAPABILITY

Japan has developed a 4-stage solid fuel rocket (LAMBA) which orbited Japan's first 46-pound satellite on February 11, 1970. A week before the accomplishment of this feat, the Japanese Space Development Agency announced successful launching of Japan's first full-scale liquid fuel rocket, an experimental rocket to be used for the third stage of a projected *Q* rocket to be used for launching a major satellite in 1972.[83]

The rocket development program in Japan started in 1963 with the addition of a Rocket Division to the National Aeronautical Laboratory. Applied research on rockets, including the improvement of the capacity of rocket engines and guidance control, and testing and research involved in the space development have been pushed.

But it was not until May 1968 (coinciding with the final stage of the elaboration of the NPT in the UN General Assembly) that Japan's space program received attention at high levels of government. On that date Premier Sato established the Space Activity Commission (SAC) as an advisory organ attached to the Prime Minister's office with the task of over-all supervision of space activities in Japan. Decisions on space programs have hence been taken on the recommendation of SAC by the Prime Minister.[84] During 1969 a solid-fuel rocket and 2 two-stage solid-liquid rockets were successfully tested. The four-stage rockets (which in the opinion of Griffin "are comparable to America's Minuteman")[85] cannot be guided from the

[82] Stewart Griffin, "Peaceful Atom Only Please," *Science News* (April 20, 1968).

[83] *Japan's Report,* XVI, No. 5 (March 1, 1970), 1.

[84] The name was changed to National Aerospace Laboratory in 1963. See Japan's report to the United Nations Committee on the Peaceful Uses of Outer Space, UN document A/AC.105/L.51/Add.2, March 2, 1970.

[85] Griffin, "Peaceful Atom Only Please."

ground once they are launched. Japan is therefore in the process of developing a ground telemetric system which would enable maneuvers to be completed through remote control.[86]

NUCLEAR ALLERGY VS. GREAT POWER

As early as 1966, when Japan's space-rocket technology was still at the planning and development stage, Leonard Beaton, the author of several books and articles on the subject, saw a paradoxical situation developing in respect to Japan's policy on nuclear-space programs: *"It is difficult to see what reasons there could be for embarking on such an ambitious program, if the decision to develop nuclear weapons has not been taken, and it is clear that no such decision has been taken."* (Italics added.) The answer should largely be sought in the present mood of the nation and the perception of Japanese leaders of their short-range and long-range interests.

A poll taken in 1969 shows [87] that 91 percent of the Japanese people supported their "Peace Constitution." [88] This has been attributed both to psychological and economic reasons. World War II, especially the experience of Hiroshima and Nagasaki, is still fresh in the memory of the Japanese people.[89] The *nuclear allergy,* a term coined to describe this mood, has already had its adverse effect on the country's pace of nuclear growth.[90] On the other hand, the Peace Constitution has been publicly identified with the "economic miracle" that has brought Japan to the forefront of the world's industrial powers.

The policy of the government has been framed with full cognizance of the nation's prevailing mood. In his speech on February 14, 1970, to the Diet, Premier Sato said "From now on, we are entering an era where Japan's national power will carry an unprecedented weight in world affairs." He added, however, "Japan is not a country to play a role in world affairs by military means." [91]

[86] *Japan's Report* (March 11, 1970).

[87] Cited by Emerson, "Japan—Eye on 1970."

[88] Article IX of the Japanese Constitution prohibits the maintenance of "Land, sea, and airforce, as well as other war potential." *Ibid.*

[89] Imai, "The Non-Proliferation Treaty and Japan."

[90] Nuclear power plant construction has been hampered on several occasions by the sharp reaction of the inhabitants around the selected sites. Emerson, p. 350.

[91] *Japan's Report,* "Excerpts from Prime Minister Sato's Speech on Feb. 14 to the Diet," Vol. XVI, No. 6 (March 16, 1970).

The Nixon-Sato Communique clearly indicates that Japan, while accepting a further share of responsibility for the maintenance of peace and stability in Asia, will press for a U. S. presence in Asia in order to be "in a position to carry out fully its obligations." [92] On December 28, 1969, Sato declared a Liberal-Democrat Party victory, in the parliamentary election in Japan, a mandate for continued close ties with the United States.[93]

If distaste for militarism is the prevailing mood of the nation and a tenet of the government's policy, a drive of self-assertiveness—a search for a role in world affairs more commensurate to Japan's potential—is becoming increasingly more evident.

Emerson most eloquently describes this emerging trend in Japan:

As a natural result of developing confidence and as a kind of reaction to "my-home-ism," a new nationalism is growing in Japan. Defeatism has given way to pride in country, and economic single-mindedness no longer fully satisfies. This spirit is not the property of any party or ideology. While it contains no nostalgia for the militarism of the past—although the Socialists warn that it does—it envisages a country with the ability to defend itself, at least to a certain degree. "Autonomous defense" is a popular phrase in Japan; *no one has clearly defined it and its significance* [italics added].

In the last few years Japan has been at pains in obtaining a voice in important international forums.[94] A great power complex has already developed, although its manifestations have not been uniform.[95]

The government has tried to build Japan's great power image on the basis of its economic strength. Based on this policy, a strategy for

[92] Nixon-Sato Communique, reproduced in *Survival,* January, 1970, p. 27.

[93] New York *Times,* December 29, 1969, p. 11.

[94] After some years of bargaining, Japan was finally admitted to the Geneva Disarmament Conference (together with Mongolia). Following the admission of these countries, ENDC was further enlarged by the addition of another 5 nations. Japan has also had trouble getting elected to the membership of the Security Council. Its representatives have often tried to invoke Article 23(1) of the UN Charter that stresses contribution to peace and security as a major qualification for election to the Council. (In practice this principle has been ignored in favor of the principle of equitable geographical distribution.)

[95] In reply to a question put to him at the U. S. National Press Club, Premier Sato remarked that though there was a segment of the population in Japan which thought Japan's no-war Constitution should be changed, he himself was opposed to such a move. *The Japan Times,* November 23, 1969.

peaceful change has been devised. (I hesitate to use the word *change* since Japan basically and despite some territorial disputes is a *status quo* power. *Change* in this context is meant as evolution of the power image.)

Foreign Minister Aichi has outlined the 3 pillars of this strategy in a speech he delivered on February 14, 1970.[96]

1. *"Further enhancement of friendly relations and mutual understanding with other nations."*

Prime Minister Sato expounded this point by saying that Japan will strive toward closer relations with the Soviet Union in trade and economic and political coexistence, "pressing [at the same time] the problem of northern territories." With regard to relations with Red China, Sato remarked that Japan will promote relations with China "with [the] expectation that China will take a more cooperative and constructive attitude in [its] external relations." [97] In the Joint Communique with Nixon he, however, said that the maintenance of peace and security in the Taiwan area was also a most important factor for the security of Japan.

2. *"Contribution towards the solution of the North-South problem."*

Again, this point was elaborated in Sato's remarks: "Japan," he said, "should be actively prepared to use [its] increasing economic power for the purposes of stabilizing world welfare." This would be done through economic aid to developing countries, particularly in Asia.

3. *"Making efforts for strengthening of the UN and for disarmament."*

For some time Japan has been seeking a stronger voice for Japan within the United Nations and a greater role for the United Nations in world affairs. Most lately Premier Sato is reported to have told U Thant (during Thant's visit in April, 1970, to Tokyo)

the UN Charter should be revised as a new era starts in international relations in the 1970's. . . . In order to strengthen the function of the world body, the so-called enemy clauses of the Charter should be deleted *and the Charter revised to abolish the San Francisco set up.*[98]

The implication seems to be that Japan wants a permanent, or at least a semipermanent, seat in the UN Security Council or some

[96] *Japan's Report,* Vol. XVI, No. 6 (March 16, 1970), see Aichi's remarks.
[97] *Ibid.,* see Premier Sato's remarks.
[98] *The Japan Times Weekly,* April 25, 1970. Italics added.

other arrangement that would put Japan on the same footing with such countries as France and Britain. By this policy Japan seeks, in the words of Premier Sato, "to solve the various inconsistencies in world affairs such as the East-West confrontation. . . ." [99]

A component part of this policy is to contrive to achieve arms-control measures aimed at nuclear disarmament. In this respect, Japan has taken a more straightforward and unequivocal position. In their declaration on the occasion of their signing the NPT,[100] Japan made it clear that it expects nuclear-weapon states to take "concrete nuclear disarmament measures in pursuance of the undertaking under Article VI." The "discrimination" inherent in the Treaty "should ultimately be made to disappear through the elimination of nuclear weapons by all the nuclear weapon states from their national arsenals."

ILLUSION AND REALITY

There are a number of questions to be asked if one is to appraise the plausibility of the assumptions behind these policies: Would a U. S. presence continue in Asia after Viet Nam or will disillusionment over the policy of containment and reaction against it generated at home lead to gradual disengagement? Will Japan then be ready to take the major share of responsibility for maintaining the security of the region or will she stick to her military inertia, relying on economic means for stabilization? What would be the margin of tolerance of the super powers toward changing patterns in power relations to be brought about by measures of nuclear disarmament, revision of the UN Charter and enhancement of its effectiveness as a peace-keeping organ? Would China take, or be permitted to take, an active interest in world affairs through participation in disarmament negotiations and restoration of its seat in the Security Council? Would Japan be able to build a world-power image on the basis of her economic power alone? Could she avoid a serious rift with the United States over issues of world markets and U. S.–Japanese trade relations?

It is beyond the scope of this article to address itself to such questions. Success or failure of Japan's peace strategy is a matter for the future. Yet one conclusion is inescapable: a great deal of optimism

[99] Statement of February 14, 1970, *Japan's Report,* Vol. XVI, No. 6 (March 16, 1970).

[100] Statement of the Government of Japan of February 3, 1970 (released by the Permanent Mission of Japan to the UN).

has been put into the formulation of this policy. Taking a more cynical look it is all but utopianism. Are Japanese leaders less than candid in advocating these policies or are they so naïve not to realize that at the end, these aims might prove illusory? My answer to both questions is in the negative. Japan is a country that has acquired all the potentials, if not all the attributes, of a great power. It is, however, a nation that has resurged from the destruction of the war and the debris of atomic weapons. There is no clear-out choice between inertia or self-assertiveness. The decade of the Seventies might well be a period of trial and transition. The policies of peaceful change will have to be tested out to see if they will work. If they do not, the choice will then be easier to make. It is wrong, however, to underestimate the foresight and the sagacity of Japanese leaders by assuming that they are obsessed by the concept of economic power, that they do not see the possibility of failure and do not make themselves ready to meet such a contingency. It is in this light that the answer to Leonard Beaton's query emerges. Japan is sincere in not wanting nuclear weapons but not so naïve as to remain unprepared for dire eventualities. Rocket technology will be perfected not only to impress the world with the space feats but for short-notice conversion into a sophisticated strategic delivery system. Fuel reprocessing plants and uranium enrichment technology will be developed not only to meet the huge and increasing civilian demand for nuclear power but also for production of the bomb, *when and if it becomes necessary.*

DECISION TO SIGN THE NPT

The signing of the NPT might, at first glance, seem a corollary of the peace strategy of the Japanese foreign policy. This conclusion deserves a digression since Japan took the step cautiously and not, so to speak, without a grain of salt. An "Editorial" of *The Japan Times* linked the decision of Japan to sign the agreement to the increasing pressure from nuclear powers. Other reasons cited were the desire to dispel suspicion by other nations and "the fear that Japan would be cut off from sources of nuclear fuel as stipulated in Article III of the NPT." [101]

Whether Japan sought to employ its option as a bargaining device in the Okinawa talks is hard to verify. The "Editorial" had exhorted the government to negotiate at Okinawa on its own merit and not to

[101] *The Japan Times,* "Editorial—NPT and Japan," November 16, 1969.

bring in NPT as a possible *quid pro quo*. The timing of the signature (February 4, 1970), shortly after Sato's Washington visit, however, suggests that some bargaining might have taken place, though no hint of a trade-off could be traced in the Joint Communique. If this be the case, Japan might hold out its ratification to obtain further concessions, presumably in talks with the Soviets over the northern territories.

But apart from basic political controversies arising from the nature of the Treaty, Japan's objections were mainly focused on the following two issues: freedom of research and development and the question of safeguards.

Freedom of Research and Development. Initially there had been fears, generally expressed, that the Treaty might curtail freedom of research and development in peaceful applications of nuclear energy. Both Japan and West Germany had taken a grave view of this prospect and have since tried to stick to a very restrictive interpretation of the Treaty provisions in this respect. Japan's concern over this issue is best reflected in her declaration on signing the Treaty:

The prohibition under this Treaty applies solely to the acquisition of nuclear weapons and other nuclear explosive devices and of control over them. Therefore, this Treaty must in no way restrict non-nuclear weapon states in their research, development, or implementation of the peaceful use of nuclear energy, or in their international co-operation in these fields, nor must it subject them to discriminatory treatment in any aspect of such activities.

There seems to be little cause for anxiety on that score especially since engagement of Japan (and that of West Germany as well) in a program of uranium enrichment has elicited no noticeable reaction from the Soviet Union. The issue, however, might deliberately be kept alive to forestall future interferences and to enhance Japan's bargaining position in obtaining material and equipment for consummation of their ambitious programs.

The question of spin-offs has also been a cause of concern for Japan. Japan does not lose sight of the fact that lack of economical military expenditure for research and development might result in great industrial disadvantages. They will remember that "gas-graphite reactors were an outcome of plutonium production facilities and light water reactors are offsprings of submarine propulsion studies." [102]

[102] Imai, "The Non-Proliferation Treaty and Japan."

Deprivation of this advantage is, however, something that Japan should accept as a fact of life. Instead, Japan will continue to press for the application of safeguards on peaceful nuclear facilities of all nuclear weapon states, supposedly to provide means of detecting innovations springing from peaceful activities of these countries. In her declaration Japan has welcomed the decision of the United States and the United Kingdom to subject their peaceful nuclear facilities to IAEA safeguards and has expressed hope that other nuclear weapon powers would undertake similar obligations.

The Question of Safeguards. Both the supply of fuel and Japan's nuclear installation will become subject of safeguards once Japan ratifies the NPT and concludes an agreement on the modalities and procedures of the safeguards with the IAEA. All appearances suggest that this will be a tough bargaining. Japan has always taken a grave view of the implications of a rigid safeguard system. In the Conference of Non-Nuclear Weapon States held in September, 1968, in Geneva, Japan was among the ardent supporters of the resolution for simplification of IAEA's safeguard procedures. Its basic position in this respect has been outlined in the following terms:

Safeguards should be subject to the principle that they should be applied at certain strategic points of the nuclear fuel cycle, and the procedure for their application must be rational when considered from the point of view of cost-effectiveness and made as simple as possible by making the maximum use of material control systems of the respective countries. Furthermore, adequate measures must be taken to ensure that the application of safeguards does not cause the leakage of industrial secrets or otherwise hinder industrial activities.[103]

Japan has also emphasized that IAEA safeguards should supersede those already applied by the United States, the United Kingdom, and Canada.

Ryukichi Imai, a Japanese scientist, who had been advocating a safeguards policy along the lines adopted by the government evaluates the effectiveness of a safeguards system in the following terms: "It is impossible to devise a system that is both effective and practical." [104] His judgment is claimed to be based on IAEA's past experience. The point he is getting at is that reliance on the technology of safeguards is not only naïve but extremely costly. Since pre-

---

[103] Statement of February 3, 1970, on signing of NPT.
[104] Imai, "The Non-Proliferation Treaty and Japan."

vention of diversion of source material cannot effectively be detected, more reliance should be put on political judgment and less on safeguard technology.

In effect, what Japan wants is a rubber-stamp role for IAEA inspectors. The admonition that Japan should not be made subject to disadvantageous treatment in respect of a safeguard agreement suggests that she would insist on terms equal with those negotiated with the members of Euratom. How this could be worked out, given the fact that Japan is not a party to a similar regional arrangement, is of course an open question.

Conclusions

Among the three countries whose nuclear policies were the subject of this study, India and Israel have more in common with each other than with Japan.

India and Israel have both a tangible problem of security; both have refused to sign the NPT; both have acquired militarily more suitable natural uranium-fueled reactors; both have tried and to a large extent succeeded in averting inspections; neither one depends for its fuel supply on the outside world; and, finally, both of these states' programs have had a more visible military orientation.

There is one thing in common between India and Japan. These two countries seem to be acquiring the potential for a meaningful strategic force through development of the civilian counterpart of the required technology. The present mood and the aspirations of the two nations are, however, diametrically opposed. While in Japan, people find distasteful anything that smacks of nuclear weapons, in India the government is under strong pressure to go right ahead with a weapons program.

Japan has less impulse yet greater potential for going nuclear. She is protected by the nuclear umbrella provided by the U. S.–Japan Security Treaty. The Sino-Soviet conflict, moreover, has provided Japan with a breathing spell in which to test out its peaceful strategy for a "new order." If this policy fails, with it the mood of the nation and the policies of self-containment might change.

Evaluation and analysis of this policy was not, however, the focus of this study. The central issue is that, far from remaining dormant, Japan is preparing herself to meet contingencies arising out of failure of its peace strategy and has pursued a vigorous program of rocketry. Japan not only has acquired a plutonium chemical separation plant but has embarked on the development of uranium enrichment technology.

India is not likely to change its present "peaceful application" nuclear policy, though submission to domestic pressure for reversal of this policy cannot be entirely overruled. India, however, will move faster in consolidating its industrial and technological base for an eventual, and seemingly inevitable, adaptation to a military program. For the time being the government shall heavily invest in conventional armaments—with a view to obtaining a maximum level of self-sufficiency as the nature of the immediate threat to India is conceived by the government to be conventional.

Israel's nuclear policy is not subject to public debate. Studies on this subject are handicapped by a lack of official data and a scarcity of available literature. There is a good case to be made against the wisdom of Israel's avowedly possessing nuclear weapons. This does not, however, overrule the possibility of concealment of a few small warheads. In all probability, however, Israel has stopped just short of production of the weapon in order to enhance its bargaining position vis-à-vis the United States for obtaining its conventional needs.

If as a result of recent Soviet moves and a lack of determination on the part of the U. S., Israel lost its margin of superiority, she might then rush into production of the bomb, still without the need publicly to unveil her decision: A nuclear deterrent posture is not likely to work in the Middle East, where the use of atomic bombs seems the last thing to which Israel would dare to resort.

Biographical Sketches

BETTE KNAPP received her A.B. magna cum laude in 1951 from Smith College where she was a Sophia Smith Scholar and received the Dawes Prize for the best undergraduate work in political science. Entering the Department of Public Law and Government (Political Science) at Columbia University in the fall of 1951 to specialize in international relations and India-Pakistan studies, Miss Knapp received her M.A. in June 1953. Her Honor's and Master's essays were both analytical studies of the organizational and political development of the Indian National Congress Party.

Miss Knapp has devoted her time since 1954 to citizen world affairs education on the community level. She was Executive Director of the World Affairs Center, Hartford, Connecticut from 1956 to 1969. During this time she produced and conducted her own local radio program featuring discussions with international affairs specialists and U.S. or foreign government officials. She also initiated and conducted study tours of Western and Eastern Europe for community leaders.

In recognition of her public service and contribution to citizen international understanding, Miss Knapp received a People to People Award in 1959 and in 1963 was one of two physically handicapped Connecticut citizens cited for "meritorious service" to the community by the President's Committee on Employment of the Handicapped. In 1963 she was invited to the Federal Republic of Germany as a guest of the Bonn Government for two weeks of discussions with leaders in politics, business, labor, education, and the media. The Federal Republic in 1965 awarded Miss Knapp the Verdienstkreuz des Verdiensordens der Bundesrepublik Deutschland.

Wishing to combine her experience in community world affairs education with undergraduate college teaching and research, Miss Knapp returned to Columbia in 1969 to complete the work for the Ph.D. in political science. Her particular interests are international relations, comparative politics, Germany, and South Asia.

CHARLES D. BETHILL graduated magna cum laude from Columbia College in 1969. He was elected to Phi Beta Kappa and awarded the Charles A. Beard Prize in Political Science. Mr. Bethill is presently a graduate student in the Department of Political Science supported by a Faculty

Fellowship and an N.D.E.A. Fellowship. His particular interests include law and American foreign policy.

PAUL A. SHAPIRO was graduated Phi Beta Kappa (1968) from Harvard College—where he held an Honorary Harvard National Scholarship from 1964–1968–in June 1968 with a magna cum laude degree in Government (International Relations). During the summer of 1968 he attended the Romanian Summer Language Institute at Sinaia, Romania, on a grant from the Romanian Government (through IIE). In September 1968, Mr. Shapiro entered the School of International Affairs at Columbia University, and he received his M.I.A. in June 1970. He has also been a member of the Institute on East Central Europe since 1968, and he is currently preparing his institute certificate essay. While at the School of International Affairs Mr. Shapiro served on the Tripartite Committee and was Editor-in-Chief of the Journal of International Affairs (Vol. XXIV:1 *Leadership: The Psychology of Political Men* and Vol. XXIV:2 *International Economic Development: Problems and Prospects for the 1970's*). A holder of a Herbert H. Lehman Graduate Fellowship since 1968. Mr. Shapiro will continue his studies under this fellowship as a Ph.D. candidate in the Department of History.

GERTRUD SVALA is a native of Sweden but has lived in the United States since 1959. During 1966–1967 she studied economics and political science at the London School of Economics. In 1968 she received a Bachelor of Arts Degree with High Distinction and High Honors in Political Science at the University of Michigan. Her academic honors at the University of Michigan included Phi Beta Kappa, Branstrom Award, and James B. Angell Scholar. At the School of International Affairs of Columbia University, where she has been concentrating on Western Europe, she was awarded the Alice Stetten Fellowship. She is a M.I.A. candidate for 1970 and participated in the United Nations Internship Program in Geneva during the summer of 1970.

GLENDA ROSENTHAL was graduated from St. Anne's College, Oxford, with an honors degree in modern history, in 1958. In 1958–1959 she studied at the College of Europe at Bruges, where she received the Diploma in European Studies. From July 1959 to March 1961, Miss Rosenthal worked as a French-English translator in Luxembourg with the special Common Market daily news service, Agence EUROPE. From Luxembourg she came to the United States and spent three years with the Press and Information Service of the French Embassy in New York, where she was head of the translation bureau and responsible for English-language publications. In July 1964 she was appointed Chief Information

Specialist and Assistant to the Director of the European Community Information Service, the New York information office of the European Common Market. Since September 1969 Miss Rosenthal has been a candidate for the Ph.D. in Political Science and the Certificate of the European Institute, in addition to serving as a part-time instructor in European history at Pace College.

KEITH J. SOURS developed his interest in Italian politics while attending the University of Padua, Italy, in 1965 on the Education Abroad Program of the University of California. Having graduated with Honors and Distinction in Political Science from the Berkeley campus in 1967, he returned to Italy to study at the Bologna Center of the Johns Hopkins School of Advanced International Studies. In June of 1969 he received his Master's degree from Johns Hopkins, having specialized in International Economics, American Foreign Policy, and Comparative European Politics.

To pursue his interest in Comparative Politics, Mr. Sours came to Columbia University as a Faculty Fellow to study at the European Institute. At Columbia he became interested in Comparative Leadership Studies. Having submitted an essay on Palmiro Togliatti for his Master's degree in the spring of 1971, he asked for a leave from his doctoral studies to teach in France and to research the life of Maurice Thorez. Upon his return to Columbia he hopes to submit a comparative study of the two Communist leaders for his doctoral dissertation.

JANUSZ A. WISNIOWSKI studied Political Economy at Warsaw University in Poland. He was chairman of the Students' Econometric Society and received the Award for Academic Achievement of the Chairman of the Department. In the summer of 1966 he worked as a researcher at the State Planning Commission in Warsaw. In 1967–1968 he was enrolled in the honors program in Economics and Political Science at McGill University in Montreal. He then transferred to the Graduate Department of Economics and the European Institute at Columbia University, where in 1969 he was appointed a President's Fellow. He has recently passed his oral examinations in mathematical economics and international trade and finance. At present he is researching econometric problems of land taxation for The Henry George School. He also serves as economics and mathematics consultant for International Arts and Science Press.

PATRICIA L. REYNOLDS was graduated from Oberlin College in 1965 with a degree in English Literature. From August 1965 to March 1968 she was a volunteer in the U.S. Peace Corps, responsible for the founding, development, and expansion of an inter-island production-and-marketing sewing cooperative among the Cuna Indians of San Blas, Panama. While in the

Peace Corps, Miss Reynolds also was co-author of a handbook for female volunteers in Panama, Cuna language instructor for an in-country Peace Corps Volunteer training program, and visited some six different countries in South America. After an extensive trip through Central America in 1968, she returned to the United States and was employed by the Inter-American Development Bank as an Accounting Assistant in Washington, D. C. In 1969 Miss Reynolds enrolled in the Latin American Institute and School of International Affairs, Columbia, where she is at present studying for a Certificate in Latin American Studies and a Master of International Affairs degree. She has been appointed a Fellow in the School of International Affairs for the 1970–1971 academic year.

DARIOUSH BAYANDOR was graduated from Teheran University in June 1961 with honors. He joined the Iranian Foreign Service after having achieved best results in the entrance examinations among all applicants. Thereupon, he was granted a scholarship by the University of Madrid, where he received a doctorate degree in Political Science with the qualification "Sobresaliente." Mr. Bayandor was assigned to the Iranian Mission to the United Nations in November 1965 where he served as an adviser to his delegation in a number of international conferences including five sessions of the U.N. General Assembly and the Conference of the Non-Nuclear Weapon States held in Geneva in September 1968.

He is currently a student at the School of International Affairs as a candidate for M.I.A. degree.